Praise for Marion Ross and *My Days*

"An autobiography as cheerful and straightforward as the author's character on *Happy Days* . . . this book will please fans with its down-to-earth account of the dedicated actress behind an adored character."

—*Publishers Weekly*

"Fans of the popular TV show *Happy Days* will recognize the name "Mrs. C." . . . Ross shares anecdotes about the show and interviews with her cast mates . . . *Happy Days* fans will enjoy, but Ross's perseverance also serves as a primer for aspiring actors."

—*Library Journal*

MY DAYS
HAPPY AND OTHERWISE

by
Marion Ross
with David Laurell

Foreword by Ron Howard

KENSINGTON BOOKS
www.kensingtonbooks.com

KENSINGTON BOOKS are published by

Kensington Publishing Corp.
119 West 40th Street
New York, NY 10018

All Kensington titles, imprints, and distributed lines are available at special quantity discounts for bulk purchases for sales promotion, premiums, fund-raising, educational, or institutional use.

Special book excerpts or customized printings can also be created to fit specific needs. For details, write or phone the office of the Kensington Sales Manager: Attn. Sales Department. Kensington Publishing Corp., 119 West 40th Street, New York, NY 10018. Phone: 1-800-221-2647.

Kensington and the K logo Reg. U.S. Pat. & TM Off.

First Kensington Hardcover Edition: April 2018

ISBN-13: 978-1-4967-1517-3 (ebook)
ISBN-10: 1-4967-1517-9 (ebook)

ISBN-13: 978-1-4967-1516-6
ISBN-10: 1-4967-1516-0
First Kensington Trade Paperback Printing: April 2019

10 9 8 7 6 5 4 3 2 1

Printed in the United States of America

For everyone—family, friends and fans—who has given me a life filled with happy days

Contents

FOREWORD

Having already had the privilege of playing the son of one of television's most iconic fathers, Andy Taylor, on *The Andy Griffith Show*, I was honored to have been given the opportunity to take on the role of the middle child of one of the medium's all-time favorite mothers, Marion Cunningham, on *Happy Days*.

As with any perfectly cast play, film or television show—and *The Andy Griffith Show* and *Happy Days* both easily qualify—it would be unimaginable to have had anyone other than Andy Griffith playing the part of Andy Taylor or any actress other than Marion Ross portraying Mrs. C.

Television aficionados and die-hard *Happy Days* fans know that the show the world would come to embrace and love first aired on February 25, 1972, as a segment on ABC's comedy anthology *Love, American Style*. Originally shot as a pilot, which wasn't picked up, the episode segment was titled "Love and the Television Set," later retitled "Love and the Happy Days" for syndication. The show was the brainchild of Garry Marshall, who believed that after surviving the turbulent 1960s and entering the 1970s with a scattered understanding of who we were and where we were going, Americans would be primed for a good healthy dose of nostalgia: a story about a family living in the simpler and idyllic postwar world of the 1950s.

It was at the outset of the filming of that pilot that I first met Marion. At the time, the cast that would eventually transition into the *Happy Days* everyone now knows included her, Anson Williams and me. I was in my senior year of high school and had taken a week off to shoot the pilot. Having acted for as far back as I could remember, I was interested in pursuing a career as a director. The thing I remember more than anything else about doing that pilot was standing on the set with Marion while they were setting up a shot, and going through my mail. I had applied to USC's film school, and there, amongst the envelopes I was sorting through, my eye caught one with the USC School of Cinema-Television as the return address. After I ripped open that letter and learned I had been accepted, Marion was the first person I shared the good news with. I recall her being just as excited as I was.

Her excitement over my acceptance to USC, along with her support and encouragement for my dream to direct, could not have been more genuine if I had been one of her own children. That real excitement and heartfelt support would be something that I, and others, would continue to experience after *Happy Days* was picked up as a series by ABC.

Marion always showed a grounded, fun, unpretentious and unforced way of cheerleading all of us during the run of the show. She was a positive and upbeat force, yet she always had just enough of a "wiseass" streak in her that she never made you feel her caring was forced or overly sentimental. The way Marion embraced and interacted with everyone was always very organic and totally genuine.

As with *The Andy Griffith Show*, the cast and crew of *Happy Days* were truly like a family. We all got along well and cared for one another, which continues to this day. I have always felt that this played a huge role in how, unlike some other child actors, I have been able to maintain my sanity in what can sometimes be a crazy business. It was that compass of nurturing care and compassion instilled in me, first by my parents and then by the people I worked with—Andy, Garry, Marion and others—that has played a major role in my ability to positively navigate my way through my career, as well as my life.

When *Happy Days* took off and exploded into a national event, we became one of the highest-rated shows in television history. And yet, in spite of all the outside noise and commotion, the excitement, the pressures, the internal business factors that are a part of any production, everyone loved working together. We loved what we achieved as a family and as a team. There was always a strong "ensemble" feel in doing *Happy Days*, no matter who had the best lines in any given episode.

I have always felt that in her own maternal and yet unobtrusive way, Marion had a lot to do with that feeling. The cast always felt free to talk to Marion, whether it was about a personal problem or a frustration on a professional level. She was a great listener and possessed the ability to defuse things in a totally uncontrolling way. Marion had an endearing way of offering advice, which stemmed from having no agenda other than being a caring and interested friend. While working with David Laurell, Marion's writing collaborator on this book, I learned that during the run of *Happy Days*, Garry would rely on her if any ruffled feathers needed to be smoothed. When David told me that, I wasn't surprised. It made perfect sense that Marion would be his go-to person to get the skinny and gain a better understanding of what was happening on the set, as well as in each of our minds and personal lives.

Today, when I think back on doing *Happy Days*, a mil-

lion wonderful memories flood my mind. Among those is
a running inside joke between Marion and me. Whenever
we did scenes together, between takes, she would lightly
brush the tips of my ears with her fingers and whisper to
me, "You should really get these ears fixed, dear. Just a little tuck is all you need, honey—just so they don't pop out
so much."

I never knew if she really meant that or not, but it became a little shared moment between us that, as with so
many other things she would do, served as a tension breaker,
made me laugh, and endeared her to me.

When I heard that Marion had finally decided to sit
down and write a book about her life, I was thrilled. *Yes,* I
thought. *I'm sure many people will initially pick up this
book simply because they grew up as a fan of* Happy Days
*and loved her as Mrs. C, but more importantly, because by
reading about her life, they will learn so much more about
this inspiring woman.*

While she made a fantastic Marion Cunningham—one
of the greatest television moms of all time—it is important
for people to know that when one looks at the totality of
her career, from the stage to the screen—large and small—
she cannot be overestimated as an actress of extraordinary
range. As they make their way through the pages of this
book, readers will learn about the days that have made up
her life and will discover that some of her most challenging and brilliantly played roles were those that played out,
not on soundstages, locations or back lots, but in real life.
They'll learn of a determined young girl who harbored a
secret dream and who blossomed into a woman who made
that dream come true; of a spouse who, like so many others, found herself dealing with the difficulties the disease
of alcoholism brings to a marriage; of a single mother with
one foot in the world of raising children and the other in

the demanding professional world of show business; of a beloved grandmother; and of the loving companion of a man who, late in her life, became her true soul mate. This is a remarkable story that will give readers insight into a Marion Ross they never knew, one who, during both her "happy days" and those that presented challenges, always handled everything with grace, dignity and wisdom, while making it all look so easy—when it clearly wasn't.

The ability to do that is the sign of a tremendously talented actress, but it is also an indication of the makeup of a woman who harbors an internal strength and wisdom that, I know for certain, will serve as an inspiration to those who get to know her better in these pages.

The story of Marion's days will reveal what those of us who have known her for many years already know: that she is a woman of great wit, a fantastic communicator who has always remained relevant, current and unfettered by false sentimentality, and a great person to confide in and seek advice from. They will discover that she possesses an insightful wisdom and a well-toned and balanced equilibrium in the way she has lived her life, both of which have formed her humanistic viewpoints.

As one turns each page of this book, it will become clear why those of us who have had the pleasure of actually knowing Marion have sought and listened to the wisdom and advice she has imparted . . . for the *most* part. While I am grateful for so much of the advice she gave me, which was greatly appreciated and dutifully applied, no matter how many times she offered one certain suggestion, it never really resonated with me. That said, please do not ask me for a recommendation if you are seeking the services of a plastic surgeon who specializes in ear tucks.

—Ron Howard

My Prologue

While the majority of my days have been happy ones, I have certainly had my share of those that were not. That's life—everyone's life. And no matter what fortunes or misfortunes we are born with, encounter along the way, or earn during the days we are given, the goal is to always make as many happy ones as possible.

I have accomplished that goal.

For as long as I can remember, from back when I was just a young girl growing up in Albert Lea, Minnesota, I have always viewed each one of my days as little empty stages that needed to be filled with all manner of wonderful adventures, stories and characters. In my bedroom, on the second floor of our little house on High Street, I would secretly dream of playing the lead role in those adventures, which would always include my taking curtain call bows in front of a standing audience, doing a dramatic scene in front of a camera with a famous actor, and signing autographs for adoring fans as I made my way into a theater for a star-studded Hollywood premiere. It was a dream that I held as a closely kept secret, because I knew if I ever made it known, my sister Alicia's laughter would never cease.

Those adventurous dreams that were played out in my carefully guarded secret became the cornerstone on which I built a life that would see those things become a reality. And, while I always fully expected those dreams to come true, so many times, and still to this day, it amazes me that those secret dreams did actually come to fruition.

And so, having lived a life in which so many of my dreams did become a reality, I found myself constantly being told by my son, Jim Meskimen; my daughter, Ellen Kreamer; my longtime personal assistant, Gwen Berohn; and many others that the days of my life—those days filled with the dreams that would take me from Albert Lea to Mrs. C, along with the ones that brought the challenges and losses we all face—would make for an interesting story. While I spent many years rejecting that premise, in the late summer of 2015 I began to think that perhaps they had a point. Maybe—just maybe—I reasoned, there were those who loved to read stories about dreams coming true and, by reading the story of my days, would better understand the fact that no matter how blessed one may be—and I have certainly been blessed—the same path that fulfills our dreams also has many twists, turns, detours and pitfalls that must be navigated.

To further convince myself that there may be those who would be interested in reading my story, I imagined the uncountable people, of all ages, I have encountered over the years who have told me how much they loved *Happy Days*. I thought of the many people who have told me I was one of the "TV moms," like Harriet Nelson, Shirley Jones and Florence Henderson, whom they had always wanted their real mothers to be more like, or, in some cases, who was what they imagined a mother they had never had would have been like. I can't tell you how many people, upon meeting me, have said, "You raised me!"

Well, I thought to myself. *Okay, if I am to sit down and write the story of my days, I would want the people who have played a part in what have been my very best days to be a part of this endeavor—my family, the people who are closest to me and, of course, the members of my* Happy Days *family.* I have always thought of the people I worked with on *Happy Days* as my family—my team. Because of that, I couldn't imagine putting the story of my days down on paper without having my family, along with my extended family and teammates, involved with the process.

That all seemed well and good, until I realized something: whether I actually sat down with them to work on this book or asked them to write their thoughts about me, I would get what I imagined would sound like a flowery eulogy. I mean, yes, I made a living performing in front of audiences, but I also harbor a fairly good-sized streak of shyness and modesty, which would make it very difficult, if not impossible, for me to sit with my children, Garry Marshall, Henry Winkler, Ron Howard or any of my *Happy Days* family and ask them, "Okay, so what do you think of me?"

To overcome that dilemma, my son suggested I seek the assistance of someone who knows their way around interviewing people, which led me to David Laurell. With a background in both broadcast and print journalism, David has conducted interviews and written award-winning stories about people from every walk of life imaginable since the early 1980s.

After bringing David on board to help with the interviews, we decided he would provide the insight on what various people thought of me, and, in turn, I would then take the opportunity to share my thoughts and feelings about them. David decided that would be best presented in an interview format, which, throughout this book, is clearly delineated from my input.

The willingness to be involved in helping me tell the

story of my days by so many of the people who mean the most to me is what truly inspired me to fully embrace this project. It is a story that, simply put, could never have been told without them, because while I may have been the dreamer, it has been each one of them, in their own very special way, that has played a role in my dreams coming true.

Chapter 1

My Beginnings

I was a strong child, both physically and in terms of will. I was athletic, was a good swimmer, and had a fiercely determined mind-set of how the world should work and the way things should be. I was also the holder of a secret—a big secret. My secret was a dream, one that has been shared by many young girls—to become a famous actress—although to me, being the determined and strong-willed person I was, it was far more than a girlish dream. It was my destiny.

While my pragmatic streak always saw me harbor my secret as a prophetic destiny, I would, at times, also allow myself to be entertained by the "dreamy" aspect of it. Those moments would usually come in my second-floor bedroom or the basement of the small Albert Lea, Minnesota, wood-framed home I shared with my parents, my older sister, Alicia, and my younger brother, Gordon. It was in those rooms, when no one was around, that I would envision my hair and makeup being done, walking out on a stage and, beyond the glare of the footlights, seeing members of the audience riveted to my every move. I remember those thoughts as being so vivid, and of me being so confident, that once they became a reality, I knew exactly how to handle each moment with ease. From taking my bows to receiving well-wishers in my dressing room, signing autographs, and then being whisked off in a big shiny limousine to my beautiful home, I just always knew that I would know how to do those things.

Why I had such an unwavering confidence of these things, and even a detailed understanding of how I would handle them, I guess can be explained only in how fiercely I was able to imagine things—to imagine a world of glittering excitement that was as far from our little Midwestern agricultural city as, well, as far as Albert Lea is from Broadway to the east and from Hollywood to the west.

It was that secret dream of my future as a famous actress that filled every cell of my body with anticipatory excitement over how things would one day be. It was a future of which I was so assured—one that I had such an unwavering knowledge would come to be—that I was able to thoroughly enjoy my childhood, without any concern for how things would eventually play out.

My childhood was a happy one, filled with many simple pleasures, which I began recording in a 1940 diary that, along with slippers and a scarf, I received as a Christmas present in 1939. Among the documented things that filled the days of my twelve-year-old, sixth-grade life were ice-skating or swimming at Fountain Lake, which was just a few blocks from our house, and going to movies, such as *North West Mounted Police*, with Gary Cooper; *Santa Fe Trail* and *Virginia City*, with Errol Flynn; and *The Old Maid*, with Bette Davis, which, according to my recording of January 4, "I enjoyed and cried."

Other "monumental" moments of those days that I felt it was important to document in my diary were working as a junior lifeguard; buying movie magazines and Cokes;

my father coming home one evening with a "nifty waffle iron," and surviving crushes that vacillated between Milton, Tom, Jim and a few other neighborhood boys, who at one point all so disgusted me that I resolved in writing to "never like a boy again."

Those written recordings of my early teenage days, which continued on for a few more years, always included three key players: Alicia and my two best friends, Margaret Larson, whom we all called Muggs, and JoAnn Youngstrom, who was known as Mert. The four of us would explore the lake in a little boat or canoe we would rent from Mr. Murtaugh's Boat Rentals, or we would roam the halls of Carnegie Library, the local public library, where I would seek out books on famous actors and actresses, hoping to learn about the path that had led them to stardom so I would know what I needed to do to follow in their footsteps.

Every one of my adventures during those days included either Alicia, Muggs or Mert, and while I loved all three of them dearly, at times Alicia and Muggs got on my nerves. Unlike me, Alicia was very careful with her toys and particular about what she wore and how her clothes were neatly hung or put away. Alicia's persnickety ways, which I perceived as being her way of showing me up with a superior attitude, infuriated me, and the last thing I needed was for her to ever get wind of my secret dream, for which I knew she would unmercifully tease me. From time to time, always in short-lived resolutions, I would also have to keep things from Muggs. In a March 1942 diary entry I wrote: "Tonight I hereby resolve never to tell Muggs any of my private affairs. All she does is mouth it off."

My little dustups with Alicia and Muggs never lasted long, and during times in which my better angels took over, I gave both of them a pass for their infuriating behavior. That was, perhaps, due to my understanding that I, too, could be equally annoying. In one of my diary entries in which I again resolved to exclude Muggs from my "private affairs," due to her "mouthing off," I also wrote: "And another thing, I am going to quit picking on everyone. Mouthing off is one of my specialties, too."

While I was so good at not keeping my mouth shut that I considered it to be a "specialty," there was always one thing I never mouthed off about: my secret dream. And, while I was always thoroughly convinced I was keeping the biggest secret under our roof, there was an even bigger one playing out, right under my nose, which I was not aware of. No one was keeping this secret from me. In reality, it was no secret at all. It was right there, out in the open for all the world to see: the fact that we were poor.

Our house on High Street, where I would dream my secret dreams, had a good-sized yard. All the houses in our neighborhood had been built on quarter-acre lots, so everyone had big yards and wonderful vegetable gardens. From the time I was very young, I was always aware that there were those who had riches far beyond ours and that there were houses far grander than ours, but those wealthy folk and magnificent mansions were simply a part of my secret dream of destiny, and the thought that we were "poor" never entered my head. And yet we were, which just made us fit in with everyone else in our neighborhood.

I was born in October of 1928, and just as I celebrated my first birthday, the Great Depression hit. It was, of course, a time of tremendous financial struggle for so many Americans that lasted well into the following decade, and it ended with the beginning of another horrible chapter in history: World War II.

I had just recently turned thirteen when Germany invaded Poland, and while the United States remained neutral until that fateful December day in 1941, we were all aware that our country was supplying our allies with money and materials to fight the war. During those early days of the war, we rented out the three second-floor bedrooms of our home to make ends meet. Because of that, my parents slept in the one bedroom we had on the main floor, my brother slept in the living room, and my sister and I slept in the basement. Now, when I say we slept in the basement, some may envision this cozy finished "family room" type of a thing. That would be wrong! It was a basement— a real basement—with a coal-burning stove, a washing machine and a very small unfinished bathroom.

Not only were Alicia and I relegated to the basement, but we also had to share the same double bed, where the verbal fight for covers would sometimes get so loud, we would engender a parental shout from the floor above, warning us to "Be quiet and get to sleep."

On either side of our bed were constant reminders of how hard my mother worked to keep her family clean and fed. On one side there were shelves where she stored all the jams, jellies and whatever else she canned. On the other side was a small heating contraption with burners. I remember my mother pumping water and then heating it on those burners so she would have hot water for the washer. She always did her laundry early in the morning, which infuriated me, because our sleep would be cut short.

Alicia and I tried to make the best of our shabby basement bedroom accommodations by plastering two solid walls with pictures of movie stars we had cut out of magazines. I have so many memories of looking at the photographs of those stars, wondering what their lives must be like, and secretly dreaming of the day that photos of me would be in a magazine. Of course, I never shared those dreams with Alicia, who would have teased me unmercifully over harboring such audacious thoughts. The other thing I never shared with anyone outside of our house was that I was dreaming those dreams in a basement. I remember, when I was twelve or thirteen, attending the Episcopal summer camp, where after it was lights out, all the girls would lie in bed and talk about how they missed their home bedrooms and describe how they were decorated. I would lie there in completely horrified silence, thinking, *Oh my gosh! I can't say that I sleep in the basement . . . in the same bed with my sister!* But that is what we did for about four years. And yet even that never made me aware of just how bloody poor we were.

Chapter 2

My Family

Although I grew up in Albert Lea, I was actually born in a Watertown, Minnesota, hospital thirty miles west of Minneapolis and lived a portion of my earliest days in Waconia, which is about thirty-five miles southwest of Minneapolis. My birth certificate listed my given name as "Marian."

As a young girl, I never gave any thought to the spelling of my name, but when I turned twelve, I was given a little Episcopalian prayer book that had my name embossed on the cover in gold letters. I would look at my name on the cover of that book and, as part of my secret dream, would imagine how it would look on a theatrical program and, more importantly, in lights on a theater's marquee. The more I looked at my name on that book, the more something bothered me. It just didn't look right to me, and finally, it hit me: my name would look so much better if I changed the spelling to "Marion." For some reason, I felt that by changing the *a* to an *o*, my name had a more pleasing appearance. That was extremely important to me, because I knew that I was destined to one day step into the real-life role of my secret dream—that I was going to be someone special and needed a name that would look good on a marquee.

The middle name on my birth certificate was "Ellen," a name, and a spelling, I was so proud of and fine with that years later I would pass it on to my daughter. I was proud of the name Ellen because it was my mother's name. My mother, Ellen Alicia Hamilton, was a Canadian, born in northern Saskatchewan, in the little wheat farming town of Tisdale, which is about 170 miles north of Regina. She was a pretty woman with blue eyes and dark hair. She was also a wonderful storyteller and frequently told tales of her parents, Irish immigrants who relocated to Canada after the Crimean War.

My mother's family was quite well educated, and they were all great fiddle players. They had originally come from Dublin and were proud of the educations they had received. Following the Crimean War, the boys in the family, who had served as soldiers, packed up their parents, siblings, wives and children and left Ireland, first for America, with their final destination being Canada. The lure of Canada was due to the country's willingness to provide a parcel of land to soldiers who had served in the Crimean War.

From what I recall, the Hamilton clan's trek to Canada was not an easy one. They somehow made it to Iowa in covered wagons, where they spent their first winter away from Ireland in a small house. As soon as the first signs of spring appeared, the men then left the women and children behind and headed north to search for their next stop. I can recall being in awe as my mother recounted the story of how the men returned for them, loaded them and whatever meager belongings they had into covered wagons, and took them to their next stopping-off point. Exactly where that was—Minnesota, perhaps, or maybe one of the Dakotas—is uncertain. The one thing my mother did remember is that when they got settled, they all took up their fiddles and played music, and everyone danced, kicking up the dust from the dirt floor of the small shelter the men had built.

While much of the story of the Hamiltons blazing their way toward Canada has been lost to the ages, from what I have pieced together, by the time they crossed the Canadian border and settled, the men had become scalawags and scoundrels of sorts. They were educated but knew nothing of farming. What they were good at was talking— telling stories and jokes. As for the Hamilton women, they also had no farming skills, so they used their education and became teachers.

My mother, who had studied English and the works of the great writers, poets and playwrights, could sit and quote Shakespeare for hours (something she continued to do for the remainder of her life). She became a young teacher with her own horse and sleigh and moved in with a fine family. Every day she would go off to a tiny school where many of the children were what was referred to back in those nonpolitically correct days as "half-breeds," half Native American and half European or Canadian.

It was a rough life, but one my mother embraced with her adventurous, can-do spirit. She was a woman who appreciated humor, had an infectious laugh, and was fiercely ambitious and driven. She had an innate passion to get somewhere in life—to become somebody—and she loved adventure. When she was just twenty-two, she used some of the money she had set aside from teaching to travel to Europe. This would not have been a typical move for a young single woman of the time, but my mother was never a typical woman.

She embarked on that trip with the desire to visit the battlegrounds and graveyards where the soldiers of World

War I had fought and been buried. I have a picture that was taken during that trip of her standing on the deck of a ship. It is a photograph that, to me, says so much about the kind of woman she was and how she raised me. It is a photo of a young woman oozing with blind ambition who believed she could do anything and was always in search of her next adventure.

Long after she returned from that trip, met and married my father, and had children, she still kept the travel trunk she had used during that trip. Inside the trunk was a little beaded dress, picture books from Europe, and a program from an operatic performance she had attended in Paris. That trip was clearly a highlight of her life, and she reveled in reminiscing about it so much that I thought, as a child, I would never hear the end of it.

My paternal grandfather, Alexander Duncan Ross, was of Scottish heritage. When he was a young man in Scotland, there were big signs posted throughout the cities that read COME TO AMERICA AND WORK. There were not a lot of good prospects for a young Scottish lad in his homeland at the time, and America was in desperate need of workers. With the promise of work and a better life, he decided to leave his country and come to America to work on the Transcontinental Railroad. There was just one problem: he wasn't a big, tough guy, by any means, which was the kind of men they were looking for to do the backbreaking work of setting railroad ties and rails into place and then hammering them together with spikes. Quickly realizing that this was work for those of a more burly constitution, he ended up becoming a jeweler—a profession far better suited for Alexander Ross, who may not have been a specimen of great physical strength but certainly cut a striking image, with his bald head and finely trimmed mustache.

His son, my father, Gordon Wright Ross, inherited his father's thin build, even thinner hair, and Scotch Presbyterian gentlemanly manners. He had served overseas as an officer in the Army Signal Corps during World War I, and when he returned home after the war, he decided to leave his family home in South Dakota and begin a new life in Canada. Buying into a parcel of Canadian wheatland, he soon thereafter met a feisty and ambitious young schoolteacher who was ten years his junior and had recently returned from an exciting adventure abroad—the aforementioned Ellen Alicia Hamilton.

I can't imagine there being anyone who knew them making whispered predictions that the electrician and wheatland owner Gordon Ross and the schoolteacher Ellen Hamilton would establish a relationship, much less get married. He was quiet—a loner—and was standoffish in social situations. She was gregarious, enjoyed interacting with people, and always managed to meet the most interesting people wherever she went. He was a conservative Republican. She was very liberal. She was always out and about and involved in various organizations. He preferred staying at home—working in the basement or remodeling rooms in the house. She was a free spirit with a wonderful sense of humor who embraced the wonders life had to offer. He, unlike his Scottish father, had hardly any sense of humor at all. He was always very serious and obsessed with exercising and seeking out all sorts of potions and elixirs to regrow his hair. She was whimsically Irish. And, while he had a beautiful singing voice and was actually quite artistic, he didn't have a dramatic bone in his body. She, on the other hand, always had a story at the ready, which she would relay with great panache, although most of them wildly exaggerated the truth, if in fact there was any truth at all to be found in them.

The biggest difference between these two polar opposites, who would go on to become my parents, was that he was content to settle in his newfound Canadian farming town, while she wanted more out of life and couldn't wait to get the hell out of that town. And yet, in spite of all the forces that should have repelled them from one another, there was an attraction that resulted in marriage and a move to Minneapolis, Minnesota.

It was the mid-1920s when the still newly wed Mr. and Mrs. Gordon Ross, now of Minneapolis, celebrated the birth of their first child, whom they named Alicia. Three years later, I came along, followed by my brother, Gordon, who was just eighteen months younger than me.

After moving to Minnesota and having children, my mother gave up her teaching career, although she always stayed active by conducting book clubs for neighborhood women, joining the local chapter of the League of Women Voters, and serving as the president of the PTA. When money and jobs got tight, especially during the early years of the war, my father did whatever he had to do to care for his family, which at one point included his acceptance of a job that took him to the Panama Canal. When he returned, he found employment at the Interstate Power & Light.

Although my parents were very different in many ways, they both considered their faith to be an important part of their lives. My father had been raised a Scotch Presbyterian, and my mother's family were Episcopalians from the Church of England, and while neither of them was religiously demonstrative, attending church was very important, especially for their children. As a child, I loved going to Sunday school and church. I was fascinated by the Episcopalian rituals: the kneeling, bowing, music, readings and the priest's ornate vestments. Those things all came together with a pageantry that had a "show business" quality I found extremely appealing, although I always kept that to myself.

Like my parents, there were also stark differences between my older sister and me. I was always very sturdy—a physically strong child who was energetic and dramatic. Alicia was more petite and slender. She was quiet, practical and serious, like my father, and tended to keep to herself, always guarded when it came to expressing her thoughts and feelings. My childhood relationship with Alicia was complicated. As much as I admired her, I also resented her. As much as I loved her, we had more than our share of fights. To me, Alicia's appearance and mannerly ways were things I saw as being lovely. She had what I perceived to be an air of distinction and sophistication, which I lacked. She looked like the movie star I secretly planned on becoming.

And as much as I may recoil at the thought, I would be far less than truthful if I didn't admit to the enjoyment I found in demonstrating my jealousy by tormenting her. She was so easy to torment, and even more so as we became young teens. Alicia's clothes were always nice and neat, while mine—both because some were hand-me-downs and because I lived a much more active outdoor lifestyle—were wrecked and torn. This resulted in my constant pillaging of her far nicer clothing and then wearing it until she caught me red-handed in something that belonged to her or she couldn't find a certain sweater or blouse and confronted me about it. I was well aware that my "borrowing" of her clothing infuriated her, which gave me the double delight of not only looking nice but also of antagonizing her.

Alicia and I also had very different views on what we found funny. I enjoyed joking around and laughing with my friends, while she tended to be aloof. She was, by all means, not a smiler. When we were kids, we would all be sitting around the dinner table and my mother would be telling one of her fanciful stories all laced with drama and humor and my father would at times be totally unappreciative of her tales and humor. "It's a joke, Daddy," I would say, begging him to understand. "It's just a joke." In her own way, Alicia also had less than an appreciation for my mother's stories. In fact, she and my mother didn't seem to understand one another much at all in any way. Whereas I was always in sync with my mother, Alicia distanced herself from her, and rarely could they find common ground on much of anything.

I knew that was the case, because from the time I was very young, I was a "watcher." Perhaps that is a somewhat typical trait for a middle child: to be watchful of how your parents and siblings interact with one another. I utilized my skills as a born watcher to get the lay of the land, so to speak, to see how certain things played out with my sister. If I saw that she got in trouble for something, then I wouldn't do that. I was seemingly full of all sorts of survival instincts and was always carefully watching how different scenarios played out. I learned a lot from watching and would then apply what I learned to the way I behaved. To a large extent, I came to realize in retrospect that I did that to garner the attention and approval I so desperately craved from my parents, especially from my father. By watching how my father negatively responded to Alicia's and Gordon's defiant refusal when he lined us up in the kitchen for teaspoons of cod liver oil, I would be almost gleefully willing to take not just my own dose but my siblings', as well. I was what you would call a "people pleaser"—a *huge* people pleaser!

Because I was healthy and strong like a boy, my father was always telling me to pick something up or to move something. I would always say, "Sure, Dad! Whatever you need, Dad!" I was obsessed with pleasing him. When he would go to the lake with me, I wanted to show him what a strong swimmer I was. I would swim out till the water was over my head and then yell back at him, "Daddy!

Look at me, Daddy! Watch me, Daddy. . . . Watch me! Please watch me, Daddy!" I just want to cry when I think back on things like that—of how desperately I craved his attention and wanted to be a "Daddy's girl," which I never was.

Was it that unrequited desire to be noticed that stimulated my secret dream to become somebody everyone would watch and admire? Well, we know what the shrinks of the world would say about that. And while, as a child, I never consciously put two and two together that it was my fervent desire for attention that sparked that secret dream, what I did know from an early age is how to "milk it."

I can remember during World War II, when I was eleven, how my parents' friends would talk about the atrocities of the war and about the young boys who were losing their lives. Inevitably, someone would say, "Oh my! Look at Marion." That was because I would be crying. Now, don't get me wrong. The stories they told were, in fact, heartbreaking and tear-inducing, but as a watcher, I knew exactly what I was doing. I knew just what I needed to do to capture their attention—to get them to look at me. I can even remember that when I was much younger— even as a toddler—I liked it when people would pick me up and say, "Oh my goodness, what a sturdy little girl you are!" I know this may sound like I'm making it up, but I literally remember being that young and being concerned if the attention I was getting wasn't all positive.

If someone picked me up, all I could think about was if I had wet pants, and if I did, I hoped beyond hope that they didn't notice. I would have been only three years old, and yet I clearly recall thinking that. It was a part of being a born watcher, I guess. I was always extremely aware that whenever someone would glance my way, pat me on the head, and say, "Isn't she cute?" it was my cue to turn it on, double down, and be cuter than ever. I always seemed to be very aware of the effect I could have on people by acting, and I was never shy about using my prodigious skills to get the attention I wanted. It always worked like a charm—except with my father, who was the one I targeted the most.

Although I never succeeded in capturing the coveted attention of my father, I was aware that he had a lot on his mind. Our nation, and the world, was at war; jobs were hard to come by; money was always scarce; and if all of that wasn't enough to divert his attention from me, the birth of my brother sealed the deal. While Alicia and I were strong and healthy children, Gordon was not. He had tuberculosis of the bone in one leg and was always in and out of the hospital and constantly in a cast or a brace. His one calf bone was soft, and when he tried to begin to walk, it bent backward. He went through an operation in which healthy bone from his other leg was placed into the diseased one to see if this could make it grow, but the operation wasn't successful.

My feelings about Gordon, like those about Alicia, were extremely mixed, but in a totally different way. On the one hand, I had tenderhearted feelings toward him and what he was going through, and yet there was also a part of me that resented him. On many occasions, I would just get sick and tired of how much attention he demanded from my parents and my sister and me. I have memories of feeling guilty about the way I felt toward Gordon. But I also remember those feelings being drained out of me as my emotional needs were completely disregarded and I was constantly being told to help Gordon do this or that, along with being enlisted to handle a variety of other chores.

While I did at times harbor resentment for Gordon, I think those feelings were really more geared toward his disease than toward him. I always felt very sorry for him and was constantly amazed that, in spite of what he went through, he developed a fairly good sense of humor. I remember when he was in his early teens, his bad leg had to be removed below the knee. They then fitted him with a wooden leg, which was difficult for him to get used to. And yet, while trying to make this prosthetic leg work, while suffering these phantom pains in the leg they removed, he would always make jokes about his situation. I recall one time, when he was a bit older and had learned to drive, that a police officer pulled him over and told him to get out of the car. He used to get us all laughing by telling us about the look he got from the officer when he told him he would be happy to comply but first had to get his leg out of the trunk. He actually got an awful lot of humorous mileage out of his wooden leg.

As I got older, into my forties and fifties, and my life and career became established, I would often find myself thinking about Gordon: what he had to deal with, how I had harbored resentment toward him, and how he managed to keep up his sense of humor in spite of his difficulties. I remember once, after being married, having children, getting divorced, becoming a successful actress and going through therapy, I had an epiphany regarding my childhood feelings toward Gordon. One day, he came over to help me paint a wall, and afterward, we sat and talked over a bottle of wine. As we talked, something just hit me, and I blurted out, "Thank God for you! If it weren't for you, I would never have become who I am! Everything I am is because of you!"

He was rather shocked by my outburst and said he certainly didn't see it that way. But I explained that I had come to realize that my desire to be someone and the way that I was able to develop the strength and the resolve to do the things I had always dreamed of doing stemmed from being so independent and having to take care of myself and my needs when I was a child.

Like me, Gordon took after my mother when it came to having a flair for the dramatic, and as an adult, he was able to secure acting roles in stage productions and television programs, such as *Renegade*; *Murder, She Wrote*; and *Trapper John, M.D.* He also landed a regular role on the daytime drama *General Hospital* in 1985 and appeared in small roles in a handful of feature films, including 1978's *Attack of the Killer Tomatoes*, 1980's *Cuba Crossing*, 1987's *Deep Space* and 1993's *The Beverly Hillbillies* (as Hank), which was the last film he did.

While he was talented, he never achieved any real success as an actor and always had difficulties that stemmed from his disability. He had a tendency to be very unrealistic in the way he approached life, and was constantly in need of help when it came to keeping his place clean and paying his bills. I think that was due to the fact that, unlike me, he had become so reliant upon others as a child.

He passed away in 1995, at the age of sixty-six, and as I've gotten older, I've found myself thinking about him more often—always with sincere fondness. He dealt with such incredible challenges throughout his entire life but was always able to laugh and make others laugh. He was a very sweet person and a very good actor.

In retrospect, I look back on my childhood as being a happy one. As I have gotten older and have thought back on my early years, I have come to terms with the fact that my parents may not have had the best marriage. But life was rough for them, as it was for so many people who lived through the Great Depression and World War II. They dealt with numerous difficulties simply to get by and to do the best they could for their children, and they remained dedicated to one another until my father died in 1960, at the age of seventy-two. I think my mother, like me, may have always held on to a secret dream of living a life in which there were no worries about money and no worries about having to care for a child with special needs. I believe she would have loved her life as a young woman to have been one in which she would travel, encounter all sorts of adventures, and then return home to host dinner parties where she would dramatically regale her guests with her adventurous tales. But I also think there was a part of her that fully embraced the life she actually lived and that she knew my father dearly loved her.

I believe that he did, and to this day, when I think about them, I have one vivid memory that is so seared into my brain, it's as if I can actually see them in front of me. There is music playing on the radio, he is holding her, and they are dancing together in our little living room. That is the way I choose to remember my parents. And I think they would both be more than fine with that.

Chapter 3

My Inspirations

We didn't have a television when I was growing up. That was not unusual. Very few families in our neighborhood did. What we did have was *Theatre Arts Magazine* and movie magazines, all of which I was obsessed with, a radio, a local movie theater and a library. It was within those entities that I escaped both to dream about my future and learn how to go about getting there—how to launch the career I was so thoroughly assured was my destiny. Every time I made my way to the Carnegie Library and climbed its granite steps, I was on a mission to find out everything I could about how famous actors and actresses had established their careers.

My greatest source for this information was these big *Who's Who* books, which gave me insight into all sorts of famous people. And while I found it interesting to learn where these people were born and what they had accomplished in their lives, the information I was desperately seeking was what happened in between their births and their accomplishments. How did they get to where they were?

At times, the search for this information took on a sense of panicked urgency. It was my destiny to live out my secret dream, and yet I had no real idea of how to go about it or what I should be doing in that very moment. That sense of urgency to start making things happen hit a crescendo when I went to a local stage production of Noël Coward's *Blithe Spirit* and then read his first autobiography, *Present Indicative*. Coward, I learned, had appeared in concert with choirs, had studied dance, and was performing professionally on the stages of London's West End by the time he was twelve years old. This hit me hard, because I was already thirteen and had done nothing.

If anyone at the Carnegie Library noticed me poring over books that detailed the early lives of Coward or Helen Hayes or Katharine Cornell, I'm sure I just looked like any other studious young lady. What they didn't perceive was that, as I turned each page, my heart would race faster, my breath would become shallow, and my stomach would begin to churn. "Here I am, thirteen years old, and I've done nothing," I would quietly agonize to myself. "I'm not getting anywhere!"

Unlike many young girls who go on to become actresses, I was never a performing child. I never took dancing lessons or put on little shows for my family and friends. I was, by no means, the center of attention in my home. That would have never been possible, because my brother needed every bit of the attention my parents had to give. It is also interesting to me, when I think back on how obsessed I was with my secret dream to act, that I never thought of acting in films, on radio, and certainly not on television. My dream was always to act onstage.

The reason I find that a bit peculiar is that it was the performers on radio and in film whom I listened to and went to see who were my inspirations. Radio was a really big part of our lives, and my favorite show was *I Love a Mystery*, which was about three detectives who traveled all over the world. I also loved *LUX Radio Theatre*, which was an anthology series that adapted Broadway plays and Hollywood films and was sponsored by Lever Brothers, who made LUX soap and detergent. These programs were performed before a live studio audience, hosted by the great film director Cecil B. DeMille, and featured stars such as Marlene Dietrich, Clark Gable, Myrna Loy and William Powell.

While I never gave any thought to radio as being a venue in which I hoped to someday perform, *LUX Radio Theatre* would, ironically, provide one of my first through-the-looking-glass moments, as when I was in my early twenties and under contract with Paramount Pictures, I was cast as a LUX Girl in a commercial for *LUX Radio Theatre*. Doing that commercial also provided me with my first residual reward, not in the way of money, but in boxes of LUX soap, which would arrive in the mail for years to come—long after my days as a LUX Girl were over. Between the arrivals of those sudsy gifts, I wouldn't give them any thought, and then another one would show up. I can't tell you how many times I saw a package being delivered and imagined that some secret suitor was sending me chocolates, only to rip it open and find another box of LUX soap.

Along with radio, I found my inspiration on the big screen. One of those who inspired me and—along with Noël Coward—had me losing sleep over how I was doing nothing to forward my dream was Shirley Temple. Because we didn't have a television, the Shirley Temple movies were my first introduction to entertainment and acting, and I was fascinated with her. Not only did I see her on the big screen, but Shirley was also, in a way, a part of our family's everyday life for many years during the Depression. My parents were in no financial shape to be able to give us expensive toys, but we were the proud owners of the grandest and most beautiful Shirley Temple doll ever made.

Our ownership of the Shirley doll stemmed from a rash of colds that had Alicia, Gordon and me all sniffling, sneezing and coughing. My father had been sent out on a mission to buy some cough medicine at the local drugstore. While there, he noticed they were running some sort of raffle in which the grand prize was this magnificent Shirley Temple doll. Knowing I was a big fan of Shirley's, he purchased a little key, which was then used to see if it would unlock the box the doll was in. And, by golly, he had bought the winning key! Along with causing quite the initial commotion when he returned home with the story and the physical reward of his win, that doll went on to become both a fixture in our home and a constant reminder to me that time was passing by without my having even taken my first step toward establishing my acting career. That reminder took on a more frantic concern that could be summed up with one thought: Shirley, who had been acting since she was three years old, who by the age of seven was an established star, and who had even been awarded a special Juvenile Academy Award, was only six months older than me!

Ironically, in a twist that was, on one hand, a part of my secret dream and, on the other, another surreal through-the-looking-glass experience, many years later I would actually meet Shirley Temple—and she would know who I was!

We crossed paths on New Year's Day of 1999 at the Tournament of Roses Parade in Pasadena. Shirley was serving as the grand marshal, and I was there to ride on a float that featured a few of the iconic mothers from famous television shows. I remember being at the Tournament House, a grand white mansion on Orange Grove Boulevard that once belonged to the Wrigley family, of chewing gum fame, and is now the headquarters of the Tournament of Roses. It was very early in the morning, before the parade began, and someone asked me if I would like to meet Shirley. I will openly admit to being a bit flustered, if not outright overcome with emotion, as I thought back to watching her on the big screen and sharing our home with a doll of her when I was a child. But yes, of course I wanted to meet her!

So I was led over to where she was standing. I was nervous and had a huge grin plastered on my face as we were introduced. I then opened my arms to embrace her in a hug, and she abruptly stepped back from me and said, "No, no! Don't mess me up!"

In that split second I felt my entire body go into a free fall, as if all my blood had drained out of me and I was in a falling elevator. I wasn't expecting that sort of a reaction from her, and it sent me off-kilter in a big way. Whatever happened in the few moments that followed, I can't say I really remember. But I do recall thinking, *Oh, of course! This poor woman has been pawed by people her entire life, and she has her hair all done up, and, and . . .* But I stepped away from her and just wanted to cry.

A short time later, my press agent, Dale Olson, saved the day. He was talking to Shirley, and she motioned toward me and asked, "Is that the woman who played the mother on *Happy Days*?" He confirmed that I was indeed that woman, which resulted in a "do over" in which I did get the chance to meet her and was totally awed that she knew who I was. As I stood there with her, the memories of watching her on the screen and of the face of that old doll flooded my mind. I thought of my father and the incredulous look he would have flashed if, when he returned home with that doll, someone had told him that many years in the future his daughter would meet Shirley Temple and that Shirley would know who his daughter was!

I have often thought it was interesting that, while it was by seeing Shirley Temple on the screen that my secret dream first bubbled up and formed, I never imagined myself acting in movies, and certainly not in television, but rather on the stage. And it was, in fact, the stage on which I made my debut as an actress—as Tom Sawyer's aunt Polly in a seventh-grade production of *The Adventures of Tom Sawyer*.

Getting a role in that play was, I'm sure, of far greater importance to me than it was to my classmates. For me, it was the beginning of what would become a life as an actress appearing on the stages of the theaters of Broadway. For my classmates, it was just another school-related activity, no different than playing a game or doing an art or science project. In fact, because of the nature of the play, with its costumes and props, many of my fellow "actors" simply saw it as an opportunity to goof around and have fun. That annoyed me—*really* annoyed me! For me, establishing my character—bringing a depth to my portrayal of Polly—was serious business. For others, it was simply a time to fool around.

As our rehearsals led to a performance, I just couldn't bear the fact that we were about to bring our audience a production that was far beneath the standard I had imagined for it. I hated the fact that all the other kids had approached this play in such a cavalier fashion. It truly hurt me, and I became obsessed with the thought that our production was not good enough. I didn't want any of my family to come and see it, because it wasn't good enough, I wasn't good enough, and the whole play just wasn't good enough! Ultimately, the show did go on, leaving me with a memory of my stage debut as one of profound disappointment. From that moment on, I knew that to make my secret dream a reality, I would have to make a move—to step out of the comfort of my family home and my life in Albert Lea.

Chapter 4

My Secret Becomes Known

As the summer of 1944 approached, I was finishing the tenth grade. I had been devouring *Theatre Arts Magazine* for years and, with my high school days being half over, had taken a special interest in the advertisements for drama and acting schools in the East, one of which I hoped to attend after graduating.

Then, one day, while poring over an issue of *Theatre Arts Magazine*, I came across an ad that riveted my attention to the page. My eyes became affixed to this one ad for the MacPhail School of Music and Dramatic Art. My heart began beating faster as I kept looking at the school's address over and over to make sure I was seeing it right. The MacPhail School wasn't in that faraway wonderland of New York. It was just one hundred miles from Albert Lea, in Minneapolis. From that moment on, what had been my closely kept secret for so many years became known to anyone who spent more than a minute in my presence. All I could think and talk about was studying drama in Minneapolis.

With my secret now exposed, the idea that my dream

was soon to become a reality consumed my thoughts. I felt assured of myself in a much stronger way than ever before, and the writing in my diary took on a bolder and more forceful look and attitude. "When I become a great actress—and I will—I will act in theatres [and will] have all the people in the world clamoring to talk to me and gush over me," I wrote. "I shall be so talented, I'll be another Noël Coward—but I've got to hurry and get started on my career, or it will be too late."

Realizing how very serious I was about studying drama and pursuing a career as an actress, my mother was very supportive. We contacted the MacPhail School, received all the information on the various courses they offered, and decided I would enroll in a summer program. We also worked out a plan that would have me work for a family that lived in the affluent Minneapolis suburb of Edina, mostly taking care of their children, in exchange for a small stipend, room and board. And so, fortified by my dogged determination and the ten dollars a month my mother agreed to supplement me with, I left the cocoon of my family, friends and Albert Lea to begin my transformation into the "great actress" I believed I was destined to become.

Each morning I would take a streetcar from Edina to downtown Minneapolis, where at MacPhail, I studied Shakespeare, poetry and elocution. During this time, I also read every play I could find and started taking some private classes with an elderly lady, who would have me recite poetry and lines from various plays. As that summer came to a close, my feelings were rather mixed. On the one hand, I felt I was moving forward by learning things that would be beneficial to my career, and yet I also felt very lonesome and homesick for my family and friends. While a part of me wanted to return to Albert Lea and resume my life as an eleventh-grade student, another part of me felt that it would be a huge step backward. Back in Albert Lea, I would have the familiarity of my home, family and friends, but I would have no opportunity to continue private drama classes.

After discussing these things with my mother, who continued to be incredibly supportive, we decided it would be best for me to stay in Minneapolis. The family I was working for was very happy about that decision. With the school year beginning, my help with their children would be needed as much, if not more, than it was during the summer. And so I enrolled in Minneapolis's Southwest High School, with plans to continue taking private drama lessons.

As a new student who came into a school in which most of the kids had known their classmates for years, and some even since elementary school, I never felt that I totally fit in. Southwest High had a student body composed of the children of many successful Minneapolitans, and I learned from my very first day that, unlike the kids I had attended school with in Albert Lea, my new classmates were accustomed to what my mother called a "spiffy" lifestyle. That was most evident in the clothing they wore, which was far spiffier than my wardrobe, which consisted mostly of simple, if not downright drab, Peter Pan–collared dresses.

While I never quite felt that I fit in at Southwest High, it didn't really bother me. In fact, I sort of privately reveled in being an outsider of sorts. Most of the Southwest High girls, I guess, would have been horrified if their clothing was not up to par with their classmates' or if, when they weren't at school, they had to take care of children or do chores in a home other than their own. That wasn't the case with me. I wasn't caring for children or attending Southwest High in Minneapolis for any other reason than it was a career stepping-stone. Sure, I knew I couldn't compete with the spiffy girls, but it wasn't them I ever cared to impress. My dream, which by that time had become my blind ambition, was to prepare myself for the future spiffiness I would be adorned in to impress those I really wanted to impress—theatrical agents, casting directors and producers.

And so I reveled in what I embraced as my "paying my dues" days—suffering with the loneliness and heartache that come with striving toward one's art, one's destiny. During that time, I became even more obsessed with reading plays, especially those by Henrik Ibsen and George Bernard Shaw, and on my focused drive to become an actress. While my drive was stronger than ever, my understanding of how things worked was still a bit shaky. In fact, it was very shaky. I was aware that the University of Minnesota's theater department staged plays, and so one day, after giving it some thought, I made my way over to the university campus, found out where the theater department was located, breezed in the door with a flair that said, "Here I am, Minneapolis's newest actress," and innocently asked how I would go about auditioning for one of their upcoming plays.

Today I shudder (and also laugh) when I recall the perplexed looks I got from the two or three people I was passed on to before one confused woman explained, as if the information was being imparted to someone from another planet, that I would have to be a student in the university's theater program to get cast in a show. I also recall exiting with the same exact flair with which I had entered the theater department, undeterred by the information I had been given and, in a way, happy about it, because the campus, located across the Mississippi River from Minneapolis, was too far of a journey to make regularly, anyway.

And so, along with my work, school and ravenous consumption of play scripts, I continued to explore what was available in private drama instruction—a business, I came to believe, that was completely dominated by extremely elderly women who were in varying stages of poor health and who lived in rather shabby dwellings. I especially remember one very old woman I studied with who lived in a hotel and whose eyes were clouded by blue cataracts. In order to reach her floor, I had to take a creaky old cage elevator—something I remember as being a tad bit scary, but also as just another spoke in the wheel of what a suffering artist must do to pay their dues.

I can still recall sitting with her on the edge of her lumpy bed, reciting poems. She would listen to me for a few lines and then abruptly stop me. "No! No!" she would say in what I felt was a rather contrived and over-the-top dramatic voice. "You can't speak the way you do!"

At first I had no idea what she meant, but then she pointed out something that up to that point in my life, I was not at all aware of: I had a Minnesota accent! *Oooo yaaa, yooo knooo.* I had that classic vowel-extending way of pronouncing words with a hard *r* and a Scandinavian-cum-Midwestern twist, which, years later, would become fodder for laughs at Garrison Keillor's radio program *A Prairie Home Companion* and at the films *Fargo* and *Drop Dead Gorgeous.*

So we dealt with correcting my accent, and when that was taken care of, she would say, "No! No! You can't breathe like that!" So between the way I talked and breathed, there were times I became so self-conscious around her, I could hardly talk or breathe at all. But her training proved to be very helpful, and I recall my time with her as being charming and magical. She would have me recite poetry, utilizing the breathing and elocution skills she taught.

What at first seemed a contrived way of speaking became more natural as I practiced lines from Alfred Tennyson's "The Lady of Shalott." "On either side the river lie. Long fields of barley and of rye," I would say, paying attention to the way I pronounced each word. And, just as with the first elderly woman I studied with, I would jot down notes and then review them over and over.

Sadly, I don't remember the name of either of those women. And yet both of them, especially the one who lived in the hotel, played significant roles in preparing me for what would very soon be a life-changing experience.

Chapter 5

My New Life in California

After experiencing my first taste of independence, living in a big city, and being exposed to those around, if not actually "in," the theatrical world, I knew it would be difficult to return to my life in Albert Lea. I loved my little hometown and all the wonderful childhood and early teen experiences it had given me, but I knew I would never be able to go back there to resume the life I once had.

Realizing my return home was imminent, I knew it would be difficult to pick up from where I had left off, and the thought of having to complete my senior year of high school was one that hovered over me like a dark cloud. *I just can't do this!* I would think to myself. *I have left that little cocoon, spread my newly formed wings, and taken my first steps toward establishing my career. I just can't take a step backward.*

And then, just as the clouds seemed to be at their darkest, a blaze of sunshine smacked the darkness away. That bright light of hope came in an announcement from my parents: my father's work as an electrician would be taking our family to San Diego, California!

My head swirled as I processed that information, and in what seemed to be a rapid blur, I said good-bye to the family I had been working for, returned to Albert Lea to help my family sell everything we owned (perhaps even our Shirley Temple doll, as I have no recollection of her after that time), and boarded a train for the two-thousand-mile journey to our new life.

While I was excited about moving to California, there was a little part of me that harbored disappointment. As it was, Albert Lea was over a thousand miles from New York's Theater District, and now living in San Diego would mean that I would be just about as far as you can get from Broadway while still being within the forty-eight contiguous states. Ironically, the one thing I never gave any thought to was the fact that less than two hundred miles north was the destination point for actors from around the world. I know that seems odd—that I wasn't totally thrilled out of my mind to be living just a few hours from Hollywood—but it just wasn't the place that held my head, heart and determination. The Hollywood-based film industry was, by all means, a place I was well aware of, but it had never been the destination point for my dream. To me, it was the streets of New York's Times Square, Broadway and the stages of its theaters that had been indelibly burned into my brain as my destiny. And yet there was an element of excitement bubbling up inside of me as we sped along the railroad tracks that, with every mile, introduced me to yet another part of the country I had never seen.

That excitement would be short lived.

If, in fact, I had any preconceived notions about what life in Southern California would be like—swaying palm trees and magnificent mansions on bluffs overlooking the sparkling blue Pacific Ocean—those were a far cry from what I found. My father was working on electrical generators for the military, and as a part of his compensation, we were provided with housing—military housing! Now, it wasn't like we came from any sort of spiffy lifestyle in Albert Lea, but to be honest, this was a step down that I didn't expect. I was terribly disappointed to find that our new "home" was in a row of dreary, nondescript cookie-cutter buildings—barracks, really—behind an old decaying theater on Rosecrans Street.

If my first impressions of our new life were far beneath my expectations (and they were!), they only got worse as time went by. I could hardly bear the way we were living and found myself pining, in much the same way as I had in the basement of our home in Albert Lea, for a better life. *Nothing is ever good enough for me in my life*, I remember thinking over and over during that time. *There just has to be more to life than living in these dreadful barracks!*

While I found our living arrangements maddening, eventually things began looking up a bit. I would go to the nearby movie theater and see films with stars like Ingrid Bergman, whom I so wanted to be like. I would also venture out to places like Point Loma, and when I was home, I continued to read scripts and memorize various Shakespearean monologues.

As it turned out, it was by memorizing monologues and scenes, especially my favorites, those involving the characters of Viola and Olivia from Shakespeare's *Twelfth Night*, that I garnered the type of attention I craved during my senior year at Point Loma High School. I remember once, in my drama class, reciting a scene in which I played both Viola and Olivia and just dazzling the class. The thing I recall most about that was when I finished, I heard a classmate say, "My God, I'm the star in this class, and now this girl comes in here and takes it away from me!"

For the first time, I realized that my years of reading plays, learning everything I could about the craft of acting, and working with Minneapolis drama coaches were beginning to pay off. I became extremely aware that I had both an understanding and an ability, both natural and learned, that made me stand out from the others in my drama class. I may not have been thrilled with life in San Diego, but I was exceptionally happy that my plan—the plan I had conceived to make my secret become a reality— was starting to fall into place.

I was no great student during my senior year of high school, but the confidence I gained in my drama class prompted me to be more "showy" than I had ever been before. And while I also became more emotional and self-absorbed than the "me" of Albert Lea or Minneapolis, that sort of paid off. I was perceived as being dramatic, theatrical, and was always being tapped to make a presentation or speech—even at my graduation.

In the weeks leading up to my graduation, with my secret to become a famous actress now fully out in the open, and my plan to make that happen coming together, I dreamed grand dreams of continuing my dramatic studies at Stanford University and then going on to New York to begin my life on the stage. There was only one hitch. Two, really. I had no money and, besides drama, had not been a good enough student to qualify for any sort of scholarship. After I rather quickly came to terms with the fact that I would not be further honing my dramatic talents on the campus of northern Santa Clara Valley's Stanford University, it was decided that I would instead enroll in San Diego State University and study drama.

The middle years of the 1940s, with World War II and the Great Depression in everyone's rearview mirror, were a time when a certain feeling of optimism began creeping into the minds and souls of Americans. Things were by no means rosy, what with the shortages of jobs and housing for soldiers returning from the war, but the promise that better times were right around the corner was palpable as a flux of marriages resulted in the beginning of the baby boom.

The San Diego State University of which I became a student had a total enrollment of around four thousand, a far cry from the forty thousand of today. We were still living in those dreadful barracks, and without a car, the mode of transportation I most often employed to get back and forth between home and school was hitchhiking. While no young woman in her early twenties with an ounce of sense would dare "thumb a ride" in today's world, back in those more innocent days of yore, hitchhiking was a common and totally acceptable practice, equivalent to catching a trolley that was going your way. I never once had a concern about accepting the kindness of strangers who graciously took me on that eight- or nine-mile ride to school or home. In fact, the only vivid recollection I have of my ride-hitching days is a conversation I had with a man who asked me what I was studying in school and then seemed a bit confused when I told him I was with the theater department, preparing to become an actress.

"So, you want to be an actress?" I remember him questioning me with seriousness. "Isn't that a very hard profession to break into?"

"Yes," I recall telling him. "Very hard. And I just don't know what is ever going to happen to the poor others who are trying to make it."

While some, if not most, of those "poor others" seemed to apply themselves and take school seriously, I had little care about majors or minors, or dances or dating, or anything else other than having the chance to perform in plays. During my time in college, I was very independent. I was more determined than ever that I was going to see my secret dream become a reality—that I was going to be someone—and that this was the path that would lead me there. That was my focus.

I never thought of myself as being a loner, but during my time in college, I was a lone wolf. I did have a small group of friends, but perhaps even they felt the way students who didn't know me felt: that I was aloof. If they did think that, I can't say I ever gave any thought or concern to it. Unlike my fellow students, I didn't have any close friends whom I did everything with. I didn't go to the dances or other social events. I wasn't popular and certainly wasn't a member of any clique. Was that by design—a part of my plan? Again, it wasn't something I gave much thought to, and when I think back, I believe had I been more of a social butterfly, I would not have been so focused on and driven about achieving my goal.

When I wasn't at school or at home, I would hang around the Old Globe Theatre in Balboa Park, which had been built in 1935 as a tribute to Shakespeare's Old Globe in London for the California Pacific International Exposition. At the conclusion of the exposition in 1937, the San Diego Community Theatre leased the Old Globe from the City of San Diego and renovated the theater. I loved everything about being in and around the Old Globe and made it a point to get to know many of the people who worked there.

During that time, I also found a few drama coaches (again, all rather eccentric little old ladies) for specific studies, was appearing in plays at school, and was constantly checking the *Green Sheet*, a local publication that listed the auditions being held at the theater groups in the area, such as the La Jolla Players, the La Mesa Players, the Lamb's Players and about five or six others. I was constantly going on auditions and got the role of an old lady with a Scottish accent in *The Old Lady Shows Her Medals*, by J. M. Barrie, for which I won my first acting award—an ashtray or some sort of coaster. To be honest, I could never really tell what it was, but I was proud of it—proud to be acknowledged for my work—and I still have it to this day. Soon after winning that first award, I was also the recipient of another, for my appearance in the La Jolla Players' production of Chekhov's *A Marriage Proposal*.

I garnered attention both in auditions and performances by being good at accents, of which I did quite a few, thanks to the training of all those little old lady coaches. Because I could do accents well, I was cast in another Barrie play, *What Every Woman Knows*, and in George Bernard Shaw's *Pygmalion*, in which I got to show off my cockney English accent.

My proficiency with the cockney accent also landed me a role as a young English maid at the Old Globe. It would be the start of what would become my long-term association with the Old Globe and playing maids. While at school, students from our drama department would work with actors from the Globe, doing scenes and plays, and when I heard they were doing Shakespeare's *Twelfth Night*, I was determined to get the role of Viola. That, sadly, didn't happen. I simply didn't have the legs for the part of the play's heroine and protagonist. And so, while some other girl, one blessed with long-legged attributes, was given the role, I did get a consolation prize and was cast as Olivia, the wealthy lady of noble birth who lives in Illyria.

My four years of study at San Diego State, augmented by the many auditions I had gone on, the roles I had been cast for, and the accolades I had received for my performances, provided me with both the assurance and confidence I would need to step out into the real world in pursuit of my "career," a word I had begun using instead of "dream" during my final year of school.

As my time at San Diego State wound toward completion, America, and most of the world, had recovered from World War II. The Cold War between the United States

and the Soviet Union began simmering, and the war between Communists and capitalists was coming to a rolling
boil.

As for me, 1950 would prove to be an important milestone. One evening shortly before finishing school, as I recall, I was having dinner with my parents at home when
the conversation turned to my future plans. By this time,
the pursuit of my dream had become the pursuit of a career, and for the first time, the evening's discussion took on
an air of seriousness and pragmatism.

"How will you support yourself?" my father asked.

"I won't need much," I recall telling him.

I knew it would be rough, and perhaps even rougher
than I let on to them. But that meant little or nothing to
me. I would soon be stepping out on the stage of life as a
fiercely determined young woman with a degree in drama
and even a little teaching credential I could always fall
back on (although falling back was something I never gave
a lick of thought to). I was certainly aware that life on my
own—really on my own—might come with some challenges. I remember thinking about the evening my parents
and I discussed my future.

*Who are my parents to question my enduring spirit in
the face of challenges?* I thought. They had certainly had
to deal with challenges of their own. My father had to
leave us to work in Panama. My mother, who had been a
credentialed teacher in Canada, had difficulties getting her
teaching credentials in the United States. She was always
taking classes to better herself, and when we first came to
California, she got a job teaching on an Indian reservation
in East San Diego. The reservation was a fairly long drive
from our home, and because of that, she had to live away
from us for a while. I remember her saying that it was a
horrible job and that she hated being away from her family, but it was one of the steps she had to take to get her
U.S. teaching credentials.

Once she did receive her teaching credentials, she got a job at a little grammar school in Rancho Santa Fe, an exclusive area of San Diego inhabited by those of the "spiffy" class. She ultimately worked her way up, gained the respect of her colleagues and the parents of her students, and was given the opportunity to serve as the school's principal. I always felt that she enjoyed that job, although it did present its share of difficulties, as she had to deal with those wealthy, spoiled kids and their even more spoiled mothers. I knew it was hard for her at times, and yet she had a unique ability to rise above the problems and personalities, and those rich folks from "the Ranch," as it is known, loved her.

I was impressed with my parents' ability to rise up and face down anything that got in their way. It was a trait that had clearly been instilled in them by their parents and grandparents. And so, with the DNA of dogged determination coursing through my body, and with a 1950 diploma from San Diego State University to boot (I was actually a few credits short but would quickly remedy that), I knew the time had come to become somebody—to fulfill my childhood dream and to make my career a reality.

Chapter 6

My Marriage

Throughout my time at San Diego State, I was determined that romance would not get in the way of my plan. During my senior year, I continued to appear in local theater, where I received a lot of support for my efforts and encouragement to venture up the San Diego Freeway or, as Californians call it, the 405, to seek film work in Hollywood.

While working in the motion picture industry was never really a part of my plan, I figured it could be a good way to capture the attention of Broadway producers, and so I started giving serious thought to introducing myself to Hollywood filmmakers. That encouragement-turned-thought soon transitioned into a plan, one that was interrupted by a force I had sworn I would never allow to interrupt me: romance!

That dreaded but oh, so alluring force of romance was made manifest in my life by a handsome young actor named Freeman "Effie" Meskimen.

I had actually met Effie somewhere around 1948 or 1949, when we were cast together in a local production of

Liliom, the Ferenc Molnár play that became the inspiration for the Rodgers and Hammerstein musical *Carousel*. Effie was cast in the lead role of Liliom, a tough, cocky carousel barker who falls in love with a young maid named Julie, played by yours truly. During the run of that show, I began harboring the second great secret of my life, one that was so secret I myself wasn't sure about it: that I was falling in love with Effie.

While I constantly tried to push that thought out of my mind, knowing it could have serious repercussions on my career, it kept oozing back in, as love tends to do. *Damn you, Freeman Meskimen*, I would think to myself during my final months of school. *Here I am, soon to have my drama degree in hand, and on my way to Broadway via Hollywood to fulfill the destiny of my first secret. The last thing I need is to allow myself—my drive and ambition— to be diverted by romance!* And yet within moments of having that thought, my mind would do a complete turnaround, and I'd slip off into thinking of the very sexy, handsome and moody Effie.

I've always had a bit of a moody streak. Because of my awareness of that, I was, perhaps, more attuned and attracted to that quality in others—and Effie had moodiness in spades, which I loved.

Effie was two years older than me and had been raised in Texas by a Scotch-Irish farm family. He didn't grow up in an environment that promoted education, and certainly not the arts, but Effie was very different from his family. He was extremely sensitive and would play his guitar and sing folk songs. He loved reading poetry and Shakespeare and books of all sorts to expand his horizons. And he had an air of moody vulnerability that worked well for him as an actor. He had served in the U.S. Navy during the war, which was something I could never really imagine. In San

Diego the naval base and its training facilities had been crucial to the American mission during World War II, and sailors were a part of the fabric of the area. Whenever I had encountered sailors back then, they always appeared to be a tad bit crude and exuded bravado, worldliness and confidence—traits you couldn't find in Effie with a microscope.

For all the sexy moodiness and sensitivity Effie naturally possessed, he had clearly missed the line when bravery was being handed out. Not only wasn't he brave and bold like all the sailors I had encountered, but he also wasn't even brave and bold like me! That never bothered me. In fact, it was just another quality that endeared him to me. I have always liked to inspire people, and I liked to rely on my own sense of courage, confidence and bravery to inspire him.

He was one of those kinds of guys who didn't like a lot of things, while I loved everything. As I look back, I think our love grew because he admired my ability to be playful and confident in every way and place except for the bedroom. I had not dated much during high school or even at college, so I was both uneducated and unsophisticated when it came to sex. I would rely on my playfulness to overcome that, and at times, right in the middle of the romance, I would say, "I don't love you, Effie Meskimen!"

He would laugh and say, "Yes you do, and we're going to go get married!"

One time after I expressed my denial of love for him, Effie's response included a coda he had never used before. "Yes you do, and we're going to go get married . . . *right now!*"

Those last two words are, perhaps, the most dangerous ones that can ever be uttered by someone who is usually not so confidently and decisively forceful to someone who is courageous, bold and playful. They are words that can prompt a naïve twenty-one-year-old woman with a love of the dramatic to grab the hand of her moody twenty-three-year-old lover and, in the middle of the night, drive from San Diego to Yuma, Arizona, to elope—which is what we did.

It was all so exciting and delightfully dramatic, although it was also all just an unreal blur. I can't recall much more about the actual ceremony other than I was wearing a little tuxedo shirt and a plaid skirt, and I have hardly any memory of our drive back to San Diego as a newly wedded couple. What I do recall is spending our wedding night in Pacific Beach, where we strolled out to the end of the Crystal Pier and then stayed in a little motel.

As for our honeymoon, we got up the next morning, checked out of the motel, and began looking for a place to live. We found a room to rent near the college, and how we came up with the money for it, I'll never know. Because of his navy service, Effie had a GI Bill, which provided educational assistance to service members, veterans and their dependents, but it wasn't much, and as for me, I had no money at all.

It was all so childlike. We had just gone off on a whim and gotten married, had a little place to live, and were off to become actors. We didn't have anything except for some plates and silverware we had received as gifts from my college friends, who were shocked and amazed that we had actually gotten married. But I remember we both seemed to be relatively content and happy in our own little naïve way—which was in stark contrast to the way my parents handled it. While I can't say that either Effie or I gave our impromptu marriage much thought, the same was not true for my parents, who, upon our return from Arizona, were devastated over the news of our less than well-thought-out nuptials.

"God damn you!" my mother seethed as my father quietly cried. "What were you thinking?" she continued, with daggers flying out of her eyes.

Although I found my parents' reaction to our marriage surprising, in retrospect, I understand it. They never saw it coming. I had never admitted to anybody that I even liked, much less loved, Effie, or anyone else. From the time I was a young girl, I had always thought and would gleefully proclaim that I was going to marry someone very important—a status no one would attribute to the man who was now my husband.

As the days and weeks following our marriage went by, my mother's anger dissipated into disappointment. However, she eventually came around to accepting that I was now a married woman, and even became helpful and encouraging. But she was never happy about it. She knew that a marriage can be the greatest interference to someone pursuing a career—especially one that demands the kind of focused determination that acting requires. I'm sure her anger and displeasure came from thinking that her daughter's dream had been intercepted by some Texas farm boy just as the brass ring was coming into view. And yet at the time, I felt her reaction to the situation was rather over the top, and being young, naïve and terribly dramatic, I rather reveled in the drama of it all (although I was smart enough to never let her know that).

In a way, it pains me to say this, but I think the truth is that I entered into my spur-of-the-moment marriage with Effie in such a cavalier fashion simply because it was a fun and adventurous thing to do. I also do believe that the dramatic aspect of it had a great appeal to me. While my mother lost many a night's sleep wondering how I would move forward with my life and career, I gave that little thought. Did I love Effie? Yes, I did. But I believe that I viewed my marriage to him in much the same way I looked at doing a play—enjoying the run and then looking forward to what was next. I never felt my determination to pursue my career had been jeopardized by marrying Effie, although I can't say I ever really gave much thought to the role he would play in my life as I moved forward.

Chapter 7

My Move to Hollywood

In the days and weeks following my marriage, I didn't think of myself as much as a newlywed as I did a student who still needed to finish up a couple of college courses. I had no money, which meant I was doing only a bit worse than Effie, who was also finishing up his studies and had what little financial benefit he received from the GI Bill.

Around that time, I formulated what I began calling my "five-year plan"—a strategy to transform myself from a young woman with a college degree in theater into an established and successful actress. Those were the only two roles in which I ever saw myself. My real-life role of being someone's wife was never one that was either a part of my plan or one I saw myself playing. And yet, as the decade of the 1950s dawned, that is what I was.

Was my marriage to Effie a conventional one, predicated on true love, the building of a life and family, and the thought of growing old together, to end only when death did us part? Not hardly. I did love him and care for him, but as I have said, entering into the state of matrimony was akin to playing a part. I never gave it one iota of the serious consideration I did to my career plan.

As the months went by, I found that my expectations of what married life would be like (if, in fact, I even had such expectations) were low—very low. My husband was a dear, sweet fellow, but one with what seemed to be a total lack of focus and ambition. I did love him, but it was a love that saw me caring for him more maternally than matrimonially. I was always trying to motivate him and encourage him, but for the most part, I seemed to always be worrying about him. At times, there would be a brief flash in which he showed me that he had the potential to become focused on doing something and becoming something. He could be very convincing in short spurts that something was going to happen. And I was always willing to buy into it and thought something was going to happen, too, but it never did.

Effie's moments of motivation were always short lived, often painfully short. His moodiness was becoming more than a temporary state and, instead, the dominating feature of his personality. He was depressed and developed an ulcer early in our marriage. He also had another problem, which, to me at the time, went without notice or concern: his drinking. It was only many years later, when I became better educated on the adverse effects of alcohol, that I came to believe that Effie had been an alcoholic from the time he was very young—by the time he left the navy.

I didn't come from a family of drinkers. They weren't Puritans, but they were Scotch Presbyterians. My father had a strong work ethic. He was a Mason, and my mom was in the Eastern Star, was a PTA president, and was always active with the League of Women Voters and her book clubs. She was also a caring wife and mother, whose pot roast, to this day, remains one of my favorite dishes. Holidays at our house weren't great, because those were the Depression years, but they were happy family times in which alcohol played no role. Our family may not have been the role model for *Father Knows Best*, but we did shun vices and embrace morality. Because of that, I was never around anyone whose life was impacted by alcohol and its abuse. As I got older, went to college, and then married Effie, I became aware that, unlike the family I grew up in, alcohol was a regular part of many people's lives.

In the early 1950s, drinking was simply a part of the culture. Even the image of the hardworking husband and father of the era was a man who would have lunchtime cocktails with his business associates and then be welcomed home with a pitcher of freshly mixed martinis and an after-dinner Scotch. Just as they smoked cigarettes, everyone seemed to drink at that time. Everyone but me, that is. I didn't drink, but it didn't bother me, because it was such an accepted part of what seemingly was the all-American lifestyle.

Because the use of alcohol was so prevalent, I never gave any thought to the fact that Effie drank a lot every day. When I think back on the early years of our life together, he was always moody and often didn't feel well. He would wake in the morning with a bad headache, go through periods of depression and, with the exception of those rare moments of motivation (usually fueled by alcohol), had no real plan for achieving any sort of career goals. He was very likely an alcoholic at the time, but I was totally unaware that such a problem existed. To our friends and others he interacted with, he acted like a tough guy, but he wasn't one—at all.

He and I were polar opposites when it came to career motivation, but that was all right with me. I was totally driven and worked so hard at finding work, pursuing roles anywhere I could find them. But Effie, while he talked about being an actor, did nothing to find work. He would always say he didn't feel like looking for work, and I thought that was fine. I liked being with this sensitive and brooding guy who some thought was a big, tough bad boy, and so for the most part, I just thought it was adorable when he said he didn't "feel like" doing this or that.

When I think back on this time, I can't for the life of me remember how exactly we thought we would manage to live or eat. It just wasn't anything that was important to me. Yes, I was a newly married young woman, but the idea of being a "wife" occupied as little thought as I gave to my impromptu trip to Yuma during which I became a wife. The only thing that occupied my mind was that I had to complete my courses and get on with my career. That was when I started to think I should go to Los Angeles. My plan was to enroll in the University of California, Los Angeles, in order to finish school, and to live in a dorm with a bunch of girls.

My decision to go to Los Angeles was bolstered by Rosa Choplin, a Spanish teacher at San Diego State who had Hollywood connections that included Tyrone Power's manager. I barely knew Rosa, but Effie had been one of her students, and she had seen me in many plays and, for some reason, believed in me. Rosa knew I was thinking of finishing my classes at UCLA, and one day she called to tell me that she was going to take me to Los Angeles on the train and that we were going to be visiting with her connections at 20th Century Fox studios. Which is just what we did.

That journey to Hollywood was all kind of a blur. We got off the train, into a cab, and before I knew it, we were passing through the West Pico Boulevard gates of 20th Century Fox, where I first set foot on the grounds of a major film studio. We then met this lovely man who was very elegant, well dressed and well spoken. He was just delightful and took us around the studio, showing us various things and introducing us to people.

If my day at that storied studio, where I walked through all these office building corridors that had been walked by Tyrone Power, Linda Darnell, Carmen Miranda, Don Ameche, Henry Fonda, Gene Tierney, Sonja Henie, Betty Grable and even Shirley Temple, was to be one that would be seared into my soul as a pivotal moment of destiny, the lightning bolt revelation of kismet never struck. I was, of course, excited and was hugely grateful to Rosa for the opportunity she gave me, but, again, I thought of working in the film industry as, at best, just a possible vehicle to help get me to my real destination: Broadway.

Still, it was all very exciting to be in Los Angeles for the first time. I recall going to a movie with Rosa after we left the studio and then heading back to the train station for our trip back to San Diego. In the days following our Los Angeles visit, Rosa made repeated calls to her contact at 20th Century Fox, inquiring about what exactly their plans were for their next big star, whom she had discovered and introduced them to.

"What do you want to do about Marion?" I once heard her say with an air of indignation over their not dropping everything and focusing on their stunning new prospect (namely, me). "What are your plans for her?" she demanded to know.

I may have always had a healthy belief in myself, but during that time, I couldn't hold a candle to Rosa, who was convinced I was on the fast-track path to stardom.

Rosa's deep conviction of my pending success, however, began to wane just a bit when her studio contact said, "Well, to begin with, she has to live up here in Los Angeles." And then, perhaps, it really crashed when she learned that Effie and I had taken off in the dead of night to tie the knot.

I think Rosa may have had more of an agenda in my becoming a star than she ever revealed to me. What that
agenda may have been—to act as my agent or manager or
something—who knows? But she did really believe in me,
and I will always be grateful to her for doing what she did
for me. If nothing else, Rosa took away any apprehension
I may have had about venturing up to Los Angeles on my
own to complete my studies—which is what I did.

Rooming with a bunch of girls while wrapping up my
necessary courses was not a conventional life for a young
wife, but, again, it was something I never gave much
thought to. Effie was completing his studies in San Diego
as I was doing the same in L.A. Once that was over . . .
Well, I can't say I had that thought out. What did happen
is we both finished college. As soon as Effie completed the
last day of his courses, he joined me in L.A., and we leased
a room in a house that offered us kitchen privileges.

Within days of Effie's arrival in L.A., in what could be
described only as a scene from some sappy drama, the
woman who owned the house where we were living knocked
on our door, announced that a letter had arrived for a
Freeman Mcskimen, and handed him an official-looking
envelope. After ripping open the letter, he read a few lines.
Looked up with a stunned expression on his face and
handed the letter to me. As a member of the Navy Reserve,
he was being called back to active duty.

Within a short time, my life in L.A. was over and we
were on our way to Vallejo, California, north of San Francisco, where Effie was stationed for a few months before
being sent to Korea. When I think back to the start of my
senior year at San Diego State, my life and my five-year career plan seemed to be so straightforward. But nowhere in
that plan was there a marriage, a move to Vallejo, a husband being called to serve in Korea, and me having no
idea what to do next.

What I did do was the only thing a young woman with no money could do—go back to living with my parents in San Diego. While I viewed this as a huge setback for me, my mother was, surprisingly, very wonderful and supportive during this time. She even provided the money for Effie and me to have a little weekend getaway at Lake Arrowhead, California, before his departure to Korea. When that weekend was over, Effie left, I settled in with my parents, and my father helped me find a job as a file clerk at Convair, an aircraft manufacturing company, where all I had to know was the alphabet.

Here I am, a college graduate with a degree in drama, and all I need to know is the alphabet, I would think to myself as I begrudgingly filed hundreds of sales slips each day and wrote and responded to what would become stacks and stacks of letters from and to Effie. While my work at Convair was depressing, my saving grace was that my evenings and weekends were free to audition and do plays with various local groups, including the one at my old stomping grounds of the Old Globe.

Although I felt my life and career were on hold, the year of Effie's service in Korea seemed to pass relatively quickly, and when he returned, we decided to once again move to Los Angeles and pick up where we had left off in pursuing our respective acting careers. Money was, of course, tight, but someway we always managed to get by. When I made the rounds at various studios, I would check their bulletin boards that had listings of people looking for people to do small jobs, usually waiting tables at dinner parties. It was during one of those dinner party gigs that for the first time, I encountered that dark underbelly of Hollywood known as "the casting couch."

During that party, which was hosted by someone associated with the film industry in some way, a comment was passed around that I was "a young lady who wants to be an actress." Soon after, as I was working in the kitchen, a man came in, handed me his card, and told me to come see him—which I did. If anyone in Hollywood had been looking for the poster girl for naïveté, I was the perfect selection, and so when I showed up at the address on his card, to find it wasn't an office but his apartment, I only shrugged and rang the bell.

Once I was inside his apartment, he made some small talk and then asked me, "How do you think you are going to get anywhere in this town?"

I told him I was a really good actress, and he laughed.

"This town is filled with good actresses, and they're lined up ten deep for every role. So, just what girl do you think is going to get that part?"

I began to feel uncomfortable. I mean, I was naïve but not completely stupid. But still, it took me forever to "get" what was happening. "I would say they will cast the one they like the best," I responded rather curtly, with this air of indignant aplomb.

"Uh-huh," he said. "And why exactly would they like one better than the others?"

That did it! I could feel my face flushing and my blood pushing on the walls of my veins.

"I'm married, and you have no character," I blurted out as I stood up.

While my heart was pounding, his face went blank, and he seemed to be perplexed and embarrassed. He seemed to be at a total loss for words and didn't quite know what to do with me.

What he did do was offer me the use of his Cadillac, although I had never owned a car and didn't know how to drive, and he also gave me a job. It wasn't an acting job, but it did provide me with a little of the much-needed money we needed to scrape by. My job was to promote a product called the Scarfinet, which was this lady's scarf you could tie in many different ways and make into all sorts of turbans. I would take my supply of Scarfinets and go to stores like Sears, where I would stand on a little platform with a light on me and demonstrate all the ways the Scarfinet could be tied.

During my Scarfinet days, I once again found myself questioning if anything like this had ever been in the five-year plan once I had that coveted drama degree secured. I, of course, knew it hadn't, and that fact found me constantly fighting off a depression that was fueled by frustration. But being the pragmatist in our marriage, I was aware we needed the money. I took the Scarfinet gig seriously, and while I sold very few of them, the shoppers (whom I always viewed as audiences) who watched my demonstrations always seemed to be fascinated. But, alas, I often thought as I dramatically did my twists and turns with the fabric, *This is what I'm doing with my degree?*

During those early days in L.A., I wasn't just trying to hawk a fashion accessory that would never quite catch on. I was also constantly making the rounds of casting directors, agents, people who knew people (or who said they knew people)—trying to make connections in what all too often felt like an impenetrable wall. During this time, I also went back to 20th Century Fox, hoping to have another meeting with the elegant chap I had met with Rosa. Alas, that idea died when I learned that he himself had died.

While all these dead ends did sometimes leave me feeling depressed and discouraged, I was never dissuaded— not in the least. My dream, my goal and my five-year plan may have had moments when they were a bit dim by the end of a frustrating day, but by the next morning, they would be rekindled and again burning brightly.

While I was proving to be a living embodiment of determination and resilience when it came to my career—or, rather, the pursuit of my career—Effie continued to be just the opposite. He also still wanted to pursue an acting career, but he didn't seemingly have any drive at all to make that happen. While I was constantly out looking to meet people and get auditions, Effie rarely ventured out at all and did nothing in the way of seeking connections or auditions or any sort of employment.

Effie had adopted this odd belief that at some point in time, in some miraculous way, someone in Hollywood would come to their senses and come looking for the elusive Freeman Meskimen and cast him in a play or a film or a television show. Most young and ambitious wives would not have put up with a husband like that, but as for me, I never really gave it a thought other than it was just Effie being Effie. We had taken a personality test together once, right after our quickie marriage, and I scored 87 percent in ambition, while Effie scored 6 percent. But that didn't bother me. In fact, in some odd way, it was kind of what I liked about him! I still found a certain charm in his brooding and mysterious Garboesque ways, which were completely the opposite of my personality traits. It is what had attracted me to him in the first place, what had made me throw all caution (and perhaps my future and career) to the wind and marry him on a whim. He was so very different than me, and as odd as it may seem, I loved that about him. *Who*, I used to think, *would ever want to be with someone who is just like themselves?*

And so Effie spent time in our meager abode, playing his guitar and on occasion talking about going back to school to get a master's degree. I, on the other hand, was always on the go—optimistic, determined and embracing each new day with anticipation. And then, one day, bolstered by my optimistic determination, I found myself in the Sunset Boulevard office of a man of small stature by the name of Jack Weiner.

While I didn't know anything about Weiner at the time, I would later learn he had been a child star who, back in the 1920s, was a member of singer Gus Edwards's vaudeville troupe, which was the early stage-stomping grounds for a very young cast of performers that included Groucho Marx, Walter Winchell, George Jessel, Phil Silvers, Eleanor Powell, Hildegarde, Ray Bolger and others who would go on to international fame. As time went by, Weiner eventually gave up performing and established a talent agency, first representing various vaudeville headliners and then film stars, including Jack Albertson, Bill "Bojangles" Robinson, Mae West, Butterfly McQueen and Linda Darnell.

But on that day, as I sat across from him, the only thing I knew about Jack Weiner was that someone who knew someone who knew Weiner had suggested I meet with him.

"Stand up and turn around," Weiner said to me after a few moments of small talk. "Jeez, you got a big can on you there, huh?" he continued as I followed his instructions. "Okay, let me see your legs," he added. "Let me see your teeth."

As I complied with each one of his requests, slightly lifting my dress and opening my mouth as wide as I could, as if I were visiting a dentist, he proceeded to tear me to pieces.

Oh, brother, I thought. *Is this going to be another one of those situations in which I'm going to have to indignantly put another guy in his place?*

But before I could even begin to let that thought process itself, Weiner told me to sit back down. He leaned back in his chair, looked me over again, and then said, "I'm not going to sign you, but I want you to feel free to use my name in any way you think may help you."

Weiner actually did more than just let me use his name. We kept in touch, and he would, ultimately, come to play an important role in my career. In the meantime, while I was doing a daily performance—as a store file clerk at Bullock's Westwood department store—I got a call from my old friend Craig Noel, who was the founding director of the Old Globe Theatre. He told me about a play that was going to be produced by the Pasadena Playhouse, and he felt very strongly that I should audition for it.

"Hollywood casting agents will need to know you are in Los Angeles and to see you in something," Craig told me. "This company has a great reputation, and you would be perfect for the role," he continued adamantly.

While I wasn't aware of it at the time, my getting to know Weiner, coupled with that call from Craig, would prove to be pivotal factors in the pieces falling in place that would make my secret dream become a reality.

Chapter 8

My Studio Contract

The play Craig Noel wanted me to audition for was Maxwell Anderson's *Journey to Jerusalem*. Written in 1940, the play tells the tale of Mary, Joseph and a twelve-year-old Jesus, who is about to learn of his destiny as the Messiah. I auditioned for and got the role of the Virgin Mary (my first "mother" role), with the part of Jesus going to Sylvie Drake, who went on to become a theater critic and a columnist for the *Los Angeles Times*, the director of publications for the Denver Center for the Performing Arts, and a good friend.

While I don't know this for sure, I have always believed that Craig spoke with some of his contacts at the Pasadena Playhouse, called in a favor, pulled some strings or, at the very least, gave their casting people a heads-up about me. He never copped to doing that, but it would have been typical of him, especially after being so adamant that I audition for this show.

While it wasn't Broadway, I was excited to be working at the legendary Pasadena Playhouse, which had been established in 1916 by Gilmor Brown, an actor and director who had formed the Community Playhouse Association of Pasadena, which would evolve into the Pasadena Playhouse Association. As the founder and artistic director of the Gilmor Brown Players, Brown played an instrumental role in spearheading fund-raising efforts to build a new home for his productions. Those efforts paid off, and in 1925 the ribbon was cut on a new Elmer Grey–designed theater, located on South El Molino Avenue in Pasadena.

Built in the Spanish Colonial Revival style, the Pasadena Playhouse soon became home to a school of theatrical arts, one that would go on to become an accredited college in 1937. Among the impressive list of actors who trained there over the years are Raymond Burr, Victor Mature, Ernest Borgnine, Eleanor Parker, Charles Bronson, Jamie Farr, Gene Hackman, Dustin Hoffman and Sally Struthers. Along with being a respected teaching facility, the playhouse drew theatergoers from all over Southern California for its critically acclaimed performances.

One night, following a performance of *Journey to Jerusalem*, I was approached by a man who identified himself as Milton Lewis and told me he was a talent scout from Paramount Pictures. He said he had enjoyed my performance, and asked if I would be interested in coming in to screen-test. By this time I had become a little less naïve, and so while I may have had an initial twinge of concern over the offer, he seemed to be very professional, and I had no reason to believe he wasn't on the up-and-up. However, I also had no reason to believe that word of my earth-shattering portrayal of the Virgin Mary had spread like wildfire throughout Hollywood and that Paramount executives had immediately dispatched Mr. Lewis, with orders to do all he could to get me under contract before any other studio could scoop me up. Instead, I just figured he attended the same temple as Jack Weiner and owed him a favor.

Whatever the reason, I did give Lewis my phone number and soon thereafter received a call from his office to schedule me for a screen test. I also learned he had been responsible for bringing many new faces into Paramount's stable of actors, including Margaret Field (usually billed as Maggie Mahoney), who went on to become the mother of Sally Field; and Mary Murphy, who, while on a coffee break at her job as a package wrapper at Saks Fifth Avenue, caught Lewis's eye à la Lana Turner at Schwab's Pharmacy and went on to appear with Marlon Brando in *The Wild One*, Tony Curtis in *Beachhead*, Dale Robertson in *Sitting Bull*, Fredric March and Humphrey Bogart in *The Desperate Hours*, and Ray Milland in *A Man Alone*.

Thanks to Rosa Choplin, I had already been on the grounds of a major studio, but when the day came for me to report for my screen test, I was a bit unnerved. It may have been Broadway rather than Hollywood that was my ultimate goal, but still, as I walked through those iconic Melrose Avenue gates of Paramount Pictures (the same ones that, ironically, many years later I would pass through on a regular basis to make my way to Stage Nineteen, where *Happy Days* was filmed), my stomach's butterflies were doing some serious fluttering.

Paramount was one of what were known as the "Big Six" film studios; and under the leadership of its founder, Adolph Zukor, who believed that big names were what it took to sell movie tickets, the studio signed many of Hollywood's early stars, including Mary Pickford, Clara Bow, Douglas Fairbanks, Gloria Swanson and Rudolph Valentino. As time went by and as the silent era gave way to the "talkies," the studio also became the home base for Dorothy Lamour, Carole Lombard, Bing Crosby, Gary Cooper, Bob Hope, Marlene Dietrich, Mae West, W. C. Fields, Jeanette MacDonald, Claudette Colbert, the Marx Brothers, Alan Ladd, Veronica Lake, Paulette Goddard and Betty Hutton.

Knowing of the long list of luminaries that Paramount had propelled into stardom, I was very serious about my screen test and made sure nothing had been overlooked as I prepared for this once-in-a-lifetime opportunity. I hired a drama coach to help me get ready and had my hairstyle and clothing selections checked and rechecked. Yes, I had cut my bangs too short, and the fact that they refused to do anything other than stick out, rather than caress my forehead, had those butterflies in my stomach smacking into one another in hyperactive confusion. But even they did nothing to diminish the pride and confidence in my stride as I walked past the soundstages to the location where I was told to report.

It will be on this day, I thought to myself as I made my way through the studio lot's narrow streets, *that I will cross a threshold and enter into an exciting new world and a new chapter of my life, one in which I will transition from being a young girl with a dream to being a young woman—an actress—actually living that dream.*

It all felt right—very right—and I savored the moment. I felt I had been methodical in the steps I had taken to get to that point, and perhaps more importantly, I also felt I had paid the appropriate dues for my dream to gently dissipate into childish stardusted memories and for reality to begin.

There may not have been a grand staircase for me to descend from, nor was there any trace of this being some sort of a deluded fantasy, and yet I did feel a bit like Norma Desmond as I stepped through the elephant door of the soundstage where my screen test was to be shot. *All right*, I thought to myself. *I'm here, and I'm ready for my close-up!*

If I was a stellar example of confidence as I walked onto that stage, within seconds that confidence took a jarring hit.

While I can't say I had totally envisioned a coterie of behind-the-scenes craftsmen, stagehands and assistants fawning over me, making inquiries as to what I may like to drink and then fighting over which one of them would get to provide me with my desired beverage while leading me to my dressing room, what I didn't envision was that there would be other girls there to screen-test. And, to make matters even less than what I may have envisioned, they weren't just *other* girls. They were beautiful girls—beauty queens—who all seemed to be "Miss This" or "Miss That." They were these gorgeous creatures, with curves in all the right places, who, unlike me, did not have bangs that stuck straight out and who were not desperately trying to use every method of makeup magic to conceal a cold sore on their upper lip.

It's all right, I recall thinking to myself as I smoothed out my dress, which, unlike the ones the other girls were wearing, was not adorned with a sash proclaiming the title of my reign. *Yes, I am a tad bit disheartened to find that this is not exclusively* my *screen test, and that I have to vie against a bevy of beauty queens, but who cares how many bejeweled crowns or satin sashes they have? I'm a serious actress.*

When my turn came to test, I was paired up with a young actor to do a scene from the Anita Loos play *Happy Birthday*. I played the role of Addie, the timid and shy librarian who is smitten with a dashing bank clerk, a role that had been played by Helen Hayes during the show's three-year run on Broadway in the late 1940s. I was extremely pleased with the selection, in that there wasn't a moment in which I didn't have the opportunity either to deliver or react to a strong emotional line. That meant also that there wasn't a moment during the entire scene in which the focus wasn't on me.

Although I was deeply immersed in the role, I was also acutely aware of the technical aspect of what I was doing—of the craft I had honed. It all felt so right. My big moment had arrived, and I was prepared and ready to face it. I felt a strong swell of confidence bolster me with energy, which wasn't even diminished when, after doing one take, I pushed up those bangs and they stayed up, looking like the brim of a cap. I gave that no thought except to believe that with the hair away from my eyes, the camera could see my reactions even more.

When the test was over and I was walking off the makeshift set, one of the grips came up to me and extended his greasy hand. As I looked up at him and took his hand in mine, he said, "You should thank your mother."

I immediately understood what he meant, and graciously accepted it as a compliment. I had projected the air of a refined young woman of proper breeding who was also capable of being vulnerable and genuine. I just knew in my bones—in my very soul—that I could not have done a better job. That fact was solidified by my capturing the attention of a grip, one of those guys who are typically more interested in getting the scene over with so they can grab a smoke or something from the craft services table rather than the actor's performance.

On that day, as I left Paramount Pictures, I was no longer dreaming of becoming an actress. I walked out into the real world as an actress and within days would be offered a studio contract.

Chapter 9

My Days Between Two Worlds

It was 1952, the waning days of the Truman administration, and while the United States was still involved in the Korean War, and polio was horrifically attacking thousands of American children, most Americans were feeling, overall, pretty positive about life. Car ownership was booming, two out of three families owned a telephone, and one in three homes had a television set. The world was on the verge of seeing faster and less expensive commercial air travel, and there was a constant stream of debuts that would change the way Americans did just about everything. A new type of restaurant that offered fast food and a chain of motels known as Holiday Inns began springing up from coast to coast.

That year the *Today* program debuted on NBC, with its host Dave Garroway, and Agatha Christie's murder-mystery play *The Mousetrap* was the toast of Broadway. As for the film world, Americans were flocking to theaters to see *The African Queen*, *The Greatest Show on Earth*, *The Quiet Man* and *Singin' in the Rain*. To me (but, seemingly, to no one else), the biggest news being made in Tin-

seltown was that Paramount Pictures had offered a contract to an up-and-coming-star—a twenty-four-year-old
actress who had risen from the unlikely place of Albert
Lea, Minnesota, and was about to take the film world by
storm before going on to dominate the stage of New
York's Great White Way.

I may have been obsessed with this big news, but for
some reason, neither *Variety*, the *Hollywood Reporter* nor
any other film industry trade magazine seemed to see it as
being worthy of front-page (or even any page) coverage.

From the moment I put down the phone after receiving
the news that I would be offered a contract with Paramount, the entire world seemed different to me. I can't say
I was shocked. In fact, I would have been far more in
shock had I not received that call. But what I did feel was
that the work of dues paying was now behind me and the
work of establishing myself as a film actress, to garner the
attention of Broadway producers, was beginning. And
there was also the more practical economic element involved, as I went from twisting and turning Scarfinets for
thirty-five dollars a week at Bullock's to being a Paramount actress who made $150 a week.

Because of my long-held belief that this was my destiny,
coupled with the methodical training and stage work I had
under my belt, I can't say I ever felt that I was floating in a
magically stardusted world of disbelief that this had actually happened to me. I was, by all means, pleased that I
could now call a major studio my employer and that, for
all intents and purposes, I could say I was a "professional"
actress (albeit one who had not yet appeared on the
screen), but it was something I accepted in a very pragmatic way. I had dreamed my dream, had been educated in
my craft, had appeared in numerous stage roles, had
worked diligently to make connections, had always (well,

at least for the most part) retained a positive attitude, and was now simply taking the next step. It was far less a "through-the-looking-glass" fulfillment of a dream than it was the practical progression of a destined and determined woman who, like any other person who had properly prepared for a career in business, medicine, law or any other profession, was now ready to apply her craft in a professional realm.

While a part of me entered into this new life with pragmatic maturity, there was, for sure, another part of me that tingled with excitement as I walked onto the Paramount lot each morning. It was an extremely exciting time to be there, or on the lot of any major film studio in Hollywood. In the 1950s, location shoots were reserved for big dramatic scenes in epic films, which meant that the great majority of scenes were filmed on the studio's stages and back lots.

Each day the lot buzzed with activity as thousands of workers each applied their specific craft to the process of filmmaking, and among the throngs I would pass on a daily basis were individuals whose names and faces were as (if not more) recognizable as those of our nation's new president, Dwight Eisenhower. Yes, I will admit that at times I did have to employ my theatrical training to conceal a gasp of wide-eyed wonder or a skipped heartbeat of excitement as I turned a corner and caught a glimpse of Burt Lancaster, Dean Martin, Agnes Moorehead, Bing Crosby, Bob Hope, Dorothy Lamour, Ronald Reagan or Rhonda Fleming on their way to meet with the studio executives, do a scene, sit in on a screening, or have lunch at the commissary. It was an exciting world—so exciting, in fact, I often found myself forgetting that it was the stages of Broadway that I saw as my final destination.

While I was now a contracted Paramount actress, I was also still something else: Mrs. Freeman Meskimen. It was, at times, like having feet in two different worlds. Effie had enrolled at UCLA, and while he was working toward obtaining a master's degree, he still seemed more interested in becoming an actor. That interest, however, still never motivated him to do the necessary work to achieve such a thing. Jack Weiner, who was by then serving as my agent, knew of Effie's desire, as well as his lack of ambition. He helped (me, perhaps, more than Effie) by suggesting that Effie change his professional name to Freeman Morse and by arranging some auditions for him. I also did my part by going to the research library at Paramount and checking out books I felt would be both helpful and motivating for him.

Still, Effie floundered when it came to really applying himself to his studies, acting or anything other than polishing off a daily bottle of Scotch. And yet Effie's drinking and moping still never bothered me. His lack of motivation may have become a little less charming and a bit more confusing for me to understand, but it was not anything I spent much time thinking about as I went off to spend my days at Paramount. To me, it was just Effie still simply being Effie.

My one foot may have been in the mundane world of being a young wife married to a brooding wannabe actor, but my other, the one that was on far more thrilling ground, was proudly promenading around the sixty-plus acres of Paramount Pictures. And it was thrilling. If I had been a slight bit nonchalant about getting a Paramount contract, that casual attitude rapidly dissipated. I got to the point where I could not wait to get to work in the morning to see what was going on and what they would have me doing. Everything was thrilling, even just eating lunch in the commissary with "the Golden Circle," the moniker that had been hung upon the studio's contracted actors. There were between twelve and fourteen of us in the Golden Circle at that time, and a few among us would go on to make our mark in the entertainment world.

One of them was Mary Murphy, who, after playing the sweet girl who, as I previously mentioned, was intrigued by the motorcycle gang member Johnny, played by Marlon Brando, in *The Wild One*, would go on to appear in many films, including *Beachhead* with Tony Curtis, *Sitting Bull* with Dale Robertson, and as Fredric March's character's daughter in the suspense thriller *The Desperate Hours*, which also starred Humphrey Bogart. She also costarred with Ray Milland in *A Man Alone* and went on to have a prolific television career in the 1960s, appearing in popular shows of the era, such as *Perry Mason*, *The Lloyd Bridges Show*, *I Spy*, *The Outer Limits*, *The Fugitive* and *Ironside*.

Another Golden Circle colleague was Barbara Rush, who was the first to break out of our little clique by winning a Golden Globe Award for the most promising female newcomer for her role in the 1953 science fiction film *It Came from Outer Space*. Like Mary, Barbara also went on to have a very successful television career, appearing in films, miniseries and the daytime dramas *Peyton Place* and *All My Children*.

A darling Texas girl, Kathryn Grandstaff, was also a part of our little circle. That name may not mean much to anyone, because she used the last name Grant and, within just a few years of being signed at Paramount, she personally (but not yet professionally) changed her last name to that of her husband's, Crosby—as in Bing. As Kathryn Grant, she starred with Jack Lemmon in the 1957 comedy *Operation Mad Ball*, and over the next few years she also starred with Tony Curtis in *Mister Cory* and played a trapeze artist in 1959's *The Big Circus*. Kathryn's acting took a backseat to raising her children, although she and the kids did appear on Bing's television show and holiday specials.

While we were mostly composed of actresses, an actor or two also completed our circle at times, most notably

Peter Baldwin. Peter played the role of Johnson in the 1953 Billy Wilder film *Stalag 17*, along with Hollywood heavyweights William Holden and Otto Preminger. He appeared in a number of films and television productions throughout the 1960s and then turned his attention to directing, where he worked with Mary Tyler Moore and Lucille Ball and directed classic shows, including *The Brady Bunch*, *The Partridge Family*, *Family Ties* and *The Wonder Years* (for which he won an Emmy Award).

Rounding out our circle of gold was an actress I will be forever associated with, in that we would both go on to play the role of an iconic mother in a classic television show. Carolyn Jones was another Texas girl, and she, unlike me, suffered with severe asthma throughout her childhood. Just like me, however, she loved to read Hollywood magazines when she was young, and she was also an alumna of the Pasadena Playhouse, where she began her theatrical studies when she was just fifteen.

Carolyn, with those big, expressive eyes, was a standout in our circle. She appeared in a string of feature films, was nominated for an Academy Award for Best Supporting Actress for her role as the existentialist in the 1957 film *The Bachelor Party*, and won a Golden Globe Award as one of the most promising actresses of 1958. While she was the only one of our Golden Circle class to receive an Academy Award nomination, Carolyn would go on to be far better known for her portrayal of Morticia Addams in the 1960s campy series *The Addams Family*, which was based on the characters in Charles Addams's *New Yorker* cartoons. The role of Morticia—the matriarch of the creepy and kooky family—earned Carolyn both another Golden Globe Award nomination and admittance into the exclusive club of beloved television moms, of which I would also become a member.

In 1953 there might have been some place in the world where more excitement was going on than what was taking place on the Paramount lot, but you would have been extremely hard-pressed to make that argument to any member of our Golden Circle. We felt as if we were at the epicenter of at least Hollywood, if not the world. I felt like I had made it. I even went to a bank and opened an account so I could cash my checks. I had never had a bank account before, so seeing my name imprinted on checks was a very significant milestone.

I never knew what each day would bring, which, of course, added more to the excitement of it all. Every morning we would all be sent over to the hair and makeup departments, where our locks would be so trimmed, curled and styled, our lips would be so built up, and the arch of our eyebrows would be so changed that we could have passed our mothers on the street without being recognized.

While it felt the way Hollywood was supposed to feel—with all the primping and pampering—it always seemed that whenever I was getting a tad bit full of myself, something would happen that would knock me back down to Earth.

I remember one day, while I was under the hair dryer, being prepared for a photo shoot, I found myself feeling rather smug about life and, specifically, my current place in it and where I was headed in the near future. I then casually turned to glance over at the girl under the dryer next to me, and it was as if the floor fell out from under me. She had beautiful features, perfect skin and, even from under a hair dryer, exuded a palpable charm in the way she gracefully and balletically positioned her arms, legs and hands. My noticing all those things hit me with lightning speed—within three seconds, the first second of which I realized my dryer mate was Audrey Hepburn.

I had known Hepburn was on the lot, filming scenes for *Roman Holiday*, but I had yet to encounter her. Along with knowing she was working on the lot, I knew she and

I were not far apart in age. And so, while I may have been feeling smug about being a Paramount contract player and a member of the Golden Circle just moments before, that smugness evaporated in a flash as my rapidly beating heart began to ache. I remember leaning back into the dryer while looking at her legs and hands. *There she is*, I thought to myself. *A few months younger than me and she has already starred on Broadway in* Gigi *and* Ondine, *for which she won a Tony Award for Best Lead Actress in a Play, and now she is starring in the role of Princess Ann in* Roman Holiday.

That, I recall, was one of only a few occasions in which I allowed an emotion that was usually foreign to me—depression—to well up within me. I also remember how, as soon as my hair was done, I maturely handled my down and dejected soul: I went right out and bought two candy bars, sat myself down on a bench, ate them both, felt guilty for a few moments, and then began to feel better as I made my way across the lot to report to Wardrobe.

Yes, the gorgeous and oh, so well-poised Miss Hepburn may have gotten her petite and perfectly shaped leg up on me, I thought as I traversed the lot. *But look where I am, as opposed to thousands upon thousands of aspiring actresses—on my way to have one of the most famous costume designers in the world dress me for my shoot.*

My time at Paramount coincided with the Edith Head era at the studio's wardrobe department. She had established herself as one of Hollywood's most important costume designers by the time I arrived, and thus it was a bit heady (if you'll excuse the pun) to go up to her salon and have her work with me in the same businesslike, no-nonsense way in which she consulted and dressed Ginger Rogers, Bette Davis, Barbara Stanwyck, Shirley MacLaine, Grace Kelly, Elizabeth Taylor and, yes, even Audrey Hepburn.

And so, while I may not have been in possession of an

impressive résumé or had laudatory hardware on my mantel (hell, I didn't even have a mantel), on any given day I, by all means, was made up and dressed to look like I could have, with my perfectly coiffed hair, arched eyebrows and Head-selected frock.

That was the way all the Golden Circle girls looked, and while I was always very self-conscious that I was a character actress who didn't possess the natural beauty or sexy glamour of the others, I would halfheartedly join in with them when they secretly reveled (and giggled) when male heads would turn in our direction as we walked in and sat together for lunch at a big circular table in the middle of the commissary. Of course, our heads would turn, too, whenever one of us would notice and then excitedly share the information that Cecil B. DeMille was sitting in a little alcove across the room from us or that Marlene Dietrich had just swept in the door.

It was always a bit of an odd feeling being a contract player—like I was lost between two worlds. I was made up to look like I was somebody, but unlike Hepburn or Dietrich, or anyone of that status I dreamed of becoming, I knew when it came to physical beauty, I was not in the league of the other girls. I was always very confident of my acting ability, but as for my membership in the Golden Circle, I often felt I was out of place, like I was a part of a group I didn't really belong in or even want to be a part of, this contingent of beauties whom I sometimes just saw as glamorously adorned set pieces, not unlike the well-appointed furnishings, beautiful paintings or fine silk drapery you would find in the studio's executive offices.

I should make it clear that when I say I didn't want to be a part of the Golden Circle, it was not just because I felt physically inferior to the other girls; it was also because my goal was to work—to act. Yes, it was nice to be draped in all manner of finery and have my hair and makeup done, but not just to be paraded around the lot, to serve as a photographer's model, or to be sent off to some publicity event. I did harbor the strong feeling that, unlike the other girls, I was a serious actress, well trained, with substantial stage work under my belt. I didn't look down on them or feel I was better than them. I think I was just constantly compensating for my lack of glamour and internally justifying to myself why I was a part of the circle.

I got along well with the other girls, who all seemed to get along well with me and one another. We were pleasant, cordial and professional toward one another, but there was always an underlying sense of competition and, whether I or they were willing to admit it, a dose of jealousy when one of the group would be tapped for a small job or be fussed over by someone.

There was a woman, Charlotte Clary, who was a Paramount drama coach that the studio put in charge of us. When we didn't have a specific reason to be somewhere on the lot, we all spent time in her office. Outside of the Paramount lot, there didn't seem to be much socializing going on among the girls. On occasion, Charlotte would invite us all over to her home for a little party. Most of the girls attended her soirees, but I did only a few times. Unlike the other girls, except for Carolyn Jones, who was living with Aaron Spelling at the time, I had a husband at home, which, along with my feelings that I wasn't in their class physically, gave me yet another reason to feel very different from them.

As the weeks turned into months, I still found it exciting to be on the Paramount lot, but my desire and my expectation were not just to be on the Paramount lot but also to be *working* on the Paramount lot. I had begun to get the sense that they (whoever "they" were) didn't really know what to do with those of us in the Golden Circle. I had become very aware in a most uncomfortable way that while

I was an employee of a major motion picture studio, which was providing me with the highest salary I had ever made, I had no real function. As more time went by, I became so uncomfortable with that fact, I began to make it a point to walk very briskly around the lot so I would appear to be late for something and always kept my head down so I would not have to make eye contact with anyone. I came to dread the occasion when I would be somewhere on the lot and would have an encounter with someone who would ask me if I worked there.

Remember, this was the 1950s, and so when I told them that yes, I did work there, the next thing out of their mouth would always be the same question: "Are you a secretary?"

I did often consider simply saying yes, that I was a secretary, but I was always in fear that they would ask me for whom or in what department and that I would get in some sort of trouble for not telling the truth. Instead, I would say, "No, I'm an actress, and I'm under contract here."

Perhaps I was a bit too sensitive, and maybe even a little paranoid, but whenever I said that, I always seemed to get the same response: a rather blank look, followed by a slightly uncomfortable nod. I always imagined the person who gave me that look and nod would then turn away from me and think to themselves, *A contracted actress? A plain and shy girl like that? I think not. She probably is a secretary, who, one of these days, is going to get herself into trouble for not telling the truth.*

I can't tell you how painful that was for me. I began to feel as if I was the only person on the lot who didn't have a real job or purpose in being there. No one ever asked me if I had gone to college, if I had earned a degree in drama, or what plays I had appeared in. If I had, at first, felt as if I was living in two different worlds, one as Mrs. Meskimen and one as a Paramount contract actress, I soon started to feel as if I was also living in a third world—one of confusion and frustration.

And yet my optimistic and determined streak—having always been far broader than my confused and frustrated one—saw me get up every morning and cheerfully return to the lot for another day, one in which I hoped my fates would change. I also always had positive feelings about what I was learning by simply watching what others were doing. From my first day at Paramount, I was extremely attuned to what was going on, especially when I had the opportunity to be near the set when filming was taking place. I was a keen observer, watching and learning everything I could about what various people did and said before, during and after the cameras rolled.

I was, however, careful never to get in the way or, God forbid, ask any questions or try to cozy up to anyone. I had actually gotten that advice from Jack Weiner, who told me to always be professional, polite and interested in what was going on, but not to behave like some of the other young contract actresses, who, when encountering someone involved with a production, were known to bat their eyes, "accidentally" expose a bit too much leg, gush over even the slightest bit of notice, or just outright flirt. While I didn't really need Jack to tell me that, being as none of those things would have been anything I would have ever dared to attempt, anyway, I did see other girls employ those tactics.

I remember once, I went over to where they were shooting *Stalag 17*. The cast was taking a break, having just finished doing a scene, and there were all these guys from the crew just hanging around on the set. I was there for only a few minutes, and I immediately knew, by the looks I was getting and some of the comments being made, that I was in a place I should not be. I was aware that there were other girls who would have handled this situation much differently as a way to get ahead in the business, but all I knew was that I needed to get the hell away from there fast—which I did.

I also remember one day, while I was sitting on a sound-stage between takes, one of my Golden Circle colleagues came walking by, and as she passed me, I heard one of the crew members say, "I know her!" and then another guy glanced over with a sly look and said, "Oh yeah! I know her, too!" As they stood there laughing, I remember lowering my head, making believe I hadn't noticed what they said, and thinking to myself, *I don't ever want anyone to say that about me.* So, while I was always watching what was going on, I was also always watching out for myself—watching and wondering just what it was I was getting out of this experience. Yes, I was learning a lot about how the film industry worked, but I had this overwhelming feeling that I was drifting.

I was certainly not doing anything to utilize my theatrical training, other than to act charming and gracious when the studio dressed us up and sent us off to premieres. And while that was a bit interesting the first time I did it, I quickly came to loathe going to them. They would send you up to Edith Head to be fitted with a beautiful gown to wear that had originally been created for one of the studio's stars, like Joan Fontaine. They would then do your hair and makeup, team you up with one of the guys from the Golden Circle, and put you in the back of a shiny black limousine and whisk you off to whatever theater the premiere was taking place in.

I know that all sounds like it would be very exciting, and like it was exactly what I had always dreamed of happening as a young girl, but all it did for me was compound my feelings that I had no real function in being at the studio, and no real reason to be at that, or any, premiere. All I could think about was whether I was ever going to get the chance to act in a film, and whether Edith Head would ever create a beautiful gown that had the name "Marion Ross" sewn into the collar.

I understood that the studio gussied us up and limoed us off to these premieres for publicity purposes—to give the appearance that every time they released a film, the beautiful, glamorous and well-dressed people of Hollywood were just chomping at the bit to be the first to see it. The problem with this was that it was humiliating. Your limo would turn on to Hollywood Boulevard and pull up in front of Grauman's Chinese Theatre. You could see the crowd start to push in around your car, and members of the press would position themselves to get the best shot of you as you stepped out of your chauffeur-driven carriage. Then the car door would open, you would step out onto the red carpet, cameras would flash for a second or two, and then, in an immediate reversal, the flashing would stop, the photographers would lower their cameras and, inevitably, someone in the crowd would yell out the most dreaded words an aspiring actor will ever hear—ones that would elicit an audible groan from the huddled masses, who thought they were about to see a big star: "*It's nobody!*"

Chapter 10

My Days of Successes and Struggles

While I had initially felt that being offered a contract with Paramount was the exciting beginning of my career, as time went by, and more crowds welcomed me to premieres as a nobody, I began to question if what I was doing had any value at all. My original contract was for six months, and when I hit that milestone, the studio renewed it for another six months. It was during that time that I was tapped for a few unbilled roles of no significance in a few feature films, including *Secret of the Incas* and *Sabrina*, which starred my old hair-dryer mate Audrey Hepburn.

Around this time, there was also a lot of excitement swirling through the Golden Circle over the fact that they were looking at one of us to play the role of the young actress Sally Carver in a film called *Forever Female*, which starred Ginger Rogers and William Holden. If there had been a "just below the surface" brewing of polite (and at times, not so polite) competition among the girls before that role was cast (and there most certainly was), it erupted into an all-out "each woman for herself" fight for that part. I felt that I had a real shot at it because it called for the talent of a real actress. Unfortunately for me and my colleagues of the circle, it was not to be. They ended up looking to Broadway and cast Pat Crowley, who would go on to win the Golden Globe Award for New Star Actress of the Year and in the 1960s would become one of television's iconic moms in her role as Joan Nash on NBC's *Please Don't Eat the Daisies.*

While neither I nor any other girl from the circle got the part we had all hoped for, *Forever Female* did provide me with my first real role in a feature film, as the main character's friend, Patty. *Forever Female* was directed by London-born Irving Rapper, who began his career as an assistant director and dialogue coach for Warner Bros. in the 1930s. Within a decade, he had become a hot commodity in Hollywood by directing a string of successful films, beginning with 1941's *Shining Victory*, which was followed by *Now, Voyager*; *The Corn Is Green*; *Deception* and *Another Man's Poison.*

Rapper seemed to take a liking to me. He always told me I reminded him of Greer Garson, and throughout the filming of *Forever Female*, he would ask my opinion on various things, always prefacing his query to me by saying, "Tell me." Then he would say in his crisp English accent, "What do you think about this, Miss Garson?" In retrospect, I think he got a chuckle out of the fact that, unlike just about everyone else involved with the production, with the possible exception of Ginger Rogers and Bill Holden, I actually had opinions and was brave enough to voice them.

It would happen over and over—that he would ask my opinion on something—and after a while I came to realize why: Everyone else on the set would seemingly just go along with his ideas or throw the question back at him, asking what he was thinking so they could then agree with him. Not me. I would render whatever opinion I had on this or that, and I believe he got a genuine kick out of that.

I really enjoyed working on *Forever Female*. *Finally*, I would think, *I am actually working, instead of just being paraded around in makeup and finery Mrs. Head designed for someone else*. I was also thrilled to be working with Ginger Rogers, who by that time had a long and legendary career as an Academy Award–winning actress behind her. She was always extremely kind to me, as was Pat Crowley. I may have been a nobody to those fans who showed up to glimpse big stars at film premieres, but while doing *Forever Female*, I felt for the first time since I had been put under contract with Paramount that things were really starting to happen for me.

I specifically recall being on the set for a scene between the two wonderful character actors Jesse White and Jimmy Gleason. The crew had built a set on one of Paramount's stages to resemble New York's Sardi's restaurant, which, in its heyday, was the epicenter of Broadway and the theater crowd. The set was so realistic, and there was a tremendous amount of bustling and activity going on with all the background people who were playing the part of diners. It was a great scene to watch, and I remember standing next to Pat Crowley as they were shooting it, feeling for all the world like I was very much a part of the production, the industry, and like I was on the path to becoming a somebody when I stepped out of a car (although Broadway was still my ultimate goal).

Oh, how wrong I was about to be about that assumption.

After *Forever Female* wrapped principal photography, it was back to the old circle for me, which was very difficult. I had gotten a good taste of working—being on the set, having a director ask for my opinion on things, interacting with big-name stars, doing my scenes in front of the camera, eating with the cast and crew—so being back in the land of nobodysville was hard to deal with.

While I believed, with my first film under my belt, offers of roles would now come pouring in, that never happened. What did happen when my second six-month contract expired was that no further extension was offered and I was unceremoniously dropped by the studio. I can't say this came as a total surprise to me. While my solid optimism had kept the belief alive that things were about to happen for me, I had also quietly, on the inside, known that after a year, the powers that be at Paramount were not going to pave my path to success.

While I had had a feeling my being dropped was inevitable for a while before the ax actually fell, when it did, I was devastated, for a few days. By the following week, after awaking to four or five mornings in which I did not have to go to the lot, I had a great feeling of relief come over me. It had become a terrible strain to go there every day, and so while I still harbored feelings of devastation over being dropped, I was also very relieved. Did I know how I was going to move forward with my career, or even how we were going to continue to pay our bills? No. But, in a way, getting the boot from Paramount proved to be a good thing. Instead of simply being made up as the starlet that I wasn't, I began going on actual auditions for real parts in real productions, some of which—small as they may have been—I got!

As a young woman now approaching my midtwenties, I spent a lot of time thinking about how I was going to bring all the pieces of the puzzle together—my training, my degree, my work at Paramount, my having actually appeared in a film—to make it all work out. *How can I make this all work*? I would sit and ask myself over and over. My answer: I'd hire a press agent!

The idea stemmed from a woman I knew named Barbara Best, who was a pioneer in the entertainment industry. Barbara was a very interesting woman who had attended the University of Southern California on a full scholarship. After she graduated from USC's School of Journalism in 1943, she landed a job at 20th Century Fox and, along with being the very rare female, was the youngest unit publicist for a major motion picture studio. After putting in six years with 20th Century Fox, she moved on to work with Stanley Kramer and then Columbia Pictures, where she assisted George Glass, who was the studio's vice president of advertising, publicity, and public relations.

After racking up over a decade of experience with the studios, Barbara decided to start her own company: Barbara Best, Inc. I had known her socially for some time and believed she would be of great help to me in putting all the pieces together. When I now look back at the list of both struggles and successes I faced as I was establishing myself as an actress, the decision to enlist the services of Barbara proved to be one that led to successes. She agreed to take me on as a client and went beyond being my press agent and took over the management of my career. She was hard on me, but I knew it was all for my own good.

Barbara and I clicked with one another right from the start. She was living with a woman, and I had my suspicions that she was a lesbian, but I never gave that much, if any, thought. I knew she was always fond of me, and as the years went by, she became completely devoted to me and my career, but she never made even the slightest unwanted advance toward me.

I found myself pushing myself harder than I ever had before, both to achieve my dream and to please Barbara. In an odd way that I really can't explain to this day, although I was her client, I always felt as if I had to do everything I could to please her. I remember getting to the point that I wanted to be successful for her as much as I did for myself. She really worked me, setting up interviews when I had nothing to talk about or sell. That would prove to be uncomfortable for me at times. Sitting with a reporter who, I imagined, was wondering just why the hell they were interviewing me brought back that wave of "nobody" nausea from my Paramount premiere days. But Barbara was always working it on my behalf, was constantly out there doing what she felt was best for me. She gave so much of herself for me that I often felt as if she was working harder on me making it than I was, which would make me work even harder, just to feel like I was pulling my weight in making something happen.

Barbara made my success her business, which was great for me, but not for Effie, who never thought much of her. When I look back on that, it makes more sense to me than it did at the time. Barbara was a classic type A personality, driven by ambition and constantly applying her high-octane methods to everything she did. Effie was, of course, just the opposite, and his feelings about her ranged from mild resentment to downright detestation, depending on the demands she placed on me, his mood, or the amount of alcohol he had consumed.

Along with Barbara, I was still working with Jack Weiner, who operated his agency out of this plain little office on Sunset Boulevard, near the Whisky a Go Go. Working outside of the contractual confines of Paramount, Jack was able to help me land some small roles in features, such as *The Glenn Miller Story*, with Jimmy Stewart. He also encouraged me to audition for television roles.

Oh my, I would think to myself. *I'm not that keen on acting in films, much less television.*

Luckily for me, without any hopes of appearing on Broadway looming on the horizon, I came to terms with television, or at least with my willingness to work in the medium.

Ironically, the television show that gave me my first real break was based on a successful play, *Life with Father*, which opened on Broadway in 1939. The play, written by Howard Lindsay and Russel Crouse, had been adapted from an autobiographical book by author and cartoonist Clarence Day. The Broadway production, which starred Howard Lindsay; his wife, Dorothy Stickney; and Teresa Wright, proved to be such a success that it was adapted for broadcast on CBS Radio's *The Mercury Theatre on the Air*, which starred Orson Welles, and for a 1947 feature film that starred William Powell and Irene Dunne, with a supporting cast that included Elizabeth Taylor, Edmund Gwenn, ZaSu Pitts, Jimmy Lydon and Martin Milner. Six years later, *Life with Father* took on yet another adaptation, this time as a television series that starred Leon Ames and Lurene Tuttle and ran from 1953 until 1955 on CBS.

In the first season of *Life with Father*, the producers put out a casting call for an Irish maid named Nora. Well aware of my ability to do various dialects and accents, including brogues, Jack sent me over to CBS Television City to audition. When I arrived at the then brand-new modern CBS production complex at the corner of Beverly Boulevard and Fairfax Avenue in the Fairfax District of Los Angeles, where *Life with Father* was shot, I had ambivalent feelings. For one thing, I felt it was just a small role in a television show, a role that consisted of not much more than saying the line "Dinner is served, sir," and one that I felt may be short lived. I was familiar with the play the show was based on and knew that maids came and went with every scene, because the man of the house was constantly firing them.

As I made my way through the corridors of Television City, I felt confident enough, but unlike my screen test at

Paramount years earlier, after reading for the part, I had no feeling of nailing the audition. I felt I had done well. My penchant for providing the proper accent certainly made me feel comfortable with the reading, and although it wasn't a role I was coveting, there was one little thing about it that did intrigue me: the show was done live.

That appealed to me because it meant the show had a live theater, Broadway-esque quality to it. Without the constant starting and stopping of a filmed production, this show had the feeling of doing what I was most comfortable with: theater. I think I may have also given thought to the fact that the show was getting a lot of publicity because it was the first live series to be aired in color. I think I may have also convinced myself that back in New York, some Broadway producer, while diverting his attention from a hard day of casting an upcoming show, may just catch an episode of *Life with Father* and, knowing it was done live, think to himself, *Aha! That girl playing the maid would be perfect! Who is that girl? Who cares! Just get her!*

And so, while I think I may have secretly wanted the job even more than I let on to myself, I didn't lose any sleep when I left Television City that day with no knowledge of what the producers thought of me.

A few days later, Jack called me to say that they liked me, but that they were looking at quite a few girls. I, again, didn't give it much thought, until I was called in for another reading. I again left without any indication that I was going to get the role, and I believe I was actually called back a few more times after that before they offered me the part. I was excited. It was work on a popular show that would, hopefully, heighten my notoriety both in Hollywood and, more importantly to me, in New York. The money wasn't great, but it was money, something I had gotten used to providing for the livelihood of both myself and my husband.

If I had been concerned that my role in *Life with Father* would be over before I knew I did it, I was wrong—very wrong. I ended up doing the show for over two years, which made me enough of a "known commodity" to land roles or appearances in a plethora of television shows, such as *The Lone Ranger, Mickey Spillane's Mike Hammer, The Donna Reed Show, The George Burns and Gracie Allen Show, The Millionaire, Perry Mason, Buckskin, The Barbara Stanwyck Show, Father Knows Best, The Outer Limits, Route 66* and *Mr. Novak.*

During this time I also landed roles of slightly more significance than I had been used to in feature films. During the last half of the 1950s, I appeared in numerous films, including *The Proud and Profane*, with William Holden, Deborah Kerr and Thelma Ritter; *Lizzie*, which was based on the Shirley Jackson novel *The Bird's Nest* and starred Eleanor Parker, Richard Boone and Joan Blondell; the comedy *Teacher's Pet*, with Clark Gable, Doris Day and Gig Young; and the Blake Edwards–directed *Operation Petticoat*, which starred Cary Grant and Tony Curtis and in which I had the role of a nurse.

With my roles in these films, I may not have seen my name in lights on any marquees or made folks from coast to coast wait in anticipation for the release of the next "Marion Ross film," but these roles were beefing up my résumé and giving this little Midwestern girl with the big dream the opportunity to work with the biggest names of the day. Yes, films that were playing throughout the United States included scenes with me and Clark Gable, Doris Day, Joan Blondell, Cary Grant and Tony Curtis.

Doing these films was exciting and yet, in a strange way, frustrating. I guess the best way to describe it would be to be a member of some sort of sports team in which the big-name players were always out on the field, scoring and getting cheered on by the crowd, while you were sitting on the bench. I was a part of the film business, a member of the cast, and yet I spent way too much time for my liking on the bench. That doesn't mean I didn't have wonderful experiences that have made for great memories. One of my most favorites was when I was doing the war romance film *The Proud and Profane*, which was directed by George Seaton and was based on Lucy Herndon Crockett's novel *The Magnificent Bastards*. I may have still been a nobody, but for a very short period of time, during the making of that film, I got the full-on star treatment.

Many scenes of that film were shot on location in the Virgin Islands and Puerto Rico, in cooperation with the United States Department of Defense, and just prior to shooting in the islands, the stars—William Holden, Deborah Kerr and Thelma Ritter—were in New York, while I was still in Los Angeles. I was scheduled to fly down to meet up with the crew, along with a lovely man from the art department who was going to be responsible for all the palm trees and fronds and shells and sand on the set. It was going to be the longest flight I had ever taken, and it was all so exciting to board a TWA Constellation for the first leg of our journey, which would take us from L.A. to Miami. It was not a direct flight, which meant we would have to make a connection, though I can't recall where. All I do remember is we missed our connection and didn't get into Miami until the middle of the night. We then met up with other cast and crew members, who had been waiting for our arrival, and we all got on a small plane that the production company had chartered to take us on to Puerto Rico.

By the time we got to San Juan, it was two or three o'clock in the morning, and this press agent, who had obviously been indulging in the airport's lounge while awaiting our arrival, was so inebriated that when I stepped off the plane, he thought I was Deborah Kerr. "Good morning, Mrs. Kerr," he slurred as he presented me with an orchid in a plastic box and this huge sombrero.

I was a bit taken aback and wasn't sure if this was a joke or if he really thought I was her. He kept going on about something, but I could make out very little and really had no idea as to exactly what was going on, but being polite, I graciously accepted his gifts, thanked him, and went along with everything he was telling me. Then, before I could ask a question or even think of anything to say, I was whisked out of the terminal and into the backseat of a big black limousine that was waiting just outside the doors.

There I was, all by myself, in the back of this shiny black limousine, with my orchid and this straw hat, which were taking up more room than I was. I may have been tired, but I was far more confused, and all sorts of thoughts started swirling through my head. *Did that fellow really think I'm Deborah Kerr?* I wondered. *Should I say something to someone? But what should I say? 'Excuse me, but I'm not Deborah Kerr'? That would be awkward. And even if I was to say it, who should I say it to?*

As I was contemplating these thoughts, we pulled into a long driveway and up to the front doors of a Hilton hotel. The next thing I knew, the door of the limo was opened and I was escorted up to this beautiful suite, where I recall the curtains being opened to reveal the sounds of the ocean and my being asked if there was anything I needed. I said something about being fine and was told to just pick up the phone and call the front desk if there was anything I was in need of.

Once I was left alone in this beautiful room, I went over to look out at the moonlit sea, and within moments the phone rang. I picked up the receiver, and a voice on the other end confirmed what I had known for the better part of the past hour: that a terrible mistake had been made and that I had been given the wrong room. The poor person calling me was very apologetic and told me that while they were going to change my room, I was more than welcome to stay at the hotel.

"Is this where everyone else, other than the stars and the director, is staying?" I asked, pretty much knowing that it wasn't.

I was told that the rest of the cast and crew were staying at some nearby hotel, but that because of the mistake, there would be no reason for me to have to change accommodations. There may have been no reason for a change to be made as far as the poor hotel night manager, or whomever it was I was speaking to, was concerned, but I knew I needed to get out of that place, fast. I was exhausted from the long trip and would have loved to have just thrown myself onto that big fluffy bed and drifted off to sleep, with the sound of the sea providing a lullaby, but I also knew that would have resulted in hell to pay from someone.

Knowing I had to get the hell out of that place, I asked if there was any way I could be helped with transportation to the hotel where I was supposed to be staying. Told that could be easily arranged whenever I wished to go, I can only remember replying with one word: "Now!"

And so, with a lack of the whisking fanfare with which I had been earlier escorted to my room, I placed the boxed orchid and the sombrero on the bed, made my way back downstairs, was again sheepishly apologized to, was packed into a vehicle that was far less shiny or long as the one that had brought me there and, just as the first rays of the sun were beginning to peek through the darkness, was deposited at my proper (and far less ornate) place of lodging.

After finally getting checked into my rightful room, with no ocean view or offer to just use the phone for any need I may have, I placed my head on the pillow of the single bed. I was bone tired, but for a few minutes before I fell asleep for a few hours, the memory of those crowds who used to groan when I would step out of limos at the Paramount premieres came flooding back into my mind. *Oh my*, I remember thinking with an embarrassed grimace. *I just know that once those people over at the Hilton realized a mistake had been made, someone asked, "Well, then, who is it that is in that room?" and someone else said, "She's nobody."*

If my first few hours in Puerto Rico made me feel like I was a nobody, that feeling continued as the days went by and we began shooting. My role was small, and so I really didn't have much to do. Perceiving my frustration, the film's director, George Seaton, who was a very kind man, would always tell me that my part was an important one. That made me feel a bit better, but it didn't stop me from padding my part when, during one day of filming, the assistant director, Frank Baur, asked if any of the actors were able to drive a jeep. I had never driven a jeep in my life, but I did not give that even an iota of consideration before my hand shot up.

"Good!" said Baur. "Let's get you in the driver's seat for this next scene."

The scene called for me to drive Kerr through this double file of marines. We did a few takes of the scene, including one that was a long master shot with the camera crew in the back of the jeep. I didn't take out any marines or lose Kerr or the cameraman, so it all turned out well, giving me a bit more screen time and the opportunity to add "jeep driver" to my résumé.

While I had the opportunity to work closely with the film's stars at times, I never developed any relationship with them. Even when I was doing the jeep scene, Kerr pretty much ignored me. She was having a romance with

William Holden during the filming, and if it was supposed to be a clandestine affair, it was the worst-kept secret of all time. They were, seemingly, rather open about expressing affection for one another and appeared to use any downtime to indulge in one another and banana daiquiris.

I remember at one point during the filming, Kerr's husband, Anthony Bartley, visited the set. Bartley had been a squadron leader and Spitfire fighter ace in the Royal Air Force and had been awarded the Distinguished Flying Cross after he scored eight victories against enemy aircraft during the Battle of Britain. From the moment he arrived, the atmosphere within the production became tense. It was palpable to everyone, but I ignored the glances and whispers, knowing it was best to keep out of anything that wasn't any of my business.

As for Holden, I found my feelings about him to be rather odd. He was an established star by that time, and yet I never found him to be awe-inspiring. I can't explain why I felt that way. He was always gracious to me whenever we briefly crossed paths, and I thought he was a good actor and extremely professional in the way he worked. But, to me, he just never had that aura of being a star.

That was just the opposite of another star I had the chance to work with: Clark Gable.

When I received word that I had been cast as Katy Fuller, the secretary to Doris Day's character, Erica Stone, in the romantic comedy *Teacher's Pet*, I was looking forward to getting to work with director George Seaton again and having the opportunity to meet Ms. Day. I was also beside myself that I was going to get to work in a film with Clark Gable.

To me, Gable was the archetype of a Hollywood movie star and leading man. This wasn't just getting to work with a big star; this was getting to work with the man who was known as "the King of Hollywood." To me, he was

Peter Warne in *It Happened One Night*, for which he won an Oscar; Fletcher Christian in *Mutiny on the Bounty*; and, of course, Rhett Butler in *Gone with the Wind*.

My mother had loved Clark Gable from as far back as I could remember. I had loved Clark Gable for as far back as I could remember. Hell, everyone I knew had loved Clark Gable for as long as I could remember. While Holden did nothing for me, it was just the opposite with Gable. I was unabashedly in awe of him and had to muster up the highest level of professionalism whenever I did a scene with him.

We were shooting *Teacher's Pet* in the spring, and as Easter rolled around, I colored an egg and wrote on it, "M.R. Loves C.G." I was far too shy to give it to him, so I gave it to his assistant and asked if she would pass it along.

Later that day, I ran into Gable in the hallway, and he broke out in that big smile of his and said, "Hey, thank you for the egg."

I blushed and managed to get out the words "You're welcome."

Throughout my entire career, I have greatly admired many of the people I have gotten to meet and work with. However, there have been a scant few who ever rendered me awestruck. Gable was one of those who did. And, while I always maintained my professionalism, there were times when it seemed surreal to be working with various screen legends—and never more so than when, thanks to my work on *Life with Father*, I was given the opportunity to work with my childhood inspiration: Noël Coward.

Having seen a local production of Coward's play *Blithe Spirit* and having read his first autobiography, *Present Indicative*, when I was a young girl, I was excited to learn that CBS was looking to cast the role of Edith, who was an Irish maid, in a live televised production of *Blithe Spirit* that was a part of a special series of dramatic productions they were presenting. A series like this was a perfect fit for CBS, which had carved out a niche by doing quite a bit of theatrical programming on shows like *Studio One*, which presented a wide range of dramas and the anthology series *Playhouse 90*. And the role was a perfect fit for me, as I had carved out a niche of playing maids.

I was aware that the network knew I was a trained actress and was out of my mind when I learned I had been recommended to play the maid in *Blithe Spirit*, which was going to be done with Claudette Colbert, Lauren Bacall, Mildred Natwick and Coward himself!

A few days later, I received a call that I was to meet with the show's coproducers, Charles Russell and Lance Hamilton, at a coffee shop down the block from Television City to discuss my playing the part of the maid. A theater impresario, costumier, actor and longtime associate of Coward's, Russell had teamed up with Hamilton, who was his lover, to create costumes for Coward's 1945 revue *Sigh No More*. Shortly thereafter, they had formed a management company to produce a touring revival of Coward's play *Fallen Angels*. They had followed that with a cabaret show starring Coward and Mary Martin at the Café de Paris in London and had then been tapped to produce the *Blithe Spirit* special for CBS.

Arriving at the coffee shop at the prescribed time, I brought something to my meeting with Russell and Hamilton that I didn't usually take along when I was meeting with producers, directors or casting people: my husband. I can't really explain why I decided to bring Effie with me, although in the back of my mind, I may have thought it couldn't hurt to bring along a handsome young man when meeting with a gay couple.

Effie, as I so hoped, was on his game that day. He was charming and personable, and Russell and Hamilton seemed as interested in him as they did in me assuming the role of the maid. It was a delightful meeting, and as we parted, they told me they would be in touch with me soon—and they were. They called me the following day and asked me a question that, even in the grandest of my old Albert Lea dreams, I could have never imagined being posed to me: Could I come to meet with Mr. Coward on Sunday afternoon at the Bogarts' home? That's the Bogarts, as in Humphrey Bogart and Lauren Bacall.

After a moment of stunned silence and a bit of confused stammering, I remember saying something like, "Okay, ah, sure. I mean, ah, yes. I mean, of course I'll be there. Oh, and what should I wear? A skirt, a sweater, a dress?"

Russell and Hamilton both laughed. "Come just the way you were the other day, dear," said Russell. "That will be fine."

When Sunday came, I drove out to 232 South Mapleton Drive in the mansion- and movie star–rich Holmby Hills section of Los Angeles. I could feel my heart pounding under my blouse as I turned into the driveway of the house that was the meeting place of the original Rat Pack, which was composed of Bogart, Bacall, Judy Garland, Frank Sinatra, Nathaniel Benchley, Sid Luft, David Niven, John Huston, Katharine Hepburn, Spencer Tracy, George Cukor, Cary Grant, Rex Harrison and Jimmy Van Heusen. Long before the more commonly known members of the pack, such as Dean Martin, Sammy Davis Jr., Joey Bishop and Peter Lawford, came along, this group became notorious throughout Hollywood for their hard-drinking all-night parties.

The Rat Pack got their name from Bacall, who, in the early morning hours of a Las Vegas party, walked in on a few of the charter members, along with Mike and Gloria Romanoff, Angie Dickinson and a few others, after they had put in a night of heavy imbibing. Bacall looked around at the bleary-eyed mess of humanity and said, "You look like a goddamn rat pack." The name stuck, and back in Los Angeles, the Bogarts' Holmby Hills home became the pack's de facto clubhouse, where they threw legendary all-nighters that included visits from Errol Flynn, Cesar Romero, Ava Gardner, Robert Mitchum, Elizabeth Taylor, Nat King Cole, Janet Leigh, Tony Curtis, Mickey Rooney, Lena Horne and Jerry Lewis.

As I stepped out of the car, all sorts of thoughts were rushing through my head, most notably, that along with the man and lady of the house, who were one of the most iconic couples ever to appear together on the screen, behind the big wooden door, which was getting closer and closer with each step I took, was Noël Coward, the man who had made such an impression on me when I was a young girl back in Albert Lea.

I remember taking a pause to smooth my skirt just prior to ringing the bell, and within moments the door swung open and a formally dressed butler asked me a question I gather most guests to that house didn't want to waste any time being asked: "What may I get you to drink?" I wasn't a drinker, so I just asked for what I knew Effie would have requested: a Scotch and water. The butler gave me a nod and led me down the hall to a large room with a parquet floor, wood-paneled walls, a large brick fireplace and, sprawled out on a rug, one of the most famous movie stars in the world, who was playing with his children.

Bogart, who was wearing a sweater with no shirt underneath, greeted me and explained that he wasn't a part of the day's reading. I stood there, not having any idea of what I should say or do and hoping beyond hope that I didn't look as nervous as I felt. A few moments later I was invited to move on to another room—a large den that housed a long table with chairs all around it and, in the corner, a grand piano with a framed photo of Ethel Barrymore sitting atop its closed lid.

And then, in a true through-the-looking-glass scenario

of the surreal that I'll never forget, a door swung open and in came Claudette Colbert, wearing a magnificent Dior suit with a fur collar. She gave me a curt nod with what seemed to be a forced smile, scanned her eyes over my sweater and skirt, and before I could even say a word, she was followed by Bacall, who was wearing a tailored gray men's suit dress with a beautiful pin. Bacall motioned for me to take a seat at the table, as Colbert, who seemed very high strung and nervous, never stopped talking. *My God*, I thought to myself as I sat in awkward silence, *will she ever stop talking?*

She finally did when the door once again opened and in walked Coward, wearing a velvet smoking jacket. He greeted the three of us and paced around the room, wringing his hands and going on and on in dramatic fashion about how he had just gotten in from Palm Springs. I had to remind myself to allow my eyes to blink and to take breaths as he went on and on about how everything and everyone out in "the Springs" was "fabulous, darling" and "marvelous, darling," phrases he seemed to work into either the beginning or the end of every other sentence.

Colbert and Bacall, who had joined me at the table, sat in rapt attention as Coward regaled us with all sorts of tidbits about this "fabulous chap" and that "magnificent dinner party." While continuing his stories, he reached into a satchel, pulled out copies of the script for *Blithe Spirit*, and placed them on the table in front of us. He continued on with another fabulous tale or two and then abruptly switched gears. "And now we'll read the play, darlings," he said.

I looked at the hefty three-inch-thick scripts in front of me and thought, *This will take hours to read.*

Coward passed on taking a place at the table and sat in an overstuffed chair in a corner of the room. For the first time since he had walked in, I had gained enough feeling in my legs to turn around toward him. And then, in a move that completely surprised me but seemingly went unnoticed by the others, I got up, crossed the room, and planted myself on the hassock adjacent to his chair. As he flipped through the pages of his script, I sat looking at him from just a few feet away.

My gosh, I thought to myself. *I can't believe I'm sitting next to Noël Coward . . . with Claudette Colbert and Lauren Bacall behind me . . . and Humphrey Bogart just down the hall, playing with his son and daughter.*

I took a quick glance behind me to see Colbert and Bacall with their noses just as buried in their scripts as Coward's was. I pretended to do the same, although I found it impossible to take my eyes off Coward. I watched as he put a cigarette to his mouth and lit it without looking up from the script.

I read this man's first autobiography when I was a teenager at the Albert Lea Library, I thought. *And now, here he is, right next to me, and I am working with him.*

Thinking about that gave me a momentary flash of confusion. As a thirteen-year-old girl reading *Present Indicative*, I had perceived Coward as being a middle-aged man, and yet all these years later, here he was in front of me, a middle-aged man. He was actually fifty-six at the time, which made me do a quick little figuring in my head. *Okay*, I thought. *That makes sense. He would have been in his late thirties when he wrote his first autobiography, so it would not have been unreasonable for a thirteen-year-old to have thought of him as being middle aged.* Still, in spite of the age calculations that were going on in my head, I couldn't take my eyes off of his face and his hands. To me, he didn't seem to be any older than I had thought of him being when I was a young girl.

When I think back on those moments—sitting there and looking at him, with only a few feet of nothing between us—I tend to think of myself as being almost in a trance-like state of awe, one that was broken when the tailcoated butler cleared his throat to get my attention and then handed me a tall glass that contained what had to have been a triple Scotch and water. Without thinking, I took a big sip of the drink, which slapped me back to reality. *God, that is just awful*, I thought as the alcohol hit the back of my throat like a burning-hot slap.

"Shall we begin?" said Coward as I placed the Scotch (which I would never touch again) on a nearby end table.

I followed along with the reading, and when my part came, I looked up, directly into Coward's eyes, and he delivered his lines with nonchalant aplomb, as if we were just having a real conversation. The reading, as I had suspected, went on forever, and through it all Coward was gentlemanly and kind as he periodically broke out of character to make an observance or give directions. After we finished the reading, we had a bite to eat, and Coward commented positively on my Irish accent, which sent me over the moon.

It was all so wonderful and exciting, and following our good-byes, I walked out of the Bogarts' mansion with my head in the clouds, so much so that I forgot to release the car's emergency brake, which, in just a matter of minutes, had my tailpipe filling the tony streets of Holmby Hills with billows of black smoke.

As we moved into serious rehearsals for *Blithe Spirit*, which had been scheduled to air on January 14, 1956, I came to like Coward more and more. He was stylish and dramatic, which I had expected, but he was also very nice to me. He was always fair in giving his time when I had a question, and was extremely patient as he worked with me to get the right emphasis on a line or to change one of my hand gestures.

While my relationship with Coward was professional

and positive, I, along with the entire cast and crew, soon realized the same could not be said for the way he interacted with Colbert, whom I rapidly came to detest. She had been what I perceived as cold, uncooperative and at times downright rude during rehearsals and even into the taping. While I, of course, hung on every word and direction Coward gave us, Colbert often interrupted him and rudely questioned his direction. Coward seemed to take her antics in stride, and knowing that he and Colbert were longtime friends who would often spend time together at his home in Jamaica, I just figured they were close enough— in the way an old married couple might be—for her to get away with that sort of behavior.

If that was the case, or if something else was going on between them, I don't know. All I do know is that Colbert never seemed comfortable during rehearsals, and by the time we got to the actually taping, she was a nervous wreck. She was constantly dropping pages of her script and fiddling with her scarf, which kept falling off. It was also apparent to me, and everyone else, that her constant interrupting of Coward escalated as each day went by. Still, in spite of the growing tension on the set, and the perceived frigid air that was forming between them, Coward retained his composure . . . for about a week. Then he had had it.

As we were taping one scene, Colbert abruptly dropped character and started yammering about something that was bothering her. When Coward asked what was wrong, she just kept interrupting him, until he finally stood up and yelled, "*Shut your fucking face, Claudette!*"

The entire set went stone-cold silent, and no one dared look up or at another.

"Shut my fucking face?" Colbert seethed back at him with a hateful glare. "*Shut my fucking face?*" she repeated at the top of her lungs.

Oh my, I thought as I stood frozen like a statue. *Now this is war.*

Once the drama of that little scene was over and we had moved on, I did all I could to avoid Colbert. Even in passing, I did all I could to keep out of her way. And when I did have to interact with her on the set, she was awful to me. As I would bend over to pour tea, she would gruffly grab my arm and push me over to where she thought I should be standing. She was downright rude to me at times, which, while it certainly added to my dislike of her, didn't really bother me that much, because she didn't seem to hit it off with anyone. I have since learned she was known for throwing tantrums from the time she was very young, but beyond that, it seemed as if something was bothering her. She always seemed extremely nervous and off-kilter from that first time I met her at the Bogarts' house right on through to the day we wrapped production.

Perhaps she was just at an odd place in her life and career. Her film work was behind her by that time, although she went on to win a Tony Award a year or two later, when she played the part of Dr. Content Lowell in *The Marriage-Go-Round* on Broadway. She also continued to do both theater and television work well into her eighties, and she won a Golden Globe and earned an Emmy nomination for her 1987 portrayal of Alice Grenville in the televised miniseries *The Two Mrs. Grenvilles*, which was based on the 1985 novel of the same name by Dominick Dunne.

So, I don't know what had gotten into her while we were doing *Blithe Spirit*, but whatever it was, it was evident to everyone, including Coward, who, from what I heard, wasn't shy about telling people that Colbert had been very difficult to work with during that show. I know he even touched on it in one of his later diaries, where, in referring to her performance in *Blithe Spirit*, he said that he had found her behavior to be "extremely tiresome." He also went on to write that while he felt she was an excellent actress and that he had "a definite affection for her as a person," working with her on *Blithe Spirit* had wilted that affection considerably, a situation he called "a sad pity."

If working on *Blithe Spirit* left me with cold feelings toward Colbert (which it definitely did), just the opposite was the case with Lauren Bacall, who I thought was divine. Bacall was only a few years older than me, but she was worldly and wise in a way that made her seem much older. That perception may have come from her being married to a man who was old enough to be her father (and who was already ill with the cancer that would claim his life the next year) and from her being the mother of two young children. By this time, she was a well-established star, having done that string of classic films with Bogart— *To Have and Have Not*, *The Big Sleep*, *Dark Passage* and *Key Largo*—and the romantic comedy *How to Marry a Millionaire* with Marilyn Monroe. But she was thrilled to be Mrs. Bogart and to be in Hollywood.

I don't think I have ever encountered someone who had such an innate sense of style, not just in the way she dressed, but in the way she spoke and carried herself, like a model, which she had been. She was warm, friendly, cooperative, and from the first day I met her, she gave me the sense that she was genuinely at ease with her life, both personally and professionally.

While I greatly admired Bacall and appreciated the kindness she showed me, we were never close. From my early days at Paramount, I was always conscious of my place in the professional pecking order and never tried to cozy up to those who were above my echelon.

Although my role as the Irish maid was neither one of

any great significance nor one that challenged me to stretch my acting chops, having the opportunity to get to know and work with Coward in the CBS production of *Blithe Spirit* was, at that point in my life and career, my greatest personal and professional experience. As the days trickled down to our final day of work, a sense of sadness crept over me that it was coming to an end. That sadness was greatly alleviated, if not completely wiped out, when Coward himself invited me to a sit-down dinner wrap party he was hosting at the home of the actor, singer and dancer Clifton Webb.

I was thrilled to have been asked to attend, and my breath was even further taken away when I arrived and learned I was to be seated at the same table as Coward, Webb and Mildred Natwick. Oh, if only I could relive that evening. Coward and Webb put on quite a show for those at our table, so much so that people from all the surrounding tables were all cramming in around ours to hear the stories. It was like watching a tennis match, with these two going back and forth, prompting each other to tell a wonderful story of such and such or to recall a juicy bit of gossip about so-and-so. I don't think I have ever laughed as much as I did while sitting at that table, and I felt as if I had died and gone to Heaven to have been right in the middle of it.

I knew that Coward was soon leaving Los Angeles for Las Vegas, where he was scheduled to perform at the Sands Hotel. Not knowing when or if I would see him again, I brought along my recording of his first Vegas appearance, *Noël Coward at Las Vegas*, and asked him to sign the cover, which showed him in a tuxedo, standing in the sand and drinking a cup of tea. Along with that treasured signed record album, I left the party that night with a beautiful bottle of perfume that Coward gave me and, more importantly, the greatest gift: the chance to have lived out the dream of getting to know and work with the man who had been such an inspiration to me as a young girl.

It was also during this point in my career that I realized another dream—one I had always perceived as being the ultimate dream—the opportunity to appear on Broadway. Yes, on the evening of November 24, 1958, I, Marion Ross of Albert Lea, realized the dream of walking out onto the boards of Broadway's 46th Street Theatre in the role of Asia Booth in the Milton Geiger play *Edwin Booth*. The show, which starred José Ferrer, told the story of the nineteenth-century actor whose brother John Wilkes Booth assassinated President Abraham Lincoln.

It seems as if this achievement would warrant a chapter of this book all unto its own—the fulfillment of the starry-eyed young girl's dream to go to New York and appear on the Great White Way—but in reality, my Broadway debut never produced the fireworks and fanfare I thought it would. In a way, the opportunity had just come to me as many other parts had, and I oddly found myself far less than over the moon about it.

My path to Broadway started when I was cast in the small role of Asia Booth, the sister of Edwin and John Wilkes Booth, when the play was being done at the Huntington Hartford Theater in Los Angeles. José Ferrer was directing the show as well as starring in the lead role. I didn't think it was a very good play, and my feelings were backed up with poor reviews and a lackluster response from the audiences. Still, in spite of its flaws, José, who by that time had been appearing and directing on Broadway for two decades, was determined to take the show to San Francisco and then on to New York. The part I was playing was not that significant, and he could have just as easily cast a local actress to play Asia, but he desperately wanted me to come along. I was all too aware that he would have liked our relationship to have been more than just a professional one, and while I did have to fight off his advances from time to time, we otherwise got along famously. I really liked him. He was charming, and once the boundaries of our relationship were finally set in place, we became good friends. And so, while I was less than enamored with the show or the role, I went out and bought myself a steamer trunk (which seemed very theatrical to me) and agreed to go wherever the show was to take me.

My memories of doing the show are sort of a blurred whirl, and while the dream of appearing on Broadway became a reality, it wasn't the way I had imagined it to be. Yes, it was interesting to be working in the heart of Broadway, on the stage of that Herbert J. Krapp–designed theater, with its innovative sloped orchestra, but that was it. It was more interesting than it was exciting. I don't recall ever feeling as if I had finally seen my dream of appearing on Broadway fulfilled. And I found it to be mundane: the entire experience was more like another job than the grandeur I had always envisioned.

The fact that I was not overwhelmed with working on Broadway was a blessing. Had it been all I had hoped it would be, I'm guessing I would have never wanted it to end, which it did—abruptly! Granted, ninety-three years had passed since Edwin Booth's brother struck down the nation's beloved sixteenth president, but, perhaps, it was still "too soon," as they say, and playgoers, who cared little or not at all about the life of the revered actor who had been tarnished by his brother's horrific deed, stayed away in droves, as I once heard a bomb aptly described. We received tepid reviews and performed to less than full houses; and after twenty-four performances, when the curtain fell following our December 13 show, the run of my Broadway debut came to an end.

Something else was coming to an end as I left New York: my twenties. I was nowhere near where I had hoped to be with my career by this point in my life, but along with the struggles and setbacks I had experienced, I had also achieved some wonderful successes. I may have been frustrated that it was all taking much longer than my old five-year plan had called for, but while I had not broken through with anything other than some minor roles, I was making a living as an actress and was optimistic and up-beat about the future. And so it was back to Hollywood, back to Effie, and the beginning of what would ultimately be two of my grandest productions: babies!

Chapter 11

My Real-Life Role as Mom

Upon my return from New York to Los Angeles, I began to accept something that I had been thinking about for a while, and that, perhaps, my less than stellar debut on Broadway had confirmed: it was not only on the stages of Broadway and in the world of "legitimate theater" that an actor could properly present their craft and find respect; those things could also be accomplished by working in film and television.

My heart may have still been in the theater, but as a practical matter, it was my work in film and television that was building my résumé, helping me make contacts and, equally importantly, if not more so, paying the bills.

When I think back on that time—the final year of the 1950s—I have memories of Effie being helpful, cooperative and understanding when, due to work, I had to be gone for long days or even for weeks at a time. He had finished college and, while still struggling over what career path he should pursue, was beginning to show signs for the first time of a willingness to consider working in a profession other than acting. He never came right out and admitted it, nor did I ever harshly throw it in his face, but I think we were both well aware that to establish a career as an actor took a dedication and a determined work ethic, which I had in spades and he completely lacked.

I can't say I ever resented it, but from the day we returned from our quickie marriage in Arizona, I always felt that I was the one who had to take the lead in everything that happened in our marriage and our lives. Along with being the sole breadwinner, I had to locate the places where we would live, and then, once we were settled, I would handle all the day-to-day things that were just the basic needs of living, from making sure we had toothpaste, toilet paper and bed linens to making sure there was food in the house and that the bills were paid.

Our marriage was never one with any sort of balance. In fact, it was always way out of balance, and there were many times when I would wish that were not the case and that things could be different. I wanted Effie to be like me, to be motivated and excited about making something of himself. He did go out on an audition from time to time, but nothing ever came of it, and he began to talk about giving up acting. *Well,* I thought, *that's all right.* I really didn't care if he pursued acting or decided to become a butcher or a baker or anything else. I just wanted him to have a career—to have a reason to get up every morning, to feel that he was accomplishing something, and to be able to partner with me in making a living.

And yet, that was neither to be the case nor a deal breaker, as it would have been to many women. I was always willing to give him a pass. I felt he was very unhappy because things had not worked out the way he had hoped. That didn't make me resent him; it just made me feel sad for him. I didn't think I could do anything to change him, and, to be honest, I was far too busy with my career to even bother trying, or to be aware of his increased drinking.

And so there I was, married to an unmotivated, unfocused, moody drinker, and yet if you had hooked me up to a lie detector and asked me what my home life was like, I would have passed with flying colors by saying it was a good life. It, of course, wasn't, but in an odd way—a way that became clear to me only many years later—it was the life I wanted. I never would have wanted to be in a weakened position in a relationship, one in which my husband totally took care of me and in which I had no power to do what I wanted to do and make my own decisions. I would have been miserable if I had been with someone who stood in the way of me achieving my dream, and with Effie, that was never an issue.

He was more than happy to let me be in control of everything and had no problem with my fervent drive, motivation and quest for a career, even if it meant that I was gone a lot. I remember at one point in our marriage, when I was doing a play, which meant I was gone from afternoon until late in the evening, our landlord questioned how I could do that—that is, be away from my husband for such long periods of time. She may not have understood it, but I did, and more importantly to me, Effie did. Crazy as it sounds, the landlady wasn't fine with it, but Effie and I were.

I think that while I may not have been really cognizant of it at the time, the reason I was always happy (or at least content) with my life with Effie was that I knew he would never get in my way. And a few years later, when our marriage finally began to crumble and I would feel so horrible about it falling apart, I would remind myself that it had been my decision to pick someone who wouldn't stand in my way. *You chose that for yourself*, I would chastise myself. *So quit moaning about your marriage not working. You chose it to be that way, didn't you? It was the way you wanted it to be, wasn't it?*

And it was the way I wanted it, up until the day I broke a bit of news to my husband that resulted in a response I had never expected: the news that I was pregnant.

For a month or so, I had kind of suspected that I might be pregnant, but I never said a word to Effie until it was confirmed by my doctor. Once I knew for sure, I was ecstatic, which, just like our polar opposite levels of ambition, was a response at the complete other end of the spectrum from his. Effie wasn't just unhappy about the prospect of our becoming parents; he was downright devastated and angry.

"*What have you done?*" he screamed at me in a rage that was unlike any he had ever displayed before.

I just kept saying, "It's okay. It's okay. Calm down. Don't worry. I'll take care of the baby," which I knew, just like everything else, I would have to.

But Effie was furious, and when I look back, I believe it was that initial reaction to my being pregnant that, for the first time, made me slowly start to fall out of love with him. If he was devastated by the news that I was pregnant, I was equally devastated by his reaction. I was dealing with feelings of frustration and inadequacy over my career not moving along as quickly as I had hoped, and now, on top of that, I had a husband who was enraged that we were going to have a child.

While I was completely taken aback, if not downright horrified, at Effie's reaction to my pregnancy, there was a part of me that felt that he just needed some time to digest and accept it. I had to remind myself I had been pretty much aware that I was pregnant for a while before I had let him know. That awareness began while I was on location at a naval station in Key West, Florida, filming with Cary Grant and Tony Curtis. I was playing the role of a navy nurse who had been stationed on a pink submarine in the film *Operation Petticoat*. I had missed a period during our first month of filming, and when I missed a second one, I was pretty sure I was pregnant. Still, I wasn't absolutely sure, and so I didn't share my suspicions with anyone, until one day, when a scene called for me to do something I wasn't sure a possibly pregnant woman should be doing, and I revealed my secret to, of all people, Cary Grant.

We were all supposed to go out to the submarine set and climb down into the sub and also do some underwater scenes. I was nervous about doing that, and as I sat waiting for us to be called to do my scene, I noticed Grant and Curtis talking nearby. After a few minutes Curtis walked away, and Grant, who a few moments earlier had noticed me and waved, came over to say hi.

"I don't think I should go down in this sub," I shyly told him.

He looked confused, because up to that point, any hesitation to do something adventurous was out of character for me.

"I think I may be a little bit pregnant," I said softly.

Well, the reaction I got from him was certainly no precursor to the one I would receive from Effie. He sat down next to me, put his arm around me, and said sweetly, "You're pregnant!" and when I looked up at him, he had tears in his eyes. This was years before he married Dyan Cannon and they had their only child, Jennifer, so he was so excited for me, and we had this marvelous moment together. I recall my eyes filling with tears, too, as one of the most handsome and famous movie stars in the world sat holding me and telling me how wonderful it was that I was going to have a baby and that I should just be careful and not exert myself too much while doing the sub scenes.

Because I wasn't 100 percent positive I was pregnant, I asked that we keep it as our little secret, and for the remainder of the shoot, he did, while I went on to do the sub scene and whatever else the script and the director called for me to do.

I really enjoyed being in Florida and working on that film. Both Grant and Curtis were so charming and very nice to me. It was also fun to be working with such a large cast, which included Dina Merrill, who was the Post Cereal heiress, and two young actors who would go on to become stars of popular television shows: Dick Sargent, who replaced Dick York in the role of Darrin Stephens on *Bewitched* for the show's last three seasons, and Gavin MacLeod, who played Seaman Joseph "Happy" Haines on *McHale's Navy*, news writer Murray Slaughter on *The Mary Tyler Moore Show*, and Captain Merrill Stubing on *The Love Boat*.

Among the memories I have of doing *Operation Petticoat* are two distinct occasions in which a strong feeling of ambivalence seemed to overtake me. The first came when I was invited to join in with some members of the cast and crew and go out on a boat for a night of fishing. We chartered a boat and arranged for a caterer to deliver all this marvelous food for our nocturnal adventure out in the darkness of the Gulf of Mexico. Janet Leigh, who was married to Tony Curtis at the time, was visiting the set and wanted to go along with us.

It had been a rather windy day as we prepared for our night at sea, and by the time we left port, the waters of the gulf were really far too rough for a bunch of adventure-seeking landlubbers. Not to be deterred, we shoved off, got an hour or two from port and, in spite of the waves and swells, attempted to do some fishing. That didn't go as we had anticipated. One by one, we all became so overtaken with seasickness that the plan to reel in some big ones was the only thing cast. Not one fishing line may have been tossed into the water, but the same was not true for the contents of some stomachs. We were all so queasy or outright sick that no one touched even a bite of all that wonderful food we had planned to dig into.

As the night went on, and we all tried to find our little

nooks on board the boat in which we experienced the least amount of rocking, a few of the guys started up a poker game. I remember sitting there watching Janet Leigh, who was just a year older than me. She had joined in the card game and seemed so happy-go-lucky and at ease with the guys. As I watched her win a hand and then lose a hand, the feeling came upon me that, even while I was doing films and television shows with the biggest names in show business, I was still a nobody who didn't fit in. I had done my best to fit in, while still being respectful of my place in the pecking order, but I constantly felt as if I was way out of my league.

That feeling made me just as nauseous as the rocking boat and my suspected pregnancy when I, along with just a select group of about twenty people associated with the production, was asked to a small dinner party being thrown by Tony Curtis. I was excited to have been extended an invitation, but I couldn't get beyond the nagging feeling that I just didn't belong.

The party was held on a ship, and when we arrived, Curtis was all decked out in a captain's uniform and was welcoming his guests aboard. He was handsome and so nice to me, and yet this overwhelming feeling of inadequacy had me in its grip. Maybe it had something to do with some hormonal changes I was experiencing from being pregnant, although I had certainly experienced waves of this same feeling long before I could blame it on that.

I just felt that my career was not moving along quickly enough. I was rapidly closing in on my thirtieth birthday, and in accordance with my old five-year plan, I should have been a star by now. Yes, I was regularly mingling with the elite of Hollywood, doing films and television shows with them and, for the most part, being treated very kindly and respectfully by the biggest names in the business. And yet I still never felt like I belonged.

I was still that player sitting on the bench who, while the legendary coaches and big-name star quarterbacks knew me and were nice to me, constantly questioned if I even had the right to be dressed in the same uniform and to be on the team. I had been in some impressive productions, including the Vincente Minnelli–directed feature *Some Came Running*, with Frank Sinatra, Dean Martin and Shirley MacLaine. But the parts I had played were all small. So small that in some cases I could have stood out in front of a movie theater, waving to people as they filed out after seeing a film I had been in, and they would have wondered who the hell this nutty lady was who was waving at them.

Not only did I feel unimportant—like a nobody—but I was also constantly around people who were some of the most important and famous people in the world. If you ever wanted to feel like a real nobody back in the late 1950s, all you had to do was spend a little time hanging around with the likes of Gable, Coward, Grant or Sinatra.

While I may have tried to blame that current wave of frustration and melancholy on hormones, the fact is those feelings constantly unnerved me from the time I signed the Paramount contract right on through until *Happy Days* had been on for a few years. It was only after about the third or fourth season of *Happy Days*, by which time it had become this cultural phenomenon, that I finally felt as if I had made it and really belonged. Up until then, even during the first few seasons of *Happy Days*, when the cast would go on these softball tours, everyone would be screaming and climbing all over themselves to see Henry Winkler, Ronnie Howard, Anson Williams and Donny Most. And then, if they even noticed me at all, they would say, "Oh yeah. You're the mother, right?"

"A hit show and I'm still a nobody," I would mutter to

myself during our public appearances and then drift into the background—back to the bench.

And so I was back in Los Angeles, and if it wasn't enough that I was fighting off these frustrating feelings of inadequacy in regard to my career, I was also facing seven months of pregnancy with a husband who embraced the idea of being a father with the same feelings one would welcome a serious case of the flu. Luckily, the weeks that followed his initial anger over my pregnancy saw Effie calm down quite a bit. I never got the feeling he was really thrilled about our pending offspring, but as with just about everything else, he seemed to lack the drive to keep up the level of anger he had displayed at first.

While one may think that this would have been an extremely trying time for me, it really wasn't. I wasn't at peace with my career, I was carrying a baby that my husband didn't want, and within a short time I would be showing a huge stomach and then meeting the needs of a newborn, both of which would hamper my getting roles for some time to come. And yet I recall being rather content and even happy during that time.

I felt very strong physically throughout my pregnancy. I really took care of myself, ate all the right things, drank almond milk, and swam every day. I felt very fit and healthy right up until I gave birth to a baby boy at Providence Saint John's Health Center in Santa Monica on September 10, 1959. While all I had ever dreamed of being was a famous actress, I was now the wife of a man whom I seemed to understand less and less as time went by and the mother of James Ross Meskimen.

We had decided to name our baby James after Effie's grandfather James Loveless, whom he dearly loved. From the moment I suspected I was pregnant, I had started to think of names and felt if I had a boy, I would love to name him Ross as a tribute to my family. I did bring it up to Effie once or twice, that I really liked the name Ross, but I never pushed it. I knew he was set on naming him after his grandfather, and I felt that, perhaps, that would be the magic to changing Effie's feelings about becoming a father.

In the days and months following Jim's birth, Effie genuinely surprised me. In a complete turnaround from his initial reaction to becoming a father, he seemed to be happy to have a son. And yet he always seemed to keep a certain distance from Jim. He was attentive and helpful, but there just seemed to be a lack of the normal connection one would expect to see between a parent and their child.

During the last few months of my pregnancy, when it became impossible for me to work or even go on auditions for future work, I started to worry about two things: our finances and my career, both of which were dwindling. Because of this concern, I made it clear to my agent that within a short time after my baby was born, when I felt I was physically ready, I wanted to get back to work. And that happened. Jim was only a few weeks old when I was called for a role in CBS's *General Electric Theater*, an anthology series that was sponsored by General Electric's public relations department and hosted by Ronald Reagan.

When I showed up for rehearsals, I felt weird: I was unfocused in a way that was out of the ordinary for me. I had trouble remembering my lines, something that had never happened before. I remember mentioning this to someone on the production, and they told me that I shouldn't worry and that it was just because I had recently had a baby. Well, I, for the life of me, couldn't figure out why having a baby would affect my memory. But I just tried to ignore it and forged on with determined diligence. I had no choice. Yes, I had a baby who wasn't even two months old. Yes, it was highly out of the ordinary for a mother to leave her baby and go back to work so soon during that time. But, no, I had no choice. We had rent to pay and mouths to feed: three of them!

I had looked into hiring a nurse to come in and help Effie take care of Jim, but the cost was beyond what I could afford. That meant I had to do everything possible to care for Jim when I could, and I had to have everything arranged so it would be as easy as possible for Effie to handle when I couldn't be there.

Fortunately, as the final months of the decade slipped into history and the 1960s began, there was a lot of television work available for an actress with my experience. I didn't feel I could commit myself to anything that was long running or demanding or that would take me away from Los Angeles, so realizing that stage and feature film work were out of the question for a while, television was fine with me. Doing work on a television series was the closest thing to having a "normal" job, and my hope was that I could keep getting work and return home each day to a more and more "normal" family life.

By the dawn of the new decade, I seemed to go from show to show without much of a break. The roles were rarely ones I could really sink my teeth into or that would make me a household name, but it was work—which translated into a paycheck and the continued building of my résumé—and it fostered the belief that every actor clings to, which is that any part, no matter how small or seemingly insignificant it may be, could lead to the coveted "big break."

The name Marion Ross may not have been one to garner something more than blank stares from most Americans, who were at the time seeing women's hemlines reach unprecedented heights, were embracing or fighting against a new genre of music known as rock 'n' roll, were watching a hotly contested presidential campaign play out that pitted then vice president Richard Nixon against then

Massachusetts senator John F. Kennedy, and were being affected personally, emotionally, or both, by the escalation of the United States's involvement in the Vietnam War, but with television set sales booming, they couldn't help but to see my face.

When I think back on that time, the shows I worked on and the roles I played are pretty much a blur. I would get up very early, get everything ready for the baby's day, get myself ready, and then have Effie drive me to whatever studio I was working at that day. I would then go to Hair and Makeup, slip into my wardrobe, and play everything from someone's daughter to a mail-order bride for series such as *The Chevy Mystery Show*, *Zane Grey Theatre*, *Philip Marlowe*, *Father Knows Best*, *The Untouchables*, *Thriller*, *Stagecoach West*, *The Barbara Stanwyck Show*, *The Loretta Young Show*, *Markham*, *Rawhide*, *The Detectives*, *Mrs. G. Goes to College* (which was retitled *The Gertrude Berg Show*), *Kraft Mystery Theater*, and far too many other comedies or dramas to mention or recall.

When I wasn't working, I loved being a mother. I was as fascinated by Jim as he seemed to be by me. I enjoyed playing with him, talking and singing to him, and showing him things. From the day I brought him home, he was a good-natured and well-behaved baby. He was curious about everything and interested in anything I showed him. Always cooperative, he caught on to things quickly and seemed to understand how to play various games without being taught. If ever there was a perfect baby, especially for a working mother, Jim was it.

While Effie never seemed totally comfortable in the role of a father, I believe he did try to interact with Jim to the extent he was capable. I'm not quite sure what their days were like when I was off working, but to his credit, Effie did seem to keep the ship running in my absence and didn't complain much when I returned. But it was clear that he lacked the paternal gene. When I was around, he was more than happy to have Jim in my care.

It made me sad that Effie just seemed to be unable to really enjoy his son, his family or even his life. But he did try, and he did have his moments. As Jim got older, Effie even began showing signs of embracing responsibilities more so than he ever had before. I would be thrilled when I saw those moments and would delude myself into thinking that things were really changing, but there was always an underlying tension, which stemmed from my being a working actress while he still drifted along without much of a plan, if any at all. And there was still his constant, and increasing, consumption of Scotch.

While Effie dealt with his demons and depression, I found myself getting antsy. It wasn't a bad time of life for me; in fact, there were some times in which we seemed like we were on our way to becoming a normal and happy little family. We were a bit unconventional, perhaps, but as I easily reasoned to myself, a conventional life would have left me quite bored.

I can't say I gave a tremendous amount of thought as to what was going on behind Effie's all too often stoic veneer, but I was well aware of what was brewing within me. I was in my early thirties, which was, at the time, a bit old for having just had a first child and way old for breaking out in starring roles as an actress. I also began to have longings that did run more along conventional lines. When I was at work, I would sit on the set while the crew was setting up for the next shot and would hear people talk about this home they were building or remodeling or decorating. I may have prided myself in not being the conventional type, but the more I heard these stories, the more I found myself falling into the role of a conventional thirtysomething woman who wanted her own home.

I became as obsessed with putting down roots in a home

as I was with noting how time was running out for me to make it as an actress. Just as I thought that having a baby would establish us as a regular family, I became convinced that the one thing that was holding us back was that we didn't have a real home to call our own. The reason for that was, of course, that we were living on the money I was making, which, while it wasn't bad in comparison to what other women (and even some men) were making at the time, was a mere pittance compared to what would be needed to purchase a home in Los Angeles. Everywhere I went, especially in the Studio City area, where we lived, I began noticing houses. For the first time in my life, I took notice of various types of architecture, the colors and textures of materials used, and how trees and gardens were incorporated into the design of homes.

During that time, Effie had taken to spending time with José Ferrer, who was preparing to direct the Rodgers and Hammerstein musical *State Fair*. José had a beautiful home with a tennis court and a pool, and he enjoyed having Effie over to play tennis with him. It seemed to be good for Effie to get out in the sun, exercise, and mingle with all the stars and fabulous people who seemed to gather at José's house on a daily basis. I was always invited to accompany Effie, but I never did. I had a baby to care for, and I greatly treasured the time I had with him when I wasn't working.

One time when José was begging me to come over, I told him that I couldn't but that there was something he could do for me.

"What's that, Marion?" he asked.

"Well, I know you are preparing for your new show, and I was wondering if you could give Effie a job."

José truly liked Effie and, like me, knew that a regular gig would do a world of good to his outlook on life, as well as to our financial situation. And so he hired Effie, not as an actor, but as his personal assistant. Effie em-

braced the work with gusto, and he and José got along so
well that he decided to cast Effie in his next show, the Saul
Levitt play *The Andersonville Trial*, which recounts the
trial of Captain Heinrich Wirz, the Swiss doctor who com-
manded the Confederate garrison at Andersonville, Geor-
gia, during the Civil War.

The role Effie was offered was not a significant one, but
it was work, acting work, and not just acting work—but
acting work on Broadway, on the stage of Henry Miller's
Theater. The cast included Herbert Berghof, who, along
with being an actor, was considered one of the nation's
most respected acting teachers and coaches; Lou Frizzell,
who is, perhaps, best known for his small role as the phar-
macist in *Summer of '42*; character actors Albert Dekker
and Russell Hardie; and a then thirty-two-year-old actor
by the name of George C. Scott, who won critical acclaim
for his portrayal of the prosecutor in *The Andersonville
Trial*.

When José first offered Effie the role, he was hesitant to
accept it. He knew it would entail going to New York for
an indefinite period of time, leaving me alone in L.A. with
an infant. I assured him I could manage and told him that
he simply must go—that it was a great opportunity that
could lead to bigger roles. And so off to New York he
went. I had conjured up and used all my acting skills to
convince him I would be just fine, although I wasn't exactly sure how I would take care of Jim and continue to
work. That concern, however, was quickly quashed when
a lovely woman who lived next door to us and loved Jim
offered to watch him while I worked.

And so it all seemed to be working out: I had child care,
consistent work, and a husband who wasn't only employed,
but employed doing what he had always hoped to do in
the world's biggest arena. I would try to manage my work-
days so that I could get home during my lunch break to

give our neighbor a break, do wash, and fold some diapers. From what I could tell from his calls, Effie seemed to be happy to be working and earning a paycheck. He even seemed proud to be able to send me a little money every week.

My feelings about Effie may have been ambivalent at times, and there was never a doubt that I just didn't understand his lack of ambition, but I did love him, and while he was gone in New York, I missed him terribly. When I spoke with him, he sounded upbeat and told me he was meeting a lot of people and making good contacts. He said that he felt New York was his ticket to finding the acting career that had eluded him in L.A., and on a few occasions he made reference to having Jim and me join him there. When he had moved to New York, he had left this big old empty steamer trunk right in the middle of our living room, and sometimes during our phone conversations, he referenced the trunk, said that I should sell everything except some essentials, pack those in that trunk, and head east.

"Broadway is what you always really wanted," he would tell me. "Forget Hollywood and television. Theater is where your heart is, what you really love. I think we could really do well here—both of us."

It was rare to hear Effie sounding so upbeat and positive, and while I hated to throw a wet towel on his newfound enthusiasm, I just could not imagine packing up my baby and going back to New York, where I would have to establish all new contacts and start at the bottom again. Heck, I wasn't that far from the bottom after all I had done in Hollywood, but at least I knew I could get work.

I was also finding myself becoming more and more head over heels in love with the idea of having my own home. When I would drive to work, I would look at all these darling little houses I would pass on St. Clair Avenue, right off of Moorpark Street. At the time, those homes, which now sell for close to a million dollars, were selling for around seventeen thousand dollars. At night, just before falling asleep, I would try to think of ways I could make enough money to put a down payment on a house. I knew getting a loan from a bank was out of the question. Banks didn't lend money to actors—any actors. The ones on my side of the financial equator were too much of a risk, and the ones on the other side—the stars—didn't need loans.

There was, however, one idea that kept recurring, and one day I mustered up the courage to act on it. I called my father, made some small talk about how things were going with Jim, my career and Effie, and then took a deep breath and said, "I would like to ask you a question. Do you plan on leaving me anything when you die? I mean *anything*, as in money."

There was a long pause and a little laugh before he told me that was, in fact, his plan.

"Well, whatever you plan on leaving me, I would like to have it right now so I can buy a house," I blurted out in such a point-blank way that my words came as a surprise even to me.

He said that he would consider it, but felt it was only fair to talk it over with my brother and sister first. After doing that and, I assume, getting their blessing, he called to tell me he would open a bank account in my name, put three thousand dollars in the account, and send me the passbook.

I was elated. I quickly found a cute little home, put a down payment on it, moved in, and began fixing it up to make it a home. Effie, who never seemed to be either happy or upset that I had bought a home, just took it with a "What the heck are you thinking and doing?" type of attitude. Well, as time went by, just what the heck I was doing proved to be a far wiser choice than joining Effie in

New York. After *The Andersonville Trial* closed, those friends and contacts Effie was supposedly making didn't exactly come through for him.

And so he returned to L.A., to a darling home, a beautiful son, and a wife who hoped this would now be the real start of our life together as a normal family. I was thrilled to have him home and enjoyed hearing all his stories about New York. He seemed more energized than I had ever seen him, and I thought that, perhaps, having had the opportunity to act in a professional production and earn a paycheck would serve as the spark that would ignite his ambition and motivate him to seek auditions and find work. That was not the case, not during the first few weeks after his return nor as the months went by. The setting may have been different—our own little home, which I just loved— but the story line was the same, as we fell back into the same routine of me working and him staying home with Jim.

It is amazing to me when I think back on this time, how, as the first few years of the sixties passed, my dream of becoming a big, famous star slowly gave way to my approaching acting as a job, in some ways not unlike being a file clerk or demonstrating Scarfinets. I was no longer a girl in her twenties with a five-year plan that would lead to stardom. I was a woman in her early thirties with a three-year-old child and a husband who, in spite of what I had hoped for upon his return from New York, was still drifting through life and was becoming more and more dependent on the bottles of Scotch he was going through at an ever-escalating pace. I was also something else: pregnant!

While the mere mention of the year 1963 conjures up all sorts of images in people's minds, from the Beatles and the Vietnam War to the elevation of Giovanni Montini to Pope Paul VI in the wake of Pope John XXIII's death and the assassination of President Kennedy, to me, that year will always be overshadowed by one thing: the addition to our family of Ellen Loveless Meskimen.

Unlike the anger he had displayed when I told him I was pregnant the first time, Effie was accepting of the fact that we would be having another child. I would have loved to say he was ecstatic or jubilant about it, but I think to say he was happy might have even been a stretch. What he was, was accepting.

While breaking the news to Effie was much easier the second time around, the actual process of bringing another child into the world was, for me, quite a bit harder. For some reason, my daughter made her entrance on to the world's stage in a much more dramatic fashion than her older brother—for me, that is. Everything about Jim was easygoing, right from my pregnancy and his travel down the birth canal to the well-mannered and cheerful disposition he always displayed. Ellen was just the opposite. They say that no matter how painful a birth may be, the mother forgets it all once her newborn baby is placed on her chest. That wasn't the case with me. All these years later, I still remember the pain. While I had given birth to Jim without much effort and little pain, my second round of childbirth was enough to have me screaming for something—anything—to help me get through it.

Having been told I had already been given everything they could give, my daughter finally popped out and a feeling of peace came over me. As I held her for the first time, I once again had the feeling that this would be the thing to change everything. We now had our own home and two children, and I was finding regular work. As for Effie, well, what can I say? Effie was Effie. His search, as well as his desire, for acting work had all but disappeared. He rarely sought work, and it had got to the point where he never even talked about the possibility of being an actor.

That was, of course, nothing new for me, and by that time I had pretty much given up on him ever changing. Just as it had never really bothered me in the past, neither did it then. It was simply the way things were. And besides, I was consumed with being a mother again, just thrilled to have a beautiful little girl, whom we named after my mother, with a middle name that paid homage to Effie's side of the family.

Jim may have been the best baby ever as far as demeanor goes, but Ellen was physically perfect. I would sit holding her as she slept and would just stare at her—in awe over what a pretty baby she was. I was also very conscientious about Jim's feelings. In the weeks after Ellen's birth, I felt this strong need to be very protective of Jim. I didn't want him to feel shunned in any way because of the new baby, and so I believe I may have overcompensated by giving him even more attention than I was giving Ellen.

When I look back at that time, I think I became so overly protective of Jim, with his sweet nature, that I began treating Ellen in much the same way I felt I had been treated by my parents. Because they had had their hands full with caring for a disabled child, I had always felt that I was expected to toughen up, fend for myself, and that I certainly should not expect any fawning attention. I had grown up feeling that because of the way I was treated as a child, I became a strong-willed woman, and while it may not have really been a conscious thing on my part, I think I felt that because she was so pretty, Ellen would benefit by being treated the same way.

"Come on. Shape up and be strong," I began telling her before she was even crawling. "You have to be a strong girl so you can grow up to be a strong woman."

Almost from the day I brought him home, Jim had been so tremendously cooperative and fun loving. I loved to get down on the floor with him and play, which would make him laugh and laugh. Ellen was very different. She had a tendency to keep to herself. She was also far more opinionated and demanding than her older brother, and yet from a very early age, she was also much more introverted and private. She is still, to some extent, that way today. When something is bothering her or she has a lot on her mind, she doesn't tell me much, and sometimes nothing. Jim is just the opposite. I pretty much always know what is going on with him.

Was that just the way they were born? Was that just the individual personalities they were bequeathed? Or did the way I raised them have something to do with that? I'm sure those are questions every mother asks herself. But I feel I worked very hard with my children when they were young, and while conceit isn't a part of my makeup, being pragmatic is: I may not have been the world's greatest mother, but I think I was a damn good one—certainly the best I knew how to be—especially when they were very young. I felt a lot of pressure to be a good parent. I was, for all intents and purposes, the one who had to be the good parent, the one who had to take care of everything— as was the case in so many aspects of our family's life.

I would not say that Effie was a bad father as much as I would say he was simply—for the most part—a nonexistent one, even when he was with Jim and Ellen. He did take care of the children while I worked, but I never felt as if he ever truly connected with them. I do believe, in his own way, he loved them, but children had never been a part of the plan for him, if in fact there had really ever been any sort of plan at all.

When Ellen was still a young baby, Effie and I began arguing more than we ever had before. There was a lot of yelling, especially when he was drinking. I think he was very unhappy and depressed, and while he had never been given to really step up to the plate and do something about that, or anything, I do believe he got to the point in which he knew, to preserve his own sanity as well as mine, he had to get out of the house and start doing something. By that time, even though he never admitted it to me, I think he knew his chances of getting even an audition, much less a role, were remote. And so, as surprising as it was, to me more than anyone, he got a job in banking—a management position with a savings and loan.

This was the first time in our marriage that Effie had an actual, real full-time job, and again, in what was a surprise to me, he seemed to fit into the work world. He would get up really early, read the newspaper, study the business page, and head on out to Encino, where his office was located. He was still handsome, and because of that, along with the brooding charm that had first attracted me to him, all the women at the bank liked him . . . a lot! I think, in a way, that was what really motivated him, and as we began to get used to having his income along with mine, he decided it was time for us to upgrade to a bigger house that was closer to his work.

And so we made the move from Studio City to Tarzana, where, for all the world, it appeared we had it all. Effie had a good, stable job, we had two beautiful children, and I was working very regularly and getting some good roles in just about every popular television series of the time, including *Route 66*, *Dr. Kildare*, *The Outer Limits* and *Mr. Novak*. I also, for the first time in our marriage, didn't feel the pressure to have to take every job and work as much as I could because I was the sole breadwinner. And yet, unlike so many other times, our life in Encino—ironically, the most "normal" one we would ever have—never gave me the feeling that now things would be the way I had always wanted them to be. Maybe that was because I had been burned too many times in the past, or, more likely, it was because there was another factor at play, one I was still, unbelievably, unaware of: Effie was an alcoholic.

How could it have been, I have often wondered, that I

didn't realize just what a negative effect alcohol had on my husband and my family during that time? I don't believe I was in denial at all about his alcoholism. I just think I was still downright naïve and not at all aware of it. I think that had been the case since he was in his early twenties and in the service. I also think I was not out of the ordinary when it came to my cluelessness. This was the early sixties; everyone we knew smoked and drank; no one, even if they were an alcoholic, discussed it publicly; and there were very limited resources—certainly nothing like today's overabundance of available information—as to what separated a person who was suffering from the clinical disease of alcoholism from someone who was just a social drinker or even a heavy drinker.

I may have grown up in a family of Midwestern Presbyterians for whom liquor played a very little role, but as a woman approaching her midthirties who had now lived more of her life in California than Minnesota, I just thought every man came home from the office and poured himself a big glass of Scotch, and then another, and then another.

And yet Effie was, as I would later learn, a "functioning alcoholic." Yes, he drank every evening until he got drunk and passed out, but he also got up early, read his paper, accepted my heartfelt encouragement as he headed off to work and, seemingly, did a good job. But, unlike other times during our marriage, the arguing and yelling continued. He also seemed to fluctuate more than ever before between being happy about life and being extremely discouraged. He had always been moody, but this was different. He had become increasingly crabby and critical of me—in fact, by his own admission, he was downright sick of me. Our sex life had become nonexistent because he was always passing out, and while he did continue to function, he got to the point where he was always either drunk or hungover.

During this time, I had begun to attend church with our neighbors. They attended a Methodist church, and I felt welcome and at home there, and so I became a Methodist. I think I found solace in the church, because I knew that the love that had once existed between Effie and me, which had been quietly leaving our marriage for some time, was now dwindling at a far more rapid pace.

Our marriage, like any marriage, wasn't all rosy and, by all means, had had its ups and downs. But where we were now was a very different place than any we had ever been in before. I remembered that shortly after our quickie marriage, which had caused such a drama, I had read a book on relationships that said something to the effect that most marriages tended to be good for two or three years before real difficulties and challenges started creeping in. *So, all right*, I thought. *We had our few good years, passed through the difficult and challenging years, and we are now, very possibly, heading toward the end.*

When we had a few people over for a party, that feeling moved from being a quiet and painful belief that things were really not going well to the realization that it would be very difficult, if not impossible, to maintain our marriage. Effie had been drinking heavily, and for some unknown reason, he flew into a rage. He picked up one of my scripts and began tearing it up and throwing the pages all over. Then it escalated, and he started throwing pots and pans around and screaming. That was the first time I had ever been frightened of him, and in the days following that event, I think we both sensed our marriage was falling apart.

We had a mutual friend who hung around with us a lot, and shortly after Effie's blowup at the party, he decided he was going to go and stay with him for a while. Shortly thereafter, our friend called me when Effie was at work and, in a roundabout way, told me to be careful and to look out for myself and the children. I wasn't totally sure what he meant by that, but what I did know was that it wasn't good. I had already been scared, and that call really struck a note with me. I began to worry about everything: my safety, my children's safety, Effie. It seemed like every ounce of my energy was going into worrying. And then, one day, Effie came home. We sat on the couch, and he told me he was an alcoholic.

As I sat listening to him, I remember thinking, *What's an alcoholic?* I know that sounds simply unbelievable, but remember, during that time the terms *alcoholic* and *alcoholism* were not ones that were familiar to most people, and certainly not to me.

He told me that he was very unhappy and that he was going to check himself into a hospital to dry out. I told him I understood (but I didn't) and went to the hospital with him. Being that I was so naïve and this was all so new to me, I remember thinking, *Okay, so he'll stay here in the hospital for a few days, until he has all the alcohol out of his system, and then that will be that. He won't be an alcoholic anymore.*

When I say I didn't understand anything about alcoholism, I really mean not anything. Even today, all these years later, the disease still has a stigma associated with it, but back then, it just wasn't ever talked about. I did, however, talk about it with a dear friend. I confided in her that Effie had to be hospitalized and was in the process of getting better. She sat quietly listening to me. She didn't seem to be surprised or to stare at me with any sort of wide-eyed wonder. She just listened, and when I told her that Effie would soon be all better, she explained to me that it wasn't that simple and that he had a very long and possibly difficult road ahead of him. Now I was the one sitting wide-eyed.

"Marion," she said quietly. "I know what he is going through, because I'm an alcoholic."

I sat in stunned silence for a few moments before saying something along the lines of that just not being possible, and then I was assured by her that not only was it possible, but it was also a fact. I was flabbergasted and began asking her all sorts of questions. She was able to provide me with answers to many of those questions I posed. I felt as if my eyes had been opened to a world that, even though it had existed right under my nose for many years, I had never been aware of.

I became somewhat obsessed with learning everything I could about alcoholism, and my friend became my go-to source for answers. She told me about Alcoholics Anonymous, that they had regular meetings both for people suffering with alcoholism and for family members who were impacted by their disease. I went to a few meetings but felt very uncomfortable being there and much preferred leaning on my friend for answers and support.

When Effie finally left the hospital, he made the decision he was not going to return home immediately. He felt that until he really had things under control, it would be best for everyone if we lived apart for a while. With his absence, I spent more and more time with my friend, who, as time went by, introduced me to an elderly friend of hers who was also an alcoholic. I spent a lot of time with them, studying them and asking all sorts of questions. I was determined to understand this mysterious disease, and one night, when the kids were staying with a neighbor because I had an early morning call to do a commercial, I decided to do some research of my own.

We had always had a good supply of alcohol in the house, and with Effie gone, it wasn't dwindling by even a drop. I remember, on this night, going over, opening up a bottle, smelling it, pouring myself a Scotch and water, and downing it. When I finished it, I poured myself another, and then another one after that. I remember feeling pretty good. In fact, I was having myself a downright wonderful time and began calling old friends I hadn't spoken to in a long time. Who knows what I may have said to them? I certainly don't, but what I do remember is realizing that I had to be up early to do that commercial and so I should really get to bed. I got up off the couch and realized that wasn't going to be as easy as I thought it would be. I wobbled around the living room, bounced off a wall or two, and could barely make it down the hallway to my bedroom, where I flopped on the bed as the room spun around me.

I had never been much of a drinker, and the three or four Scotches I had that night were by far the most alcohol I had ever consumed in one evening. Heck, it was more than I had ever had in any given month! I don't remember anything else about that night, but I do have a vivid memory of my alarm clock going off at some ungodly hour, reaching over to turn it off and, for the first time, experiencing the excruciating wave of nausea, the throbbing headache, and the feeling that my tongue was stuck to the roof of my mouth that come with a night of overindulging.

I had the worst hangover I have ever experienced, and the fact that I somehow pulled myself together, got to the studio, and did that commercial is a testament to the strength a human being can somehow summon to accomplish what seems to be an impossible feat. I felt as if I had been run over by a train, which had then dragged me along and finally deposited me in a hot and dusty field where both the ground and the horizon were unsteady and even the slightest sound or movement caused pain in every inch of my body.

My God, I thought to myself as I somehow got through that day. *If this is what drinking does to you, why in the world would anyone ever do it?*

I do remember, as the day wore on and my pain somewhat subsided, reminding myself that this had all been done for a noble reason: as an experiment to educate myself on the effects of alcohol. "Fine," I recall muttering to myself as I drove home from the studio. "My experiment was completed, and now I shall swear to God, on the lives of my children, to myself, and to anything else I should be swearing to that I am still in too much pain to think of, that I will never do that again."

Chapter 12

My Luckiest Airplane Ride

By the time Ellen had celebrated her first birthday, my marriage was anything but normal or conventional, if, in fact, it could even still be considered a marriage. Effie was constantly coming and going—living at home for stretches and then gone for days or even weeks at a time. When he was at home, there was a lot of arguing and yelling, and whatever help he may have received at the hospital had been washed away with Scotch. He was still working and, to some extent, assisting me financially, if not physically or emotionally, in keeping our household running. I also continued to work, which was becoming more of a stressful situation as I tried to balance my career with the raising of a five-year-old and a toddler on my own.

The chinks in our marriage were clearly evident by this time, but the first real fissure of consequence, which would prove to be a harbinger of what would lead to its end, occurred when I experienced the first loss of my life. During the final years of my father's life, he lost his hearing and experienced the health issues that come with age. When I received the call that he had died, it was the first time I had experienced the death of someone very close to me.

None of us know how we will deal with a difficult situation, challenges or the loss of a loved one until we actually face those issues, and while I was crushed by the news of his passing, I found myself handling it with a sense of calmness and acceptance. I never really thought about it at the time, and I honestly never really gave it much thought until I began working on this book, but I have always seemed to deal with bad news, even the loss of dear friends, family members and beloved pets, in a very matter-of-fact way. That is not to say I haven't experienced the horrible pain and deep sadness that come with a loss, but I have always had the capacity to process the news of a death very quickly, accept it, adjust, and move on. I have never been the type to fall into a deep sense of grief over a loss. In fact, I don't know if I ever really knew how to grieve in the way I have seen others handle a death. I don't know what gene I may either have or be lacking that makes me that way, but it has always been a part of my makeup—to be pragmatic, keep my chin up, and just deal with whatever needs to be dealt with.

In the case of my father's death, the thing that needed to be dealt with was to get to San Diego to be with my mother and assist her in the planning of his funeral. I wanted Effie and the children to go with me, and since I just expected Effie to be there for me, I was shocked when he told me he didn't want to go. We had very young children who needed to be cared for while I tended to all the issues surrounding my father's death, and Effie's attitude toward me was cold and uncaring in a way that made it clear to me that whatever love we may have had for each other had deteriorated to a point that it could not be saved.

With my father's death serving as the impetus for the beginning of the end of our marriage, I did find myself experiencing bouts of depression. It wasn't a depression that I ever considered to be debilitating in any way, but rather one that left me in a fog of deep disappointment, melancholy and anxiety. I had always felt, from the time when I was very young, that I had the strength to handle things on my own, and yet there was something about the anxious feelings I was experiencing that told me I should seek professional help, and this realization was coupled by the urgings of a few close friends.

Just as the experts at Alcoholics Anonymous relieved me of the guilty confusion I was feeling by explaining that I was powerless to change an alcoholic's behavior, the psychiatrist I went to see made me feel better when he told me it was completely natural and normal to be feeling the way I did.

"There's nothing crazy about being upset over a crumbling marriage, financial concerns, the fear of losing your home, and the well-being of your children," he told me. "If you weren't feeling anxious and depressed over these things, then you would really have a problem."

While Effie and I didn't formally divorce until 1969, our marriage and life together had been over for years before that. When we did officially separate, the children were old enough to understand what was happening to some extent and took it hard. We all did. They continued to live with me in Tarzana but did go and stay with him at times. When they would return from spending time with him, they would say that he had told them he loved me and wanted to come back and live with us again. At one point, after the children returned and pleaded with me to let him come back, we did try a brief but ill-fated reconciliation. After that, we both knew it was really over, and Effie and I sat down and talked about it like civilized people. I got the impression that even though our marriage was over,

Effie was in no hurry to make it final. I knew if I let it linger on, it would just keep both of us and the children in a state of limbo, which I didn't want to put any of us through. And so, just as with everything else that happened throughout our marriage, I was the one who had to take the initiative, contact an attorney, and handle the arrangements that would bring the marriage to an end.

In the weeks and months following our divorce, I began taking more jobs than I had in some time and felt confident that I would be able to continue to support myself and the children without Effie's help. I even rented out a room in our home to a college girl for sixty-five dollars a month to help me get by.

It was a time of strange emotions for me. On some days I had that springlike feeling of renewal many people experience following a divorce. I felt as if I was at the beginning of a new chapter of my life that could be exciting and rewarding. And yet there were also days when I couldn't get over the mess I had gotten myself into. On those days I cried a lot and felt like such a failure. Divorce, for anyone, brings with it the knowledge that you were a tremendous failure at something that should have been your highest priority to make work.

I had wanted my marriage to work. I had wanted us to be a family like the ones I did parts in on shows like *Father Knows Best*. And I had wanted to have succeeded at making my dream—the one I had been so dedicated to from the time I was a child—a reality. All those things had been very important to me, and yet here I was, no Mrs. Hotshot, no Mrs. Big Shot or Mrs. Big-Time Actress. In fact, I wasn't even a "Mrs." at all anymore. I had failed at two of the things that had been the most important to me: my career and my marriage. This nagging sense of failure soon saw the bad days overtake the good ones, and had it not been for the love of my children and my dedication to them and their care, I think that psychiatrist I had gone to see would have reversed his analysis about my not being crazy.

While it was a very difficult time for me, I did everything I could to shield my despondency from my children, the people I worked with, and just about everyone I encountered, other than a few close friends. I began going to church a lot and immersed myself in reading the Bible. I really felt I was finding strength and hope in various scriptures, and I embraced Christianity in a very personal and deeply spiritual way. That really began one Sunday, after coming home from church. I was feeling down and hoped I could soak away some of my blues by taking a nice hot bath. As I slipped into the tub and let the water envelope me, I became extremely emotional and started crying uncontrollably. I remember lifting my hands upward and saying, "I give up, God. I can't do this anymore. I repent." I just kept saying it over and over until I cried myself out.

During this time, I saw my sister more than I had in many years, and we often talked about our faith and religion. She was, however, the only one I talked to about my faith. I didn't want anyone else to look at me as one of those people who, after hitting rock bottom, finds Jesus and constantly reads the Bible and prays. But, during that time, that was very much who I was.

I was trying to do all I could to lead a Christian life. I was tithing my income, even when it was derived from an unemployment check, and I thanked God for my children and for the gift I believe He had given me to perform. Now all I needed was for something to break for me to be able to share that gift in the way I had always hoped to. I was tired of feeling like a failure, of constantly struggling, of worrying as each job ended when the next one would come, and of wondering if I would ever get the opportunity to, if not realize my dream, at least feel as if I was successfully accomplishing something—anything.

We have all read or heard the inspiring stories of people who have turned their lives around and overcome great disappointments, setbacks and failures. Many of those stories include grand moments of awakening—dramatic epiphanies in which lightning bolt strikes provide clear intuitive perception and insights. My moment—the one that shook me out of my depression—wasn't quite so monumental. In fact, it simply took place one afternoon, as I sat at my kitchen table, aimlessly staring at the floor.

Maybe the piece of linoleum that caught my eye had just broken, or maybe it had been that way for months. I had no idea. But there it was, sticking up in a curl that made it look like it was staring back at me with this big old snarling evil grin. I knew we had some leftover linoleum out in the garage, and after rummaging through a few things, I came upon a nice big square of it. I went back in the house, cut the big old snarling grin away, cut the new piece to fit the area to be replaced, heated it up in the oven, slathered it with glue, and pushed it into place.

Maybe I just got lucky when it fit in so perfectly I couldn't even find the seams, but handling that repair so quickly and adroitly gave me a boost like I hadn't had in a long time. I stood back to look at my handiwork, and this wave of strength and determination came over me. "Well, well, just look at you," I said to myself. "Boy, oh boy, you not only fixed it, but you did a great job."

It wasn't nailing an audition for a great part, getting cast in a leading role, or stepping out of a limousine and having the crowd yell, "*It's Marion Ross!*" but at the moment, it just may as well have been. They don't give out coveted awards for fixing linoleum floors, but the way I started singing and dancing around my house, you would have thought I had just collected an armful of Oscars, Emmys and Tonys.

It was in that insignificant and mundane moment, inspired by a little piece of curled-up linoleum, that I felt like my old self for the first time in a long time. *All right,* I thought. *I may now be a woman in my early forties with kids in grade school. But I also have a substantial acting résumé, and so why can't a woman who can so magnificently repair her kitchen floor still realize her dream of becoming a star!*

I began making a lot of calls, touching base with my agent and old contacts, letting them know I was very actively seeking work. I even went as far as to hire a press agent to help me shape my career and garner some publicity. When I look back on that time, I have no idea where I came up with the two hundred dollars it cost me to retain her each month, but somehow I did. And it was money well spent.

I began getting calls for various television series and show pilots, but I needed something more to happen than that. I was now the sole breadwinner, and while that was a role I had been accustomed to playing in the past, this time it was different. It was no longer simply providing for my husband and myself and coming up with the rent for a little apartment. I now had to handle the mortgage on an Encino home, along with supporting two children. My life-changing linoleum moment may have gotten me back into the game, but I was still finding myself either sitting on the bench or getting third- or fourth-string roles—neither of which could maintain the lifestyle I was living, much less transform my dream into a reality.

I was out there scrambling, making the rounds, calling everyone I knew, and really hustling for roles. If I got wind that someone was doing a pilot or a film, I did all I could to get in touch with their casting people. One of those peo-

Here I am with my mother, Ellen Ross, by Lake Waconia, Minnesota, in 1929. *(Author's personal collection)*

With my sister Alicia (left) and brother Gordon (right) in 1930. I was two. *(Author's personal collection)*

With Alicia on a trip to
Saskatchewan, Canada.
(Author's personal collection)

With Alicia in Minnesota --
note the bathing suits!
(Author's personal collection)

"Watch me Daddy!" My brother Gordie is on the inner tube. *(Author's personal collection)*

Posing with Gordie.
(Author's personal collection)

Easter Sunday with
Alicia, Dad, Gordon, and me.
I had just had my appendix removed.
(Author's personal collection)

With my mother and brother,
about 1942.
(Author's personal collection)

San Diego, 1948. I won the S.D. Journal Award for Best Actress,
Little Theatre Tournament, for Checkhov's *A Marriage Proposal*.
(Photo permission granted by Amy E. Allison, Director of Administration, The Old Globe)

Under contract to Paramount, 1952. (I made $150 a week!
I had been making $38 a week filing at Bullocks!)
(© Paramount Pictures. All Rights Reserved.)

From *Life with Father*, CBS.
I was Kathleen the Irish maid.
(Photo courtesy of CBS Broadcasting Inc.)

The Glenn Miller Story, starring Jimmy Stewart and June Allyson, 1954.
(Photo courtesy of Universal Studios Licensing LLC)

With Cary Grant during the filming of *Operation Petticoat* in 1959.
(Photo courtesy of Universal Studios Licensing LLC)

Clark Gable and Marion,
Teacher's Pet, with Doris Day.
Clark signed it:
"To Marion--Let's Do It Again."
(© Paramount Pictures.
All Rights Reserved.)

With Tony Curtis while filming *Operation Petticoat*. "Am I thrilled!" *(Author's personal collection)*

From my appearance on *Perry Mason*. *(Photo courtesy of CBS Broadcasting, Inc.)*

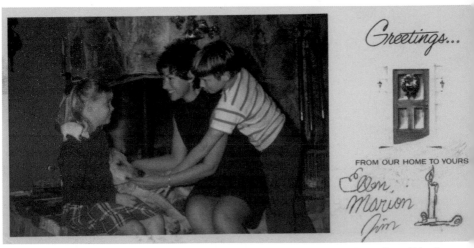

Christmas 1968 (I was divorced), with Ellen, Jim, our white rat, and our dog, Abigail.
(Author's personal collection)

Happy Days:
Marion and Tom Bosley
as Laurel and Hardy.
*(Photo courtesy of
CBS Television Studios)*

Happy Days Ball Game,
Garry Marshall at the fence.
Note my wedgie shoes!
I could hit!
*(Photo courtesy of
CBS Television Studios)*

With Garry Marshall. *(Author's personal collection)*

Paul and Marion in 1988. *(Author's personal collection)*

Marion and Gwen Berohn, Marion's assistant for 26 years. *(Photo credit: Dennis Hennessy)*

Marion and Rosa Salazar, Marion's housekeeper for 25 years. *(Photo credit: Gwen Berohn)*

Christmas 2016 with the family! My children, their spouses and my wonderful grandchildren! *(Author's personal collection)*

Happy Days cast at Marion's seventieth birthday party, 1998: Don Most, Scott Baio, Henry Winkler, Ron Howard, Marion Ross, Erin Moran, Ted McGinley, Cathy Silvers, Clint Howard, and Anson Williams.
(Author's personal collection)

Jim Meskimen, Marion, Rance Howard, and Ron Howard on the set of *How The Grinch Stole Christmas*, 2000. *(Author's personal collection)*

Erin Moran and Marion at the Motion Picture Academy. *(Author's personal collection)*

At my house, Happy Days Farm, 2017. Memorial supper to honor the passing of Erin Moran: Scott Baio, Cathy Silvers, Marion, Anson Williams, Ron Howard, Don Most.
(Photo credit: Cathy Silvers)

As Lorelai Gilmore the First on *Gilmore Girls.*

A very special photo from Ron Howard. *(Photo courtesy of Imagine Entertainment)*

ple was the writer and producer George Seaton, who was casting for a film he had written and would be directing called *Airport*, which was based on Arthur Hailey's 1968 novel of the same name and in time would prove to be the impetus for the "disaster film" genre, which would become so popular throughout the 1970s.

I didn't know much about the film, except that it would star Burt Lancaster and Dean Martin, that Seaton would be directing it, and that I made the fortunate decision to stop by his office with a résumé and photo. Once I was granted the opportunity to meet with him, it all went much the same way as the hundreds of other similar meetings I had been in with casting people and directors: a quick exchange of pleasantries while being looked over from head to toe and a thirty-second spiel on what I had recently done. The one thing that made this meeting different was the way it ended. Unlike my typical closing spiel of "I'm very grateful for your time," I instead blurted out, "I'm recently divorced, with two children. I really need this job, and so, please, can I have your card?"

Seaton sat with his mouth open for a second or two and then said, "What do you want my calling card for when it's a part that you want, right?"

I shook my head in agreement.

"Okay, then," he continued. "Show up for casting."

A week or so later, I made my way to the Universal lot, where I had been told to report, and made my way to the soundstage where they were casting for *Airport*. As I walked into the stage, a wave of nostalgia (and not the good kind) swept over me as I realized it was a "cattle call," not unlike the one I had experienced at Paramount all those years earlier. There were all these actors just sitting around, waiting for that minute or two in which they hoped to distinguish themselves from the crowd. I hadn't been on an audition for a part like this in some time, but it was clear to me that nothing had changed. There was that same look on all the actors' faces, one that every actor knows all too well: the old "I desperately need this part" look. As is always the case with these things, there was very little, if any, small talk as we all just sat there, staring at the stage floor and avoiding eye contact with anyone.

When my turn came, I did all I could to wow them with my newfound linoleum-repair-inspired enthusiasm, subtly shaded with what I hoped was just enough pity-inducing despondency that Seaton would remember me as the pleading divorcée who had kids to feed. In retrospect, I think none of those things meant anything. They were looking for actors with genuine acting chops. My résumé showed that I fit that bill, and soon thereafter, I received a call that included the sweetest four words any actor can ever hear: "You got the part."

I was thrilled, although my agent, my publicist, some friends and a handful of others, who were all looking out for my best interests, were far less than happy about it.

"You can't take that part," I recall someone (if not everyone) telling me. "It's a nonspeaking extra role that is way beneath what you have been doing."

Maybe so, I thought (but didn't ever actually come out and say to anyone), *but it's work—paying work—in a feature film, and I need it.*

Yes, it was a nonspeaking role of an airline passenger, a role that most directors would have filled with an extra, but Seaton had opted against that for a reason. He knew that the people playing the parts of the passengers would be far more highlighted than a typical extra simply walking through a scene in the soft-focused background. He was also aware they would be closely interacting with the film's stars and would be clearly reacting to the horrific situation they were caught in.

Everyone around me may have thought I was making a

mistake by taking that role, but maybe, just maybe, God wasn't one of them. Maybe all those prayers I had been praying had finally gotten through to Him, and in the mysterious ways in which He liked to work, what seemed like an insignificant role to everyone would prove to be the most pivotal turning point in my career and my life. The characters in that film may have found themselves in a disastrous situation, but for me, landing a role in *Airport* would prove to be the luckiest airplane ride I would ever take. Had I not gotten that role, the chances are more than good that I would have never been cast in *Happy Days*, that my lifelong dream would have never come true, and that at this very moment, you would be reading a book by someone other than me.

While everyone had rolled their eyes at my taking the part in *Airport*, and while I had no idea that my involvement in that film would prove to be a major stepping-stone toward the big break I had always dreamed of, I really enjoyed working on that production.

Prior to filming, all the actors who were playing the roles of passengers were shown a film about what happens to people when a plane loses pressurization and oxygen. When we actually got on the set, which was the fuselage of a plane, I was positioned two rows in front of the distinguished Academy Award–winning actor Van Heflin, who played the bomber, D. O. Guerrero; and Helen Hayes, who played the stowaway, Ada Quonsett. It was exciting to get to work with someone of Hayes's stature, even though I had no direct interaction with her. She was, of course, a legend. She had established her career as a performer before I was even born, and had won a Best Actress Academy Award while I was still an Albert Lea toddler.

While I would have loved to have had a role that gave me the chance to really do scenes with members of that impressive cast, I found it to be enjoyable and relaxing just to work with my fellow passengers by doing reactions and to get to know so many of them during what seemed to be quite a bit of downtime between scenes. We would all sit around the set and tell one another stories about our lives, our families, our careers and our hopes. We became a close little group, and it seemed as if each day, the stories being shared brought about more drama—either laughter or tears—than what we were emoting when the cameras were rolling.

One of the actresses, Sandra Gould, who was playing the part of a passenger, became an especially good friend of mine. She was a few years older than me, and her early career had been very similar to mine in that she had done small roles in numerous films and television shows. But unlike the rest of us uncredited passengers, she had landed a role that provided her with regular work and a recognizable face. Her name may not have resonated with the public, but during the time we were shooting *Airport*, she was also in the midst of what would ultimately be an eight-year run for the hugely popular ABC situation comedy *Bewitched*. Gould played the part of the shrill-voiced, nosy neighbor Mrs. Gladys Kravitz, and five years after *Bewitched* was canceled, she reprised the role on the one-season spin-off, the ABC series *Tabitha*, which starred Lisa Hartman as the grown-up witch daughter of *Bewitched*'s Samantha and Darrin Stephens.

I enjoyed Sandra's company very much. We became fast friends, and in the crazy and unpredictable world that show business is, she unexpectedly played an important role as another piece of the puzzle—another vital stepping-stone—in making my childhood dream come true by inviting me to join her for dinner one evening. When I arrived for dinner, I learned that Sandra and I would be joined by another one of her friends, Millie Gussie, who was a casting director. We had a wonderful evening together, and as the night wore on, we began talking about our upcoming projects. Sandra was looking forward to the next season of *Bewitched*; Millie had so many irons in the fire, my head was swimming; and I, embarrassingly, had nothing to share.

"Well," Millie said slowly in response to my shrug over having nothing planned, "I would like you to come by my office. I'm looking to cast a role that I think you may be perfect for."

Chapter 13

My "Lovely" Big Break

The role Millie was looking to fill was that of an all-American-type 1950s mother and housewife for a pilot that had been written and was being produced and directed by a man by the name of Garry Marshall. Garry, I would quickly learn, had been a joke writer for various comedians, including Joey Bishop and Phil Foster. He had also been a writer for *The Jack Paar Tonight Show*, *The Dick Van Dyke Show*, *The Joey Bishop Show*, *The Danny Thomas Show* and *The Lucy Show*.

A few years earlier, he had created and produced a sitcom for NBC called *Hey, Landlord*, which starred Will Hutchins, who was best known for the role of lawyer Tom Brewster in the popular Warner Bros. Western television series *Sugarfoot*, which aired on ABC from 1957 to 1961. In *Hey, Landlord*, Hutchins played a man who inherited from his uncle an apartment building filled with colorful tenants, and while the show lasted only for one season, it set Garry up for what would be his first major success: the ABC television series *The Odd Couple*, which starred Tony Randall and Jack Klugman and was adapted from

Neil Simon's play by the same name. As a 1968 feature film, *The Odd Couple* had been a box office hit for Jack Lemmon and Walter Matthau.

Enjoying the success of *The Odd Couple*, Garry knew the iron was hot to strike with another show, and with the turbulent 1960s behind us and the United States still embroiled in the very contentious Vietnam War, he reasoned Americans were primed for a show that would take them back to the simpler times of the 1950s. The new show he created, which Millie was casting the mother for, was called *New Family in Town*. Garry was green-lighted to do a pilot of the show, with its idealized vision of life during the Eisenhower administration, for Paramount. Millie and Garry obviously thought I had the wholesome maternal look they were searching for, and I was cast in the role of Marion, the mother of a Midwestern family known as the Cunninghams.

After finishing my work in *Airport*, I was still in desperate need of work and continued to get small roles in various television series until Garry was finally ready to shoot the pilot for *New Family in Town*. Along with me, the cast included Harold Gould, in the role of my husband, Howard; Ron Howard and Ric Carrott as my sons, Richie and Chuck; Susan Neher as my daughter, Joanie; and Anson Williams as Richie's best friend, "Potsie."

I knew of Gould's work, which paralleled mine: extensive work in theater and a string of small roles in films and television shows. I was also well aware of Ron, who had been a fixture on television since he was five years old and had played the part of the little boy with the lisp in the 1962 film version of *The Music Man* and, of course, Opie Taylor in the hit CBS sitcom *The Andy Griffith Show*. As for the other cast members, Ric and Susan had done very little professional acting work, and Anson's only claims to fame were appearing in theatrical productions at Burbank

High School, where he had also been the captain of the track team, and appeared in a few commercials including one for McDonald's.

By this time in my career, I had appeared in enough pilots that had never seen the light of day to know better than to get my hopes up. To me, Marion Cunningham was just another role, although I believe I may have, for a fleeting moment, let myself revel in the idea that Garry was right, that Americans were ready for a little soda-shop-sweet nostalgia, that the show would be picked up and would become a hit, that my financial woes would be forgotten, and that my dream of becoming a star would finally become a reality.

If, in fact, I did allow myself that foolish pleasure, it was short lived. Paramount passed on *New Family in Town*, and as was done in those days, the pilot was recycled with a new title, "Love and the Television Set" (later retitled "Love and the Happy Days" for syndication), for the television series *Love, American Style*. Hearing that a pilot was turned down is always disappointing, but shooting a pilot is also something every actor (perhaps as a defense mechanism to ward off depression) goes into knowing that the odds are against it getting picked up. And so it was back to the grind of finding television work, which, for the first time in a long time, began to get less and less frequent.

I'm not quite sure as to why I hit a dry period of television work, but for whatever reason, I had to find something—anything—and fast. Whenever actors hit a period like that, they think back on everyone they have ever worked with or for and then attempt to reach out to them. It was no different for me, and as I went through my contacts, I thought of a conversation I had had with some of my fellow passengers while doing *Airport*. We were having the typical type of conversation that actors have about the agents, casting people, producers and directors we have

worked for, and as we chatted away, it came up that I had
been involved with the Old Globe Theatre and knew Craig
Noel. There we were, sitting on this fake airplane between
scenes, and all these actors were contorting themselves
and bending over their seats to hear what I was saying.

"Oh my! You know Craig Noel," I remember one of
them saying in disbelief.

"I do," I replied. "And he told me anytime I wanted to
do a play, I should just let him know."

The other actors seemed to be in a state of shock.

"He really said that to you?" I recall one of them asking me.

Well, he did say that to me, and while I hadn't given
that offer much, if any, thought in quite some time, with
television work now scarce, I began thinking, *Boy! I've
got to take advantage of that contact.*

I began doing some research on what the Old Globe
Theatre had on its slate, saw that they were going to be
doing Tennessee Williams's *Summer and Smoke*, and called
Craig and told him that I was interested in taking him up
on what I hoped was still a standing offer, and that I
would like to return to my old stomping grounds in San
Diego and do the role of Alma Winemiller.

There was a short pause and more than a bit of surprise
and hesitation in his voice as he said something like,
"Huh! What? Oh! Alma, huh? Well, ah, yeah. I mean,
sure, all right. Alma? Really? Well, yeah, I guess. Okay.
Uh-huh."

Anyone else may have been a bit put off by his stammering, but I had two things on my mind that made me
impervious to his lack of enthusiasm over my return to the
boards of my old haunt: one, that he had given me a standing offer to perform at the Old Globe and, two, that I was
taking him up on it because I needed a job! So I glossed
over Craig's surprising reaction, and then we arranged for

a meeting to discuss further my taking the role of Alma. It was a good thing I didn't know then what ensued right after we hung up.

He announced to everyone in the office—all of whom remembered me—that he had just spoken to Marion Ross and she was interested in the role of Alma. According to the reports I received much later, everyone in the office looked at him in stunned silence and then at each other with blank stares.

Yes, I was aware that I was a bit on the old side for the role. Okay, I'll come out and admit it: I defiantly conjured up more of the image of the motherly Marion Cunningham than I did of the high-strung unmarried minister's daughter, who, by the play's end, had emerged from being a girl "suffocated in smoke from something on fire inside her" and was pleading for a steamy romance with the young doctor who lived next door, but, hey, I needed a bloody job!

After my meeting with Craig, we decided that under his direction, we could make it work. He showed me how he wanted the part to be played and cast me as Alma. I made arrangements for where I would stay in San Diego, and while I did at times feel like I wasn't really comfortable doing the part, mostly because I had been away from the stage for so long, I was glad to have the work. It also made me feel good to know that, no matter how far away I would ever roam, if I returned like a prodigal daughter after things went wrong, Craig would always be there to catch me and welcome me home.

And then, one day, in my dressing room at the Old Globe Theatre, as I was preparing for a performance, it happened—the break I had been dreaming of and working toward for over thirty years.

I don't really remember if there was just one or two people present or if the entire office had crammed into my dressing room to break the news they had just read in the paper that the pilot I had done for Garry Marshall, the one that had aired as a *Love, American Style* episode, had been picked up by ABC. Here's what I do remember: I turned around in my chair and screamed, "What! Please, get me that paper!"

How I managed to concentrate on doing the show that night, I'll never know. And if how I did that was a blur, things got even blurrier over the following days, when my agent informed me that they did, in fact, plan on staying with me for the role of Marion.

"Now we have just got to get you out of that play," said my agent.

My manager disagreed. "No, stay in the play! There's no reason you can't do both. It's a half-hour flight between Los Angeles and San Diego. You can fly up to L.A., get over to the studio, say, 'Oh, Richie, you're not eating, dear,' and then return to San Diego and do the play."

Of course, that was an oversimplification, and in reality, it would never really work out logistically. And so, Craig, who was more than thrilled for me, released me from my contract, and back I went to where my Hollywood career had started all those years ago—the Paramount lot.

Wow, I thought as I said good-bye to everyone at the Old Globe and headed back up to Los Angeles. *How lucky I am to have taken that nonspeaking role in* Airport, *which led to meeting Sandra, who introduced me to Millie, who thought I'd be a good fit for Marion.*

I just constantly shook my head in amazement as the freeway signs kept indicating that L.A. was getting closer and closer. *Maybe all that dreaming, hard work and prayers are about to pay off,* I thought. *Maybe this will really prove to be the big break I have craved for so many years. Maybe my time has finely come to leave being a nobody behind for good, to really do something with my life, and to never again have to worry about how I am going to pay the bills from month to month.*

As I neared L.A., I could see the Hollywood sign on Mount Lee out in the distance.

"Wouldn't that be just so lovely?" I kept repeating over and over as I headed home to Encino. "So very lovely."

Chapter 14

My Dream Becomes a Happy Reality

In much the same way that all the pieces of the puzzle came together for me to be selected for the role of Marion Cunningham, various elements had magically merged and made the powers that be at ABC decide to pick up Garry's pilot.

That all started in 1972, when, before he would become world renowned for the *Star Wars* and *Indiana Jones* franchises, a young filmmaker just a few years out of the University of Southern California named George Lucas decided to produce a screenplay he had written about his teenage years growing up in Modesto, California, in the early 1960s called *American Graffiti*.

As Lucas began to put together the cast for his film, which would ultimately include the then unknown Richard Dreyfuss, Harrison Ford, Mackenzie Phillips, Cindy Williams and Suzanne Somers, he remembered seeing the *Love, American Style* episode about a 1950s family. Lucas did a little digging, found out that it had originally been a Garry Marshall pilot, called Garry's office, and asked if he could view it. That arrangement was made, and Lucas was so impressed with Ron Howard in the role of Richie Cunningham that he cast him to play the recent high school graduate Steve Bolander in *American Graffiti*.

Released in August of 1973, *American Graffiti* became a huge blockbuster hit—one of the top grossing films of that year—and then went on to receive five Academy Award nominations, including Best Picture. In the wake of *American Graffiti*'s success, coupled with the success of the musical *Grease*, which had opened on Broadway that summer, a wave of 1950s and '60s nostalgia swept America, and ABC, which had previously snubbed Garry's belief that the nation was ready for a good healthy dose of simpler times, was now desperate to get a nostalgia show slated for January of 1974. The call went out to Garry, a meeting was hastily arranged to view the pilot again, and the green light was given to bring back the Cunningham family in a show they retitled *Happy Days*.

As soon as Garry knew it was all a "go," I was contacted, as were Harold Gould and Ron Howard. Ron was available and interested; Harold was interested but not available. Committed to doing a play in Europe, he had to pass on reprising his role of Howard Cunningham, which meant Garry had to find a new actor to take on the role of the family's patriarch.

In what I thought was an ironic bit of fate, Harold's loss of the role in *Happy Days* was the second time in less than a decade he had appeared as a father in a show's pilot, only to have the show recast after being picked up. In 1965 he had originated the role of Lou Thomas, the Brewster, New York restaurateur father of the actress Ann Marie, who was played by Marlo Thomas, in the pilot for *That Girl*. Alas, when the show received the green light from ABC and was slated for the fall of 1966, the producers recast the father's role with Lew Parker.

I had felt bad that Harold missed out on getting the part

on *Happy Days*, but in the ensuing years, fate would once again provide yet another twist when he was cast to play Martin Morgenstern, the father of Rhoda Morgenstern, played by Valerie Harper, on *Rhoda*, a role that earned him an Emmy Award nomination. Harold, who really chalked up a wonderful career, having done over three hundred television shows; twenty feature films, including *The Sting*, with Robert Redford and Paul Newman, which won Best Picture; and hundreds of stage plays, continued to work into his eighties, gaining renown as Miles Webber, the suitor of Rose Nylund, played by Betty White, on the hugely popular NBC series *The Golden Girls*.

Faced with recasting Howard, Garry decided to offer the role to Tom Bosley. Tom had achieved great accolades, which even included a Tony Award, in the late 1950s and early 1960s for his role as former New York mayor Fiorello H. La Guardia in the long-running Broadway musical *Fiorello!* He then went on to appear in about a dozen feature films and numerous television shows and specials, including the TV film *Arsenic & Old Lace*, which aired on the anthology series *Hallmark Hall of Fame*; *Car 54, Where Are You?*; *Bonanza*; *Bewitched*; *Get Smart*; *The Streets of San Francisco*; *The Virginian* and many others.

While Harold Gould had been reserved and very much the gentleman, I found Tom to be difficult to work with. From our very first meeting and table read, he had a lot of opinions and was forceful with Garry and the writers that Howard Cunningham would be a dominant figure in every episode. *Okay*, I remember thinking. *He's a pushy little fellow, huh. Well, it will be interesting to see how far they let him go and how long they will put up with his input and demands.*

As for me, I was just thrilled to be a part of it all, even though Marion's role in the beginning was small and unimportant. My lines were usually not much more than an occasional "Oh, Howard," "Oh, Richie," "Dinner is almost ready," or "What time will you be home?"

Along with Ron, who was playing my son Richie, as he had in the pilot, the producers brought Anson Williams back to play Potsie Weber. To round out the new cast, they hired a darling young girl named Erin Moran to replace Susan Neher in the role of my daughter, Joanie. Erin's parents were free-spirited types who had been pushing her into an acting career since she was very young. By the time she was six years old, she had done some commercial work and had been cast in the CBS series *Daktari*, an adventure show that was based on the 1965 film *Clarence, the Cross-Eyed Lion*. On *Daktari* she played an orphan who was taken in by the veterinarian and conservationist Dr. Marsh Tracy, who was played by Marshall Thompson, at his Africa-based Wameru Study Center for Animal Behavior. In 1968 she appeared in the feature film *How Sweet It Is!*, with Debbie Reynolds, and by the early years of the 1970s, she was getting regular work on shows like *The Don Rickles Show*, *The Courtship of Eddie's Father*, *My Three Sons* and *Family Affair*.

The producers also brought in two New York actors, Donny Most and Henry Winkler, to play my son Richie's friends Ralph Malph and Arthur "Fonzie" Fonzarelli. Donny was a quick-witted redhead who was very sweet but had very little professional experience. Henry was a very quiet fellow who always wore a Windbreaker and at first struck me as being moody and unfriendly. He had done some commercial and theater work before coming to Los Angeles, where he had landed small roles in episodes of *The Mary Tyler Moore Show* and *The Bob Newhart Show*. I was also told he had just completed shooting a feature film called *The Lords of Flatbush*, which had yet to be released. In the film he played a 1950s "greaser" type, which was what put him on the radar screen for the producers of *Happy Days*.

As we began shooting the first episodes of *Happy Days*, if I ever felt as if my role was small, I would just look at poor Henry. Although he would go on to become the breakout icon of the show, during that first season, he hardly had any lines. They would just have him strut into the bathroom at Arnold's Drive-In, take a look at himself in the mirror, see that his hair was perfect, put his comb away, and walk out. That was about it.

As is the case with most television series, especially ones that are fortunate to be successful and live on for many seasons, *Happy Days* began with a basic premise and then grew in different directions as the years went by and the characters developed. Just like in real life, television characters are organic creatures that find themselves growing and maturing—doing things, saying things, experiencing situations, and going in directions that had never been thought of by the producers, writers or actors when the show was first created.

Our show had a lot of young writers, guys in their late twenties who were, to a large extent, street kids out of New York, just like Garry. They were a very lively bunch who, like most television writers, looked out for themselves and were highly protective of the ideas, character developments, plotlines, and especially the sight gags and laugh lines they brought to the table. In the production of a television sitcom, it's very rare that the producers and actors don't know exactly which writer brought this or that idea to the table, especially if something is successful, works well, gets a big laugh, or takes the show or a character in a new direction. The reason for that is simple: the writers themselves never miss an opportunity to remind everyone over and over that it was their idea.

Every week we would get our new scripts, do a table

read with the full cast, all the writers and the producers, and then begin a week of rehearsals in our home—Paramount's Stage Nineteen—which would take us up to taping the show in front of a live studio audience on Friday evenings. (Our first two seasons were filmed without an audience, using a single-camera setup and a laugh track. From the third season on, we used a three-camera production and shot in front of a live audience.) As soon as we got our scripts, I would do what every actor in every television show has ever done and will ever do when they first get their hands on a freshly written script: quickly go through it to see how many scenes I was in, how many lines I had, what they had me doing, and, most importantly, to make sure what I was doing didn't involve my planning a long trip away from home, accepting a job in a new town, getting ill, or having some sort of a mishap that involved a bus, a cliff, an explosion or anything else that may indicate a search for new work may be looming.

As soon as I had each new script in my hand, right after making sure Mrs. C was safe, I would then highlight my lines, rev myself up, and just read the bejesus out of each word from our first table read to our final run-through. I felt that to keep my job, I was constantly auditioning before Garry, the other producers, the directors, the writers. Hell, I was consumed with proving myself to everyone, including the technical crew, production assistants and craft services people. I was really rather shy and reserved, especially during the early seasons of the show. I was also one of only two females in the principal cast (the other being a girl barely in her teens), and let's just say, at times, the testosterone was pretty thick on Stage Nineteen, what with Tom running the show and taking weekly, if not daily, umbrage with the writers and even the producers.

Whenever things would get a bit tense, Garry would usually do something to break the tension, which, typically, was caused by Tom. I quickly learned four things during our first season: one, that there is an interesting and multifaceted dynamic going on within the creative team of a television show; two, that in order to compete and survive that dynamic, you had better learn how to hold your own; three, that our boss, Garry, was a true sweetheart; and last but not at all least, that working with Tom was very difficult.

When we first started, none of us knew one another well, but I'm sure it was clear that I wasn't a big Tom Bosley fan. Other than an eye roll here or there when he was being his most contentious, I did try to keep my feelings below the radar screen, but I think it would have taken the combined acting skills of the Lunts, Gielguds, Oliviers, Hepburns and Brandos of the world to have concealed that fact.

The man who was our script supervisor, perhaps, knew this best. He was always very close to us when we were on the set, listening to our every word, making notes, or prompting us with a line, and so he was on the front line when it came to noticing what I thought were my subtle facial expressions in response to Tom's behavior. Whenever Tom would really blow up over something, which would result in his huddling up with the director, the producers and the writers, I would just stand there while they worked it out, and the script supervisor would sidle up to me and whisper in my ear. "You know you really love him," he would say. That would always break the tension I was feeling, and I usually employed no acting techniques whatsoever to conceal a laugh.

If I had reservations about Tom (and I certainly did), I felt that he was not keen on me at all. I began to wonder if he had wanted someone other than me cast in the role of Marion and if he resented me because he hadn't gotten his way. I really had no idea why he was cold and distant toward me and, God knows, I tried to get him to warm up to me. Sometimes between takes when we were doing a scene together, I would put my hand on his arm or shoulder.

"Don't touch me!" he would say in a way that let me know he wasn't kidding.

To this day, whenever I see an episode of *Happy Days* from the beginning of the first season, and we are sitting on a couch together, looking all warm and cuddly, I laugh to myself and think, *That is really some great acting you did there, old gal!*

Along with his aversion to my making any sort of physical contact with him, Tom also seemed to be irritated by just about anything I did or said. I remember times during rehearsals when the cast and some of the technical crew would all be sitting around telling stories and laughing. It seemed that whenever I told a story, Tom would grunt and say, "Who gives a shit, Marion?"

Well, I may have spent a lot more time in Hollywood than I had in Albert Lea, but I still possessed those deeply engrained Minnesota values and Midwestern manners that I had been raised with, and when he would say that, I would sort of laugh it off, clam up, and then just sit there looking at him, while thinking, *Yes, I'm nice, but you have no idea what I'm really thinking about you.* I know that my upbeat, optimistic and, perhaps, sometimes Pollyannaish personality got to him so much that at times he seemed to want to kick me to the moon. But I couldn't change my style—who I was—and I certainly wasn't going to change anything for him.

During that time, I was still seeing a shrink but had made a marked improvement, as the depression from my failed marriage had dissipated and my financial situation had at least stabilized. I would have a session and get high marks for my improvement from the doctor, only to return for my next visit and have her ask me why I had seemed to take a few steps back.

"You were doing so well when you were last here," she would say. "What happened to cause this setback?"

It was due to the stress at work, much of which I felt was being caused by Tom and the writers. It was a hard-hitting, rough-and-tumble atmosphere, and not, by any means, the tea party people may have thought working on such a wholesome and fun show would be. There was what I perceived to be a crudeness to the environment, and a lot of complaining and questioning. At least, that was how I saw it. What I really didn't understand was that this dynamic is very common with a weekly show. Up until that point, my work had been periodic: it had entailed working on a show for a few days or weeks, doing a series in which I had only a day or two of work each week, or doing a film for a few months. *Happy Days* was different. It was a weekly grind of long hours, during which tension and stress levels got high.

While my shrink had been extremely helpful to me in so many ways, the thing that finally snapped me out of the feelings of inadequacy and discomfort I was experiencing on the set of *Happy Days* was something I worked out on my own. It happened on this one day when a loud argument broke out among the writers. It escalated to the point that it was close to being a downright brawl, and I retreated to a side of the stage, where I tried to calm my frayed nerves.

But then, just as quickly as it had all started, it settled down, we did our scene, and these guys, who had earlier been at one another's throats, were all laughing, had their arms around one another, and were happily heading off to lunch. It had taken me a while to get it, but something went off in my head when I saw that. *Okay*, I thought to myself. *Now I get it. The pressure on them is high to do a really good job, and at times it just gets to a boiling point, erupts, and then quickly passes. I get it! I get it!* It wasn't personal. It was just the working style of these young testosterone-raging New Yorker writers and, of course, also of Tom.

While I had had my issues with Tom at first, as the months went by and I got to know him better, I actually began to feel myself warming up to him and, surprisingly, I also began to see some cracks start to form in his hard shell. I slowly began to realize he possessed a warmth that could be just wonderful. Yes, he was, by all means, this peppery and feisty little guy who could get on your nerves, but he also had another side to him, and he could be this very dear sweetheart.

Realizing that Tom could be such a great guy, I began to let my guard down around him and feel more comfortable. The problem with that was all of a sudden, out of nowhere, he would get irritated over something, slam something down, start swearing, and jolt me back into thinking, *My God, how can he be so nice and then turn around and be so damn difficult?* I didn't understand it. I didn't understand him. And, most importantly, I didn't understand what he was going through in his personal life.

Unbeknownst to me at the time, and seemingly to everyone else associated with the show, with the possible exception of Garry, Tom's wife, Jean Eliot, who had been a dancer, was ill—very ill. She had been experiencing excruciating headaches, and as time went by, she began displaying erratic behavior that made it difficult, if not impossible, for her to care for herself or their young daughter, Amy. As Jean's pain increased, she became more and more depressed. This, obviously, caused a tremendous amount of anxiety and stress for Tom. He was angry about what was happening to his wife and extremely frustrated that the cause of her illness seemed to be a mystery. At first, her doctors believed she had epilepsy, but as things got worse, they learned she was suffering from an inoperable brain tumor.

Tom was dealing with all those issues at home and then,

somehow, managed to get to work and appear to *Happy Days* viewers from coast to coast as this cuddly little father figure with a touch of cantankerous charm. Yes, we who worked with him knew that the cantankerous streak of Howard Cunningham was nothing compared to the one of Tom Bosley, but when I think about what he was going through, I have no idea how he conducted himself as well as he did.

I would later learn that as Jean's illness progressed, Tom himself began experiencing the dark depths of depression. I remember him once saying, many years later, that as his wife faded, his depression grew. Of course, that made sense. How could someone not become severely depressed when they had to work at a demanding job all day and then return home to care for a very sick spouse and a young daughter? Tom did just that until Jean died during the fourth season of *Happy Days*. In the wake of Jean's death, Tom's depression continued as he coped with raising Amy, who was only eleven years old when her mother died.

In today's world, Tom may have been more open with his friends or coworkers about what he was going through and may have gone for treatment, but back in those days, men kept that sort of thing to themselves. They were supposed to be these strong and macho tough guys who could deal with anything and who certainly weren't supposed to give in to sadness or depression. And so, like so many other men of that era, he suffered in silence and did all he could to hide his travails from as many people as possible. I can't even imagine what it was like for Tom to be this role model for American husbands and fathers, when in real life he was falling into an ever-deepening depression.

Many years later, long after *Happy Days* was over, he opened up about what he had been going through while doing the show, and often credited his work, the interaction he had with his cast mates, and the love of his daughter as the things that helped him get through that difficult time, recover, and go on to become an advocate for depression education and awareness. As he got older, he participated in various campaigns to educate people on the signs and symptoms of depression and on its treatment. One was called "Happier Days in Mature America," and I know it helped a lot of people by explaining that depression is not a natural part of aging, and that if people become depressed as they age, they should not keep it to themselves, as he did for so long, but rather should discuss their symptoms with loved ones and seek help from medical professionals.

Because Tom had been extremely private about what he was going through while we were doing *Happy Days*, he received very little understanding from those he was working with when he would become difficult and demanding. But as time went by and we all began to know one another better, we did learn about what he was going through.

I may have once had mixed feelings about him, but I really did come to love him, and he and I—both as Tom Bosley and Marion Ross and as Howard and Marion Cunningham—became a wonderful pair. We worked well with one another and off one another. It became a perfect match, one in which we truly harmonized with one another, me playing my sweet little piccolo to his boisterous tuba.

The more I got to know Tom, the more I learned that he possessed a great intelligence. The writers, who may have been leery of his interference at first, also came to terms with him and realized that if they were ever stuck when trying to come up with a good punch line to end a scene, Tom was the go-to guy for coming up with something.

As the seasons of *Happy Days* passed by and I came to understand him better, my relationship with Tom evolved into one of great love and care for one another. One time when we were all honoring him for something, I remember how after I had delivered my tribute to him, he got up, looked over at me, and said, "You know, Marion, I have a little secret to share with you. I *do* give a shit about you and what you have to say!"

After *Happy Days* ended, Tom and I always kept in touch, and he and his second wife, Pat, invited me to many parties at their home. I was always honored to call him my friend and was very proud of the way he raised Amy, who went on to become a highly successful studio executive and to own her own entertainment development, production and consulting company.

When Tom died on October 19, 2010, Pat asked me if I would say a few words at his funeral. I was honored, and while I did tell a few stories of our times together, there was really only one thing I wanted to say: that he was a lovely and kind man whom I loved very much. . . . And one thing I thought privately: that he really *did* give a shit about me.

Chapter 15

My Happy Days

By the evening of January 15, 1974, the night *Happy Days* debuted, I was a forty-six-year-old divorced woman who was the mother of an eleven-year-old girl and a teenage son. My father had been gone for ten years, and in 1971 I had lost my mother. I have been asked on occasion if it bothers me that neither of my parents lived to see my dream come true. Well, it would have been nice, but it was not to be, and being the type of person I have always been when it comes to dealing with death, I have never really given it any thought.

I was thrilled that *Happy Days* had been picked up, and more than grateful that they had decided to stay with me for the role of Marion. I had given my character a lot of thought from the moment I heard we would be doing the show, and on the night of our debut, as I sat watching it, I couldn't help but think that while I may have looked the part, there was a world of difference between Marion Cunningham and Marion Ross. Marion Cunningham didn't have a career outside of the home, didn't drive, and always made sure her hair was perfect and that she had on a clean and freshly pressed dress as she cared for her children, her home, and her husband, who ran his own small business. I knew women like that from when I was a child growing up in Albert Lea, but that had never been me.

At first, she was rather ditzy, but as time went by, she would grow into a more grounded character. But as I sat and watched that first broadcast of the show, I had no idea I would ever get the chance to see her evolve. I never allowed myself to think the show would become a big hit; none of us did. It just wasn't the kind of dream any of us would allow ourselves to dream. I think we all knew that the timing was right for a show like *Happy Days*, that the cast was really good, and that the writing was very solid, but we just could not let ourselves become convinced the show would become a success, since we would then have to live with the crushing disappointment if it didn't.

I loved having steady work, and while my salary was nothing to brag about, it covered all the bills, left me with a little for some very simple luxuries for myself and the children, and allowed me for the first time to stash away a little to tide me over if things didn't work out.

When we first started, we did the show like a film, shooting with one camera and no studio audience. It was kind of a scattered mess at times, with scripts still being worked on as we went into rehearsal and Tom being difficult. But things would soon change.

I remember we were about six months into our first season and none of us really knew how we were being received by the viewing public. And then one day, we were all summoned into a room by one of our producers, Bill Bickley, who, after doing *Happy Days*, would go on to produce such successful shows as *Family Matters*, *Perfect Strangers* and *Step by Step*. None of us knew why we were being called together, and while no one said it, I can't imagine I was the only one who was worried that we were about to get word that we had been canceled. I recall all of us sitting around with these wide-eyed looks as Bill took his place in the middle of us.

"Okay, everybody, I need you to listen to me," he began. "You're all doing a great job, but we have got to start really buckling down and cooperating with one another and really taking this serious, because we have a big hit on our hands!"

We all broke out in applause, and while I don't remember much of anything else he or anyone else said during that meeting, it was the first time I allowed myself to really believe that my dream of being a star of a television show was becoming a reality.

Our ratings were strong, and by our third season, when we were a genuine hit, the producers came to each of the cast members and, instead of having us sign back on for just another season, asked us to sign for two seasons. By then, we had moved on from doing *Happy Days* as a one-camera show to doing it with the traditional three-camera setup in front of a live studio audience. Many television aficionados know that it is widely believed that Desi Arnaz created the three-camera system for *I Love Lucy*, but television historians have argued that this system actually goes back to the late 1940s, when it was employed in the filming of such shows as NBC's *Public Prosecutor*, CBS's *Silver Theatre* and a few others.

No matter who really gets the credit for that multi-camera format, all I know is incorporating that concept, along with doing the show in front of a live audience, dramatically changed both the way *Happy Days* was done and how it was presented to viewers. The dynamic of doing the show in front of an audience shifted the tone and gave it a heightened energy, a different texture and a different pace, which were all for the better.

All of us in the principal cast, with the exception of Ron

and Erin, had worked in the theater, so even though doing a television show, with the many stops and starts, is very different than doing a play, having the chance to be in front of real live people—to feed off their energy and reactions—was something we all loved. Garry also loved having the audience as a sounding board. He was always very in tune to the audience's reactions to everything, and if ever a line or a joke or a scene wasn't working, he would engage the audience, asking them for their thoughts, opinions and input. I always thought he was very smart to do that.

As much as we all loved having an audience, oh, did they love having the opportunity to come in and see how it all came together. We always seemed to attract a young crowd for the tapings, and as the years went by and Henry broke out as "the Fonz," becoming America's heartthrob and one of the country's biggest stars, our audiences became younger and wilder. They would line up for hours before being escorted into Stage Nineteen and would just go crazy when, before we began taping, Garry would welcome them and introduce the cast members. We were all received with love and warmth, but it was a completely different thing when it came to Henry. It was like Beatlemania, with all these young girls screaming and going wild.

Fonziemania had swept the nation. Henry had gone from being a secondary character with hardly any lines to being the central focus of many episodes. And his image was on everything, from posters and lunch boxes to pillows, drinking glasses and just about anything else they could figure out how to put a person's image on.

Most actors by nature are born with healthy egos, and while I always felt that we all kept ours in check during the run of *Happy Days* and that there was never any serious resentment over the fact that Henry had risen to be the show's breakout star, it did at times make the rest of us feel like we were supporting players. His fame was, of course, great for all of us, but along with being humans, we were still those actors with healthy egos, and at one time or another each of us went through "Fonzie overload." I will never forget the day when, though the show was sitting strongly in the number one slot in the ratings, a dejected Ron Howard came into my dressing room and flopped into a chair, looking like he had lost every friend he ever had.

"What's wrong?" I said as this brief pulse of fear shot through my body and I wondered if anything had happened to any of our cast or a member of his family.

"Ya know, Marion, there are just some mornings that I hate having to get out of bed and come to work," he said with this out-of-character look of disgust on his face.

"Why, dear?" I said, turning to him. "What's bothering you?"

"It's just all about the Fonz. Every damn day it's the Fonz this and the Fonz that. There are other people involved with this show other than him, ya know!"

I know that, just like the rest of us, it was difficult for Ron to express that, because he held no resentment toward Henry. It was not Henry, but the character of Fonzie, whom we all at times resented, because he sucked the air out of everything associated with the show. While I know each of us felt that way from time to time, we rarely really came out and verbalized that complaint to one another, and certainly not to the producers, who were simply capitalizing on having a show that was giving the world one of the most iconic characters in television and pop culture history. We all, pragmatically, knew and understood the fact that a big part of our show's success had to do with the character of Fonzie, and that was why we usually let our personal feelings about the character overshadowing everything just pass. One of the things that made that much easier to do was that Henry was such a sweetheart about it all. He never thought of himself as anything other than a part of our team. He never acted like he was the star or was better than anyone else. That sort of thing just wasn't a part of his personality, of who he was as a person, a person whom we all loved.

While Henry, along with Ron, Anson and Donny, had all become highly recognized stars by the time we were into our fifth season, that same lightning had not struck for me. Unless it was some planned and publicized *Happy Days* event, I was, for the most part, able to go to a market or out for dinner without being noticed. That slowly began to change after our sixth season, when the writers began to beef up Marion's role. I began to notice more and more people either glancing in my direction and whispering when I was out in public or just coming up to me and asking for an autograph and telling me how much they loved the show. Yes, there were times, especially when we would all be out doing what had become our famous *Happy Days* softball games and tours, that, while I had become very well known to the crowds, I was never the hot item the guys were. But I got that, and it was okay with me.

I had made it. I had seen my dream become a reality, felt that I was doing something important, and secretly allowed myself to revel in the fact that I was no longer a nobody. Had I realized my dream of becoming one of the stars of a hit show when I was in my twenties, I think I would have handled it differently. I don't mean to say that I would have let it go to my head and would have started living some wild Hollywood lifestyle. That was just never a part of who I was. But I do think I would have taken it much more for granted. The fact that my success as an actor didn't come until I was in my early fifties made me more grateful for it and also allowed me to handle it in a more mature fashion.

When that success finely came, I felt odd about it at

times. I was, on one hand, extremely happy, grateful and satisfied, and yet, on the other hand, I felt it was a bit anticlimactic. Maybe the best way I can describe my feelings is the way lyricist Fred Ebb does in the song "A Quiet Thing," which he wrote for the 1965 play *Flora, the Red Menace*, which starred Liza Minnelli. In that song he writes that when your dreams come true, you don't hear bells ringing, choirs singing, fireworks going off, or crowds cheering. That the happiness that accompanies a realized dream sort of tiptoes in as "a very quiet thing."

That was how it was for me, and even the show's huge success—when we were the undisputed number one in the ratings—didn't change me much. Although it was satisfying to have accomplished what I had always hoped to accomplish, and to feel more secure financially than I ever had in my life, my personal world—my life at home with my children—was not that different.

It was a happy time for me, although, as with any successful show, there was also a lot of stress to deal with, as everyone from the network executives on down became obsessed with maintaining our success. I know I dealt with that stress far better than I would have had I been in my twenties. I felt that all I had gone through both professionally and personally had left me with a good dose of solid maturity, and I was at peace, feeling that I was doing what I was supposed to be doing—that I had achieved what I had always felt I was put on this planet to do. It was not the happiest time of my life, but it was an exciting and gratifying time. I was on a hit show, I greatly loved the people I was working with, and I just came to enjoy it more and more as each season passed.

In the years following *Happy Days*, many interviewers, reporters and talk show hosts have seemed surprised when I have said that I didn't consider the days when we were in production to be my happiest. But I think when you are actually in the middle of something—in the eye of the hurricane, so to speak—you just can't appreciate things in the same way you can when it is over, when some time has gone by, and you have a better perspective and understanding of just how lucky and fortunate you were to have been in a hit show, and you are able to really enjoy the benefits that come with having been a part of something so special.

Although I loved doing *Happy Days*, and we really did all become like a big close-knit and loving family, it was still work in which things would go wrong and the tension and stress were always present. While the people who loved our show—or any television show—might have watched it and thought that doing it was all fun and games, I can tell you that is simply not true. Putting out a weekly television show, especially one that is operating under the pressure of maintaining its quality and extremely high ratings, and is also making the network and a lot of other people huge sums of money, is a really serious thing. You are never just playing around when you are associated with a hit show, believe me! The pressures are big on everyone involved.

I know that while I always felt good about the way I handled the pressures of doing *Happy Days*, there were just those times when it would take its toll on me, and by the time I got home to the kids, I would be pretty crabby. I can clearly recall evenings when I would step in my front door and scream, "Everybody! Get out of my way!"

I think the reason for that stemmed from the fact that I had been an angel all day. I rarely complained about anything, and if I did, I never made any sort of a big issue about it. I was extremely cooperative and good at doing whatever it was I was told to do. I never got into any arguments or debates over anything, was always prompt and professional, and then, on top of all that, when the cameras rolled, I played the archetype of maternal perfection. Who could keep that up day after day and not get so anxious and exhausted that once they were in the cocoon of their own home, their entire demeanor would change and, like an uncaged wild animal, they would be ready to strike out at anything that was keeping them from getting undressed and into a tub filled with warm, sudsy water? If there is such an angel, it wasn't me!

While I have always felt I was a nurturing mother (both to my real children as well as to Ron, Erin, Henry, Anson, Donny and any other *Happy Days* cast or crew member, no matter what their age), I know there were too many times when I would return home after putting in a long day and be the complete opposite of the loving and caring mother I had played all day and that Americans had come to know me as.

Perhaps, had I been doing a different role, I would not have found myself contemplating that fact so often and then feeling so much guilt because of it. Every week people from all over the nation would tune in and watch me portray such a picture-perfect mom that the most repeated line I got in my fan mail was, "I wish I had a mother just like you!" And yet, in reality, my own flesh-and-blood children were left in the care of someone else all day and then learned to duck and cover when I returned home like some sort of a spinning-out-of-control whirling dervish.

I would, at times, feel so bad about this double life I was living that I would bring Jim and Ellen to the set. They both even played small roles on *Happy Days*, Ellen as a candy striper in a hospital scene and Jim in an episode that became one of our most famous (or should I say infamous?) and went on to coin that television industry and pop culture phrase "jumping the shark." That took place in 1977, during our fifth season, when one of our writers, Fred Fox, wrote an episode titled "Hollywood: Part Three." In that show, our central characters were visiting Los Angeles, and Fonzie accepted a challenge to water-ski up to a confined shark and then jump over the dangerous sea predator. If you ever catch a rerun of that episode, watch for the young fellow running down the beach, yelling, "It's a shark! It's a shark!" That's my son, Jim. I enjoyed the days that the kids joined me on the set, although it did bother me when Ellen once told me she didn't like coming to the set, because I was so different there than I was at home.

That is not to say I was ever a bad mom. Neither I nor either of the kids ever thought that. I was just different from the mothers their friends had, in that I had a demanding job and seemingly everyone in the country, other than my two children, thought that I, like Mary Poppins, was practically perfect in every way. On weekends and when *Happy Days* was on hiatus, things were much better. I loved raising my children and spending time with them, seeing them grow and develop their unique personalities and curiosities and interests in various things. They would have their friends over, and to all of them, I wasn't the perfect Mrs. C. I was just good ole Mrs. Meskimen.

Although *Happy Days* brought about many changes in our lives, the kids and I were always keen on trying to keep many things the same (although both Jim and Ellen would have liked it if I had loosened up the purse strings a lot more). I made it a point to try to keep things perfect at home, which, of course, they never were—not in our family, or any family. When I first got the part of Marion and began getting used to a regular paycheck, I saved every penny I could. I was making a decent living but, unbeknownst to me, nowhere near what I should have been making.

One day, a few seasons into our run, one of the producers pulled me aside and told me I was not being paid enough. I delivered that news to my agent, and after we did a little research, it was decided that we would ask for more money. The answer was no. So we waited a little longer and asked again. The answer was still no. That was when we made the decision that I would not show up for the next Monday's table read and would continue to be a no-show until they upped my salary.

When that Monday came, I, in fact, didn't show up to work, and sometime around noon I received a call from Ron, who told me that during the morning table read, the producers announced to the cast that I was being replaced. At that time, the character of Mrs. C wasn't as entrenched in the show as she would be in years to come, so if they had to change out the actress playing the mother, it wasn't a big deal. There was even a precedent for doing so: on *Bewitched*, the producers replaced Dick York, who had fallen ill, with Dick Sargent in the character of Darrin Stephens without hurting the show's popularity or ratings.

If the powers that be at the network and the producers of *Happy Days* thought they could call my bluff by announcing that they were going to recast the role of Marion, they were 100 percent right! After speaking with Ron and then calling my agent, I panicked and was back reporting for work on Stage Nineteen bright and early the next morning.

That did change a few years later, when the show had become such a huge hit and Mrs. C had become such a beloved character. It was during our hiatus that my manager called to tell me that negotiations were about to begin to get me a raise. I was advised that things would probably get rough and that I should not worry about anything except heading off on the cruise I had planned. I did just that, and when I returned, Garry called me and said, "I'm going to the network to fight for you. Tell me what you want, and tell me what you need. I'll fight for what you want and won't settle for anything less than what you need."

I wasn't greedy or out of line in what I was asking. I just

wanted what the other kids were getting, and Garry and our other producers were on my side. They knew that in the grand scheme of things, when you considered the kind of money *Happy Days* was making for the network, the increase I was asking for wasn't even half of a drop in the bucket. What was said between Garry and the network representatives, and just how rough it may or may not have gotten, I have no clue. All I do know is Garry kept his promise, he fought for my getting a raise, and I finally got it.

As the seasons of *Happy Days* passed, I had the chance to work with and get to know so many wonderful actors who they brought in to play new characters, including Scott Baio as Chachi Arcola; Al Molinaro as Al Delvecchio; Pat Morita as Arnold; Ellen Travolta as Louisa Delvecchio; Cathy Silvers as Jenny Piccalo; Ted McGinley as Roger Phillips; Roz Kelly as Carol "Pinky" Tuscadero; singer Suzi Quatro as Leather Tuscadero; Lynda Goodfriend as Lori Beth Cunningham; Lyle Waggoner, who guest starred as one of Marion's old flames; and, of course, Cindy Williams and Penny Marshall, who as Shirley Feeney and Laverne DeFazio, brewery worker friends of Fonzie's, were such a hit with viewers that Garry spun them off into the successful series *Laverne & Shirley*.

Since the early days of television, we have all heard and read stories of how cast members of various shows were either archenemies or like a loving family. Just as any real family, we at *Happy Days* had issues arise from time to time. But, as for the principal characters, we all developed a deep love and respect for one another. We truly did become a family, and as is the case with any family, we matured and our lives evolved and changed. That happened with each of the main characters on our show and with each of us who brought those characters to life. We all brought so much of ourselves to those characters that, although each of us has a résumé that includes other fine work and honors—including Ron winning two Oscars for his 2001 film *A Beautiful Mind* and being presented with the National Medal of Arts by the United States Congress, and Henry being awarded the Most Excellent Order of the British Empire, an order of British chivalry that rewards a person's contributions to the arts and sciences—it is, and always will be, our roles on *Happy Days* that indelibly burned the names and images of each of us into popular culture and television history.

No matter what we have done, or will ever do, the world will always think of Tom Bosley and Marion Ross as Howard and Marion Cunningham, Ron Howard and Erin Moran as Richie and Joanie Cunningham, Henry Winkler as Arthur "Fonzie" Fonzarelli, Anson Williams as Potsie Weber, Donny Most as Ralph Malph, and Scott Baio as Charles "Chachi" Arcola. When we began our eleventh and final season, we all knew that we had been a part of something very special—something that would define us for the rest of our careers and lives. We were all very proud of *Happy Days* and grateful for the opportunity we were given to be a part of that show and to bond so strongly with our fellow cast members.

It has been the sad case that some television shows have ended without the producers and the cast being aware that they had done their last episode. I have always thought that was terrible, that there was no resolution for either the actors or the fans. That, fortunately, was not the case with *Happy Days*. We all knew that the last two weeks of November 1983 had been slated for the taping of the final two-part episode of *Happy Days*. Up until that time, during our last season, we all knew the end was coming, but it really began to hit us as a reality during those final two weeks, and each of us took turns being weepy. We all knew that when we said our final lines as the characters we had become so associated with, it would be the end of an extremely important time of our lives.

Our last show—the wedding of Joanie and Chachi—wrapped production on the evening of November 28, 1983.

In our final scene, my last line as Marion was, "Wouldn't it be lovely if someone made a toast on this happy occasion?"

Then Tom, as Howard, made a beautiful toast in which he talked about how, when you come to one of life's milestones, like a wedding, you have to look back and reflect on what you have done and what you have accomplished. He then put his arm around me and talked of watching Richie, Joanie and their friends grow into adulthood, and of how the time had come for me and him to have the pleasure of watching the love we gave them be passed on to their children.

As we were doing that scene, I could feel my lips begin to quiver, and when Tom looked at me with tears welling up in his eyes, he said the line "I guess no man or woman could ask for anything more."

If you ever catch the final moments of that episode, you will notice Tom's voice cracks slightly as he says the word *more*. The emotion you see on my face is very real, and I remember taking a hard swallow and pursing my lips tightly so I wouldn't lose my composure.

Tom and I then both broke the fourth wall, looked directly into the camera, and he addressed our viewers: "So thank you all for being a part of our family." I took another hard swallow and my eyes filled with tears as he raised his champagne glass and delivered the very last line of the show that made my lifelong dream come true: "To happy days!"

In what I thought was a masterful touch, they then dissolved into a montage of clips from our eleven-year run as the song "Memories," by Elvis Presley, was played, and then, in the last few seconds before fading to black, showed all of us watching Joanie and Chachi cut their wedding cake.

After that scene, we were all emotional and crying, although our work was far from over. The very next day we were all scheduled to board a plane at Los Angeles International Airport that would take us to Okinawa. We may have wrapped *Happy Days*, but we still had a softball game scheduled against the United States Marines.

The members of that cast were also the members of my softball team and will always be my extended family. I would have never achieved my dream without Garry and each one of them. That is why, after my hesitations to write this book were quashed, I agreed to write it on one condition: that every member of our cast, our team, our family, would be involved.

It broke my heart that Tom, Al Molinaro and Pat Morita were gone, but I was thrilled when every other member of the principal cast agreed to be a part of this book. Although, little could I have known that between the time I started this book and finished it, we would lose two more members of our family: Garry and Erin.

Chapter 16

My Boss Garry

Everyone, if they are fortunate—very fortunate—has a person who comes into their life, changes everything for the better, and makes their dreams come true. Of all the good fortune I have experienced in my professional life, nothing will ever top crossing paths with Garry Marshall.

Without Garry, there never would have been a *Happy Days*, a Mrs. C or the fulfillment of my great dream.

Along with having played an instrumental role in my life, Garry always impressed me by being one of the kindest people I have ever known. I know some people thought of him as this gruff New Yorker with the Bronx accent, but that would not be those who really knew him. I have seen how he cared for his mother and his sisters. I've seen how he loved his wife and children. And, of course, I have seen how he loved the cast he assembled for *Happy Days*.

Ever since I first met Garry, when I auditioned for him for the pilot of what would become *Happy Days*, I have always pictured him as a little boy walking down a New York street, kicking a piece of paper, and finally picking it up and opening it and reading what it says: "You will be in charge of everything and everyone." That is the image that always comes to my mind when I think of Garry.

While everyone who worked on *Happy Days*, from the cast to the entire crew, played a part in the show's success, to me, 100 percent of the credit for that show becoming such a huge hit goes to Garry.

He had always been attuned to people—what they were about, how they would fit into his life or on one of his shows, or how they would work out as a player with one of his legendary softball teams. Garry was the most unconventional television or film producer I have ever encountered. If there is some sort of a guide or playbook for producers, I'm guessing Garry never read it. He operated in a different way than most people in the television or film industry. He always seemed to have a good "feel" for someone, and throughout his career he hired people who would have never gotten a chance otherwise. He was a genius when it came to putting a team together, whether for a show, a film, a play or a softball game. And if you were fortunate enough to be a part of his life and one of his teams, you would find that your teammates always had fascinating stories of how they came into Garry's world. You would find out that a writer's dad had owned a cab service and, having Garry as a fare, had mentioned that his son wanted to get involved with television. Garry had said, "Fine. Send him to see me."

Garry had always been a "gatherer" of people. He had a very trusting nature. But I think that trust was based on a keen perception of a person's soul (along with their softball prowess). From the time he first started out in television, he gave so many people a chance—their start. He made people's dreams come true. He completely changed their lives—made them rich and made them stars. What a lovely life that must be, to put your head down on your pillow every night and know that you have so dramatically changed people's lives.

When I am asked to share any specific memory of working with him, I always think of the times when I would be doing a line or an action of some sort and it just wouldn't work, just didn't feel right for some reason. Garry's finely tuned perceptive intuition would kick in during those moments. He would stop everything and come over to me and say, "That's not working for you, is it, Marion? Let's fix it." That sort of understanding and care is not just rare in the entertainment industry; it is rare in our world—period!

I always thought the world of Garry. And what did he think of me? Well, God forbid I would ever dare ask him that question. For that, I turned it over to my writing colleague, David Laurell, who, in what would prove to be Garry's last interview about *Happy Days*, just a few months before his death in 2016, was far more adept than I could have ever been in getting the answer.

"You've heard the term 'a hot mess'? Marion Ross is just the opposite of a hot mess!" —Garry Marshall

David Laurell (DL): You cast Marion in the role of the mother for the pilot that became the *Love, American Style* episode. Did you know her prior to casting her?

Garry Marshall (GM): I didn't know her at all. We found her through an open casting call. And I remember when she came in to read for the part. Right away I thought she was perfect. She had that bubbly housewife personality. She had the right look, and she also had a certain sexuality and nurturing quality. Marion had a pedigree as an actress, and there was also a star quality about her. I remember she really popped with me in the audition. She came in wearing a bright red dress. I asked her about the dress. I mean, how could you not? It was blinding me, it was so bright [laughing]. *She told me she always tried to wear a red dress or something very bright and colorful when she went on an audition. She said that she had chosen to be an actress because she wanted to be noticed—to be seen. Well, in that red dress she had on, you couldn't miss her.*

By the way, David, you were correct about it being a pilot that became the Love, American Style *episode. I know everyone thinks it was the other way around—that* Happy Days *evolved out of a* Love, American Style *episode. But that wasn't the case. It was shot as a pilot, and back in those days, when a pilot didn't get picked up, they didn't want it to go to waste—to lose the money is what it was— so they would recut the pilots and give them some title and use them for* Love, American Style, *because anything could go on that show.*

DL: When *Happy Days* was ultimately picked up by ABC, you went back to Marion for the role of Mrs. Cunningham.

GM: *You know, when* Happy Days *was picked up, the show's original title was* Cool. *Then the network tested it, and everybody thought it was a show about cigarettes, so Tom Miller, the producer, was the one who came up with the name* Happy Days. *And yes, when we put the cast together, we went with Marion and Ron Howard and Anson Williams—the only three who had been in the pilot.*

That was a no-brainer—going with Marion. She and I bonded right away because we are both Scorpios. She was born in late October, and I was born on November 13. So we got along, and she was just perfect for the part. She perfectly portrayed the solid mother of the 1950s, and she also had the ability to deliver a joke. In the beginning, when we started out, her role was pretty small, and yet she got big laughs with lines that weren't really even jokes.

Sometimes she got a laugh with just a word or a look. And as the years went by, Mrs. C became one of the show's most popular characters. The character of Mrs. C grew— evolved—and that was all because of Marion.

DL: When you think back on doing *Happy Days*, what memories do you have of working with Marion?

GM: She was never a problem. And believe me, over the years I've dealt with my share of actors who were prob- lems, but never Marion. One of the things that was always great about working with her was that she wanted to dis- tinguish herself, within her role, but she never came to me with crazy ideas from the moon. I've worked with actors who have come up with all sorts of crazy things they wanted to do with their character or the plots that would have ruined the whole show. That wasn't the case with Marion. She was good at coming up with things that really worked for her character.

DL: On television shows, especially long-running sit- coms, some things that work tend to just bubble up during rehearsals and even during tapings. Did Marion bring shadings to the character of Mrs. C that the writers then elaborated upon?

GM: That kind of thing does happen all the time. I re- member [laughing], there were ten writers or so on Happy Days, *and one day, Marion comes down to my office and asked me this odd question: "Who is the writer assigned to doing my lines?" I told her that wasn't the way it works, that we don't assign writers to a particular character. We don't have a guy who just writes for Fonzie or for Mrs. C. They all write for everyone, I told her. So I never knew where the hell she was going with that, but she seemed to be satisfied with my answer, and that was that.*

A lot of actors look at the scripts and just turn to their lines and complain about not liking this or that. But Mar- ion was always the type who looked at her lines—even if it

*was just a word or a direction the writers had written—
and asked herself how she could deliver them well. How
to make it work. She was never the kind of actor who was
looking to the writers to give her lines that worked. It was
the other way around with her. She felt her job was to take
their lines and make them work. She could make things
work no matter what she was given.*

*But you mentioned how things happen—come up—that
aren't in the script that work and then the writers incorporate that. That can be just a word or a look or the way an
actor does something with a prop. I think one of the
things that naturally evolved with Marion was Mrs. C's relationship with Fonzie. There was always this underlying
thing between them. Fonzie loved her and looked to her as
a parental figure because he didn't have parents. Those
two characters formed a special bond, which was never
planned out by the writers. That all just evolved. To everyone, Fonzie was this cool tough guy. But that was never
the way Mrs. C saw him. She saw him in a different light,
and to separate the way Mrs. C perceived Fonzie from
everyone else, she was the only character on the show who
called him "Arthur." Marion was always a person with
great dignity, and I think she saw the character of the Fonz
as she did every character—that they should be treated
with respect and dignity. That relationship between those
two characters was always where we would go when we
needed the "aw" moment. We would do a scene with
Fonzie putting his head on Mrs. C's shoulder.*

DL: That affection—that love between those characters—seemed to translate to all the actors behind the characters on *Happy Days*. We always hear of so many shows
in which cast members don't get along and there's a clash
of egos. That didn't seem to be the case with *Happy Days*.

GM: *I have never worked on a show that was more like
family than* Happy Days. *They all ate together. They cared*

about one another. They hugged a lot. That's what I wanted: for that cast to be like a real family, and that's what happened. Tom Miller once said to me, "Sometimes you get really blessed, and you were really blessed with Happy Days." I have never worked on another show like that. On the set of Laverne & Shirley, *there was always fighting going on. My kids always tell people that when they were little, they were allowed to visit the set of* Happy Days *but not the set of* Laverne & Shirley, *because of all the fighting and foul language. On* Happy Days *they all just melded together. It was a great time for all of us. We had a hit show.*

All these kids, who ranged in age from eighteen to twenty-four, were making a lot of money. They had become stars, and yet they were all real people—they were kids who were growing up, and falling in and out of love, and getting married. I remember Marion holding court with all of them when they were dating badly and breaking up badly and spending money badly. We all shared in each other's real lives. During the show Tom Bosley's wife passed away, and we were like any family, seeing life and death and marriages and everything that everyone deals with in life. That entire cast always stuck together, and I think Jerry Paris, the director, was a great influence behind that happening. They all knew him and respected him— his goodness, as well as his faults. He was the kind of director who really understood his cast, and I think that was a big part in how, over eleven seasons, we all really got to know and love one another.

DL: And, unlike so many other shows, this cast has remained close as the years have passed.

GM: *That is true and, of course, everyone loved Marion. What's not to love? But I think for the kids who grew up doing that show, they also always trusted Marion. I think whenever you do a film or a play or a television*

*show—whenever you do anything, in any line of work—
you need someone to go to in case of problems. I've done
eighteen movies, and Héctor Elizondo was in every one of
them. Why? Because we're such great friends? No. Because I always have to have someone in the cast I can go
to in case there's trouble. In* Laverne & Shirley *it was Phil
Foster. In* Mork & Mindy *it was Conrad Janis, and with*
Happy Days *it was Marion.*

*If there was ever any trouble, if I ever had to call the
cast together for some reason, I needed a mature person—
the adult in the room—who they all trusted. No matter
what you're doing, someone has to be an adult, and Marion was the adult on that show. I always relied on her to
be the sane one. To keep everyone sane, including me! So
they all trusted her, and I trusted her. Marion was always
the most grounded one—always there for all these other
people who were having their problems and troubles. But
she never gave me the least bit of trouble. I went through
eleven seasons with her, and I never even knew who her
agent was. I've done shows with actors where I've had to
ban their agents from the set because they drove me so
crazy.*

DL: As people read this book, I think they may be surprised to learn that, while Marion created a character who
became the archetype of the all-American mom, she herself constantly questioned her real-life role as a mother.

*GM: It's not an easy job, being a mother. I grew up with
a working mother, so I understood what she was going
through. And it's even harder when you are a single parent
who is working a job. I know how hard it was to be a father doing that, and Marion and I would talk about that
once in a while—the difficulties of raising our kids. I think
that maybe she learned some things about being a good
mother from playing Mrs. C.*

We did the show in the 1970s, and during that time

there were a lot of changes going on with women and the way they were being perceived by themselves and by society. The housewife she was playing—Mrs. C—was a thing of the past by that time. But Marion had lived through that time—the 1950s—and she saw how things had changed, and how women were changing, and she wanted to bring some of that change to Mrs. C. As the years went by, Mrs. C branched out. She wore slacks instead of a dress and even went out and got a job. But as far as how she raised her two kids—Jim and Ellen—I think she did a really great job as a real mom.

DL: Garry, with all the memorable characters and shows you have given the world, you will go down in history as one of the great storytellers of the late twentieth- and early twenty-first century. Will you share one or two of your favorite stories about Marion?

GM: One of my favorite stories about Marion has nothing to do with acting or show business. It has to do with softball. I always put together softball teams with the casts and crews from all my shows. So with Happy Days, *everybody on the show played—the entire cast. So she had to play, too. Our* Happy Days *team played all over the country—all over the world. Ronnie Howard and Donny Most were real ballplayers. They knew what they were doing. But Marion turned out to be a good player, too. She went out and got a glove and a bat that she was comfortable with, and I tell you, she could hit pretty good. She could hit and catch. I would always tell her how wonderful she was, and once she asked me why I gave her so many accolades on her softball playing but not on her acting. Well, she was a terrific actor, so I didn't have to bother telling her that. I remember once she told someone, "My boss wants me to play softball! There's my dream—softball!" But she was fearless, as an actor and as a softball player. I remember I used to tell her it was nice that such a great softball player also had a nice little hobby in acting.*

The other story I have of her is a play she did for me. I had written this play and asked Marion to read it because I thought she would be good in it. It was called Shelves. *It was my first play, and I ended up changing the name of it to* Everybody Say "Cheese!" *She read the script and agreed to do it in Chicago, and she was wonderful in it. She really did me a gigantic favor by doing that show, and because of her, it got rave reviews. She certainly didn't have to leave her home and family to do it. It was at a dinner theater, where she had to compete with people while they were eating their roast beef. But she did it for me as a favor, and I will always love her for doing that.*

I remember during the rehearsals for that show, the director wanted her to enter from this area where there was a table. So they had to move this table by the side of the stage, and all hell broke loose. The manager, or whoever the hell it was, said we couldn't move the table. So I'm from the Bronx. I know how to handle these things. I asked him how much they would make on that table every night. He told me, and I said, "Fine! I'll pay the money you'll lose. Just get the table out of here." So I bought the table so Marion could make her entrance. That's what you do when you love someone. You want them to do well and be happy.

One of the happiest times for me was when Marion met Paul. They were perfect together, and it made me very happy that she was happy. I also remember when she got her star on Hollywood Boulevard. I walked away from that ceremony and thought, Wow! She's really come a long way.

DL: As you know, Marion put off writing a book about her life for many years. Now that she has decided to do it, what do you hope readers will learn about her that they otherwise may have never known?

GM: *In her field, the genre of the television moms, Florence Henderson and Shirley Jones, the mothers from all those classic shows, like* Ozzie and Harriet *and* Leave It to Beaver—*they are the women people think of when they think of mothers. Marion and those other actresses who played the famous mothers did more for motherhood than anybody else. Marion was always a solid actress. She could always deliver whatever was asked of her. She could be the face of white-bread America in* Happy Days, *or she could do an ethnic role on* Brooklyn Bridge, *playing a Jewish woman.*

But, beyond being a talented actress, nobody ever found her in bed with someone in some sleazy cheap motel in Minneapolis. She wasn't drugged out and insane. Now, maybe she would have sold more books if that was the case [laughing], *but that wasn't her. She was always sensitive when it came to people's feelings, and she survived the difficult times she went through in the nicest way. She always lived her life in the way we would all want our mothers to live their lives. I have always admired Marion for making her way through the rough times in her personal life and through this business with her integrity intact. Marion got through working in this crazy business without a bit of a mess. You've heard the term "a hot mess"? Marion Ross is just the opposite of a hot mess!*

Chapter 17

My TV Son Ron

The pride I have in what my two children, Jim and Ellen, have accomplished in their lives is as great as any mother's. But, honestly, I don't think if you could actually measure the level of pride I hold for what Ron Howard has achieved, it would prove to be much lower than what I harbor for my biological offspring.

When I was cast to do the pilot for *New Family in Town*, Ron was the only other actor I was aware of who was slated to work on it. I, of course, knew him for his role as Opie Taylor in *The Andy Griffith Show* and was also aware he had played Winthrop Paroo, the little boy with the lisp, in the 1962 film version of *The Music Man*, which starred Robert Preston and Shirley Jones. What I learned after getting to know him was that by the time I had become aware of him as Opie, he had already chalked up numerous television appearances on shows such as *The Twilight Zone*, *Dennis the Menace*, *The Many Loves of Dobie Gillis* and *The Cheyenne Show*. He had also played the part of Henry Fonda's character's son in the ABC series *The Smith Family* and Jodar in *Land of the Giants*.

Another thing I learned about Ron, because he talked about it all the time, was that while he enjoyed acting, his true passion was in filmmaking. He had wanted to become a television and film director since he was very young, and by the time we were cast together in Garry's pilot, he was finishing up his senior year at John Burroughs High School in Burbank, with hopes of going on to film school. I knew he had applied to the USC School of Cinema-Television to study filmmaking, and it was while we were shooting that pilot that he received his letter of acceptance. He was ecstatic, as was I, although I kind of felt a tad bit guilty that I was there to share that moment with him rather than his own parents, Rance and Jean.

I knew Ron was very serious about his future, and while we were doing *Happy Days*, I realized it was from Rance that he had inherited that seriousness. His father was all business when it came to Ron's work on *Happy Days*. He made it a point to remain aloof from the cast and was always just quietly watching everything that was happening. He also made sure in those first few years of *Happy Days* that as soon as we were wrapped each evening, it was back home to Burbank for Ron. While Ron was of legal age by that time, Rance was not going to hear of his son going partying and getting into any child actor mischief. The Howards were staunch family people with roots in Oklahoma, and both Ron and his younger brother, Clint, who was also a child actor, best known for the role of Mark Wedloe in the television series *Gentle Ben*, which was based on the Walt Morey novel, were raised in a loving yet strictly disciplined environment.

I have many times said that two of the greatest blessings of my life are my children, but whenever I have said that, I have always caught myself and thought that I was fortunate to have those blessings doubled by also being a "mother" to Erin and Ron. I have been so proud of what he has accomplished as a filmmaker, and I'm just amazed when I think of the films that, under his creative leadership as a director, have been brought to life, classics such as *Splash*, *Cocoon*, *Backdraft*, *Apollo 13*, *How the Grinch Stole Christmas*, *A Beautiful Mind*, for which he won two Academy Awards, *Cinderella Man*, *The Da Vinci Code*, *Angels & Demons*, *Rush*, *In the Heart of the Sea*, *Inferno*. The list just seems to go on and on.

"Marion possesses an equilibrium that can balance things in a calm fashion, and she is capable of exuding that calming balance to people who come into her orbit."
—Ron Howard

David Laurell (DL): Ron, do you recall your first meeting with Marion?
Ron Howard (RH): It was when I showed up to my first day of work on the pilot for what would ultimately become Happy Days. *The pilot we shot had a very different tone than what the show became once it had been picked up. For anyone who has ever seen the pilot, which aired as an episode of* Love, American Style, *they know it was more to the theme of the film* Summer of '42 *than* American Graffiti. *It was shot in the single-camera format on film, so it had the look of a feature film, and the entire tone of it was softer and very nostalgic.*
DL: When you think back on doing *Happy Days*, what are the things that come to mind?
RH: That we really all got along and cared for one another. We did that through the run of the show, and that has been something that still continues to this day. I was lucky in my career to have been involved with two experiences like that. The way the cast cared about one another was the same on The Andy Griffith Show.
DL: There are, sadly, way too many child actors who

achieved various levels of success in the business and then, for myriad reasons, saw their lives take a horrible downturn or worse. How did you manage to avoid the pitfalls that took down so many others?

RH: *I'm asked that quite a bit. A lot of people are curious as to how I navigated the business, grew up in it, and maintained my sanity. My answer is, first and foremost, that I had great parents who never let me or my brother get out of control. Then I was, again, so lucky to be involved with the shows I did, both of which provided me with such a nurturing environment. I know that people in Middle America don't think of Hollywood as providing a nurturing environment, but it does happen. It's just like anything else. There are bad players in the entertainment business, just like in every other business. I have been in show business for as far back as I can remember, and I have found that there has always been a lot of really good people in this business.*

That was especially true about Happy Days. *Here was a show that took off like a rocket. It exploded and became kind of a national event. We were one of the highest-rated shows ever for a really long time. And yet, in spite of all the commotion and outside noise, all the changes, the excitement, the pressures, the various voices and the business factors—the internal business part of doing a show—everyone associated with* Happy Days *loved working together and loved what we achieved as a team. There was always an ensemble feel to that show, no matter who had the best part in any weekly episode. Even when Henry just exploded as the Fonz, and that kind of took over for a while, we may have gotten frustrated at times, but we all kept that in perspective and knew it was great for all of us in the bigger picture.*

I think that in her own winning and unobtrusive way, Marion had a lot to do with creating that ensemble feel

*and the collegial perspective. Of course, our director Jerry
Paris was responsible for that and, of course, Garry Marshall also set that tone—Garry in his energetic and sometimes outrageous way. He was probably the greatest boss
I'll ever come across. He was a remarkable leader. But I
think Marion did a lot, not just to make* Happy Days *such
a great show, but to help everyone from Garry on down to
approach our work, and one another, in a way that would
not have happened without her there.*

**DL: What was it about Marion that created that envi-
ronment?**

*RH: Oh gosh, David, so many things. Marion possesses
an equilibrium that can balance things in a calm fashion,
and she is capable of exuding that calming balance to people who come into her orbit. She has great wisdom that
she applies with a very humanistic viewpoint. I think,
when you take those qualities into account, you can understand what those who know her really well know: that she
is a fantastic communicator and a great person to confide
in. She was always such a positive force on the set, even
when tensions got high. She always maintained this great
tone that was positive and upbeat, but also just wiseass
enough that it never felt forced or overly sentimental. I
don't think I have ever met a person whose positivity is as
organic as Marion's.*

**DL: You say she was a great person to confide in. Did
you ever share any of your concerns with her?**

*RH: I think everyone did! People went to her with
tough questions to get good answers. She was always a
great listening board, whether it was a personal problem
or some frustration with the show or over some professional career matter. She is one of the best listeners I've
ever known, and I think the greatest quality she brought
to our show was that she knew how to defuse things in an
extremely uncontrolling way. She never stepped in and
took charge—that would not be her at all.*

But she had this way of going around to individuals, very quietly, like a little hummingbird or something going from flower to flower, and giving each of us a little dose of whatever she felt we needed to calm down and move forward. She never had any sort of an agenda other than being a caring, interested friend. My bet is that, at one time or another, every cast member, heck, maybe everyone involved with the show, went to Marion for advice on one thing or another. She was never judgmental, just endearing and always very encouraging.

DL: You know that Garry, on occasion, when things got a bit hairy, would seek out Marion to help him calm the waters.

RH: *I didn't know that he actually did that, but I'm not surprised that Garry would have gone to her. I'm not surprised at all that he would seek her out to get the skinny on a situation or on someone and understand what was going on in their head.*

DL: It seems that, to a very large extent, Marion has had almost the same level of interest and pride in you and your career as she has had with her own children.

RH: *I think that was true of all the younger members of the* Happy Days *cast. She was definitely that way with me. She had been with me when I opened the envelope and learned I had been accepted to the USC film school, and from then on she was always encouraging and supportive of me. She knew that while being on* Happy Days *was a great opportunity for me, my real passion existed in directing. So, in 1980, while we were still doing* Happy Days, *I got my first chance to direct a film. It was this low-budget movie I did for Roger Corman called* Grand Theft Auto. *Marion was so excited that I had gotten that chance, and I asked her if she would be willing to play a role in it. We paid her a tiny fraction of what she was making for just one episode of* Happy Days, *but she didn't care. She was there for me on this crazy film, where we had her run-ning around and falling down in the desert. She gave it her all in that movie, and she was so proud of me.*

DL: Let's talk about Marion as an actress. What do you think she brought to the role of Mrs. C?

RH: Well, she has become one of the most iconic television moms in history. I think that was because she made Mrs. C a multidimensional character. Tom Miller, who was our executive producer, just loved Marion. He loved the character, and he always felt that the mom was as im-portant as anyone in the show. Tom had been born and raised in Milwaukee, and so he knew real-life Mrs. Cs and what they were like and all about. I remember when we were first starting out with the show, he told me a lot about her that I hadn't known. He had seen her do a Ten-nessee Williams's play and had been really knocked out by her performance. He considered her to be a great stage ac-tress, and he was thrilled that they had gotten her to play Mrs. C.

As for what she brought to the role, like I said, she made Mrs. C a multidimensional character. She gave her an impish side that was even a little flirtatious. Because Marion had such great acting chops, she knew how to shade a character and give her depth. She gave Mrs. C a wit that kept her relevant and current and unfettered by false sentimentality. Marion had been trained as a dra-matic stage actress, and yet she embraced the sometimes slapstick and broad comedy of Happy Days. *She had a tremendous résumé as an actress, but she really didn't have much experience in comedy. She wasn't a comedic actress, but she had a sense of humor that, with no prob-lem, had her holding her own with Jerry Paris and Garry Marshall and Henry Winkler, guys who had these great wits and who could be incredibly funny.*

If Marion only had three lines in the episode, she was

the same as if she was carrying the entire episode. She was a consistent and consummate professional. I never heard her complain, not a single time. Yet if other people complained, which we all did [laughing], she could be totally nonjudgmental, empathetic and understanding.

DL: It is rather amazing, when you look beyond her portrayal of Mrs. C, how versatile Marion was as an actress.

RH: Oh my, yes. Marion is an actress in the purest sense. She loved the process of acting—that was always evident. To her, acting was a means of expression, and also a way of life. I don't mean it was all she cared about, but having the chance to create a character and perform meant a lot to her. She loved the work of being an actress and was always very ambitious about getting work. After Happy Days, *she went on to do some great roles, and that wasn't because she had an ego-driven desire to prove that she had more to offer than the role she was so well known for. It was because she loved the art and work of acting. Even when we were at the height of our popularity with* Happy Days, *when we would go on hiatus, she would go and grab a play just to keep stretching herself as an artist.*

DL: You know, perhaps as well as anyone, that Marion was extremely hesitant about writing this book. As someone who has known her so well for so long, what would you hope people will learn about her from reading this book that they otherwise would not have known?

RH: Well, I'm very glad that she did decide to write this book, because she has a life story that is inspiring to anyone who has ever had a dream. Everyone, of course, knows that she made a fantastic Marion Cunningham and will always be known as one of the greatest television moms, but there is so much more to her than Mrs. C. I would hope that readers would learn about her career both before and after Happy Days *and see that she cannot be un-*

derestimated as one of the great character actresses of our time—a true artist with an extraordinary range. I hope they will also learn that she was a real team player, on the show and also on the softball field [laughing]. She put on that uniform and got out there with the same gusto and enthusiasm as the guys. I don't remember her driving in any key runs or making any game-saving diving catches, but just as in our work on the show, she was there for all of us, being a part of our team and always cheering us on. I think it is also important for people to know that she had a difficult private life and had to deal with a lot of challenges as a single mom with one foot in a very demanding professional world. She navigated it all with strength, grace, dignity and wisdom, and when you look back at her life, in its full context—both personally and professionally—you've got to be amazed at how she made it all look really easy. But how easy could it have been?

Chapter 18

My TV Daughter Erin

In April of 2017, I was deeply into writing this book. I had completed the first draft and was going back over each chapter, line by line, making sure I was comfortable with everything. Just a few months earlier, my writing colleague, David Laurell, had spent time with Erin Moran, whom, just like the rest of my *Happy Days* family, I wanted to be involved with my book.

Erin had called me shortly before speaking with David, and although we hadn't talked to one another in a while, we picked up right where we had left off and had a wonderful "catch-up" conversation. As I said good-bye to her and hung up, I felt so much better about her than I had on so many other occasions over the years. She seemed to be not only upbeat but also at peace with the demons of depression, drugs and alcohol she had wrestled with for many years.

To be brutally honest, had I received the news that Erin had died at any point in time during the prior two or three decades, I would have been crushed, but not surprised. Every time I had seen her or spoken to her in the years following *Happy Days*, I had hoped and prayed that her demons would never get the better of her and that we would see one another again. By that April, I no longer gave that any thought. As hard as it may have been for me to believe, the cute little girl so many Americans grew up watching on *Daktari*, *Happy Days* and *Joanie Loves Chachi* was now older than I was when I played her mother. She had turned fifty-six the prior October, and it seemed that she had beaten the odds, had put her demons behind her, and had settled into a peaceful life with her second husband, Steven Fleischmann, in Indiana.

I think it was because of that last conversation, in which she sounded so good, that when I received the news of her passing on the afternoon of April 22, 2017, it hit me much harder than it might have ten or twenty years before. Within a short time, the news of Erin's death was being reported on various television networks and, I'm sure, many people who knew of her history just surmised that drugs were involved. My phone began ringing off the hook with news producers who wanted to send reporters and camera crews out to my house to talk about Erin and my feelings about her passing.

Because it was a Saturday, my longtime personal assistant, Gwen Berohn, was off, and I just couldn't bring myself to deal with all the calls, much less have camera crews come to my home. I did, however, speak with a few reporters by phone. At that time, I was as much in the dark as anyone else as to the cause of her passing, so all I could say was that it was a tragedy that we had lost someone who was so kind and talented. I kept being asked how I felt, and what could I say? I was obviously heartbroken, but I was also a bit annoyed at being asked that question. Erin's passing wasn't about me or my feelings. It was about the loss of a woman who had brought so much joy to people from the time she was very young.

My feeling that Erin's death was a tragedy only grew stronger when I later learned that she died due to complications of stage four squamous cell carcinoma of the throat, and that the toxicology tests showed no illegal narcotics were involved in her death. From what I heard, she first experienced symptoms of the problem just shortly after her fifty-sixth birthday, deteriorated rapidly, had poor medical treatment, and may not even have been aware herself of just how badly the cancer had metastasized.

In the weeks following Erin's death, I thought of her every day. I thought back to those days when she and I were the only "girls" on the show, and recalled how close we had become during the *Happy Days* years. I have the most lovely memories of her coming to my dressing room between scenes, where we would have tea together and we would talk. She was just a few years older than my daughter, Ellen, so I was always very interested in learning what Erin was going through so I could get ready to deal with that sort of thing with my own daughter as she got older. She was such a darling girl, and she fit in so well with the rest of the cast.

That, however, wasn't always the case with her parents, who loved to be onstage when we were rehearsing and on the nights we taped. And they especially loved cast parties. They were big partyers and were always the last to leave. They were this young and attractive couple who were a little wild, and I know they caused Garry some frustration at times. And then there was her grandmother, who was very keen (maybe a little too keen) on Erin being in show business. Erin was not brought up the way I was. Her parents were, seemingly, not serious about anything. They were fun-loving and free-spirited, and I just never felt that Erin was properly grounded because of that. But everybody loved her. She was always eager to please and was a very good actress to boot.

After *Happy Days* was over, I stayed in touch with Erin. I genuinely cared about her and often worried about her. She had gotten involved with Scott Baio romantically, and that was not good for her. She would call me crying, and I would talk to her and offer some advice, but I don't know if she was really capable of understanding some things, because she had never been taught how to cope with the realities of life. She was always making friends with the strangest people and getting herself into odd situations, which I think stemmed from a lack of guidance. But I sincerely hope that in the end, she was doing as well as she sounded the last time we spoke.

Not too long after her death, I had a very small gathering at my home—the Happy Days Farm—to pay tribute to Erin. I knew Henry was out of town and would not be able to make it, but I was adamant that the guest list be very intimate, just Ron, Anson, Donny, Scott and Erin's very close friend Cathy Silvers, the daughter of Phil Silvers, who played Jenny Piccalo on *Happy Days*. I tried to keep that very hush hush, but word leaked out, and I said no to everyone outside of our little *Happy Days* family. I even turned down the pleadings of my own son, Jim. I just wanted it to be us—the *Happy Days* family members who knew her and loved her.

We had a wonderful time reminiscing and telling stories, so many of which we had forgotten. When they left, I felt so much better after being around the guys and Cathy, although a while later, I found myself sobbing uncontrollably as I read and reread the interview David did with her for this book not long before her death.

"Marion is a Scorpio, so she has a very stable personality. She is grounded and has a strong foundation." —Erin Moran

David Laurell (DL): How did *Happy Days* come into your life?

Erin Moran (EM): I had done quite a bit of television work and was doing a play with Anson Williams right around the time they were casting for Happy Days. I had this big crush on Anson, and I knew he had already been cast, so I tried out for the part of Joanie, but I didn't get it. Then the girl that did get it didn't work out for some reason. Anson gave my agent a call and said I should come back for another reading. I did, got the part, and the rest is history.

DL: Do you remember the first time you met Marion?

EM: Yes, it was on Stage Nineteen on the Paramount lot, which became our home. On my first day I was introduced to the whole cast, and right from the start, everyone was so nice. I was happy to be working with such wonderful people, who, in such a short time, became like a second family to me.

DL: I know that it will mean a lot to *Happy Days* fans to learn that you really all did, and do, love one another.

EM: Oh yeah! We really bonded, almost immediately. There was no negativity on that show. It was just all positive and warm. Right from the start it was like we all had known each other for years. I was really lucky. I had been working in the business since I was four years old, and had never had a bad experience. Then the icing on the cake was getting to do Happy Days. I deeply loved those people and have always thought of them as family.

DL: Talk about your personal relationship with Marion. Did you ever go to her seeking advice?

EM: She was the one I went to. We had gotten very close over the years, and when we were rehearsing, I would go over to her dressing room, which happened to be right next to mine, and we would have tea together, like two neighbors. We would sit and just talk and talk. She would tell me about her kids, and I would tell her about my family. We would talk about what I was going through at any given time, and she would give me advice on stuff. We would get so lost in our deep conversations that we would forget we were doing a show. Then they would come and knock on the door and say, "Come on, come on. Marion, Erin, places!" Marion and I would look at each other and laugh and laugh, because we would get so caught up in talking, we would actually forget we were at work.

DL: Marion has said your parents were rather free-spirited. How was your real mom different than your television mom?

EM: *My parents were not your typical stage parents, but I think they had more fun than anyone by being involved with* Happy Days. *My mom was the type who was very outgoing and didn't appear to be strict with me, but at home she was. I was not close with her, and so if I had something bothering me, I would go to Marion. I know that on many occasions she felt uncomfortable—that it would have been out of place for her to interfere in some personal family situation, and she would feel she needed to back off. When that was the case, she would say, "I really don't know. You should ask your mom about that."* When she would say that, I would think, I don't want to ask my mom. That's why I'm coming to you. *I didn't want to ask my mom, because I knew she wouldn't answer me. Talking with her the way I talked with Marion just was not where our relationship was.*

I was kind of hurt when Marion put me off, but then, as time went on, I noticed she did that with other people who went to her for advice. When I saw that, it clicked. I re-member one time thinking, Oh, okay! That's just what I needed to see to get it. Now I understand. *She was very wise, and because of that, she wasn't going to step out of bounds and cause problems or disruptions within families or between people. She was one smart lady. We had this wonderful talk one time, long after* Happy Days *was over and I was an adult. I think it was shortly after my mother passed away in 2008. Marion told me that there had been so many times she wanted to tell me something or give me some advice and help with all the questions I had and answers I craved, but she just felt it wasn't her place to do so.*

DL: As you may know, Garry was very aware that Marion was a calming force who had a stabilizing influence over the cast members. He said that when there would be cast meetings, he looked to her at times because she was the real adult in the room.

EM: We would all know that. Marion is a Scorpio, so she has a very stable personality. She is grounded and has a strong foundation. We were always kind of in awe of her. She always had a wonderful answer for everything— very clean cut and to the point. If you ever had a question for her, the answer would be right there on the table for you to take.

DL: You know that Marion was very hesitant about writing this book. How do you feel about her deciding to finally do it?

EM: I have to say I'm surprised. I never thought she would do it, because years ago she would tell me, "I'm never going to do an autobiography! Never!" I never really knew why she was so adamant about never writing a book, but I'm so very glad she finally decided to do it. If anyone ever had a reason to write a book, it's Marion. She has so many stories about how she came through difficult times and how she never gave up on her dream of becoming an actress. People forget, she wasn't well known before Happy Days. *She didn't become a star until she was in her fifties. Most actresses I know would have thrown in the towel a long time before that. She is a great inspiration to people who know her, and I think by writing this book, she will be an inspiration to all those people who only know her from television.*

DL: What do you hope readers will take away from this book?

EM: I hope they will get a real understanding of just how nice of a person she is. She has such a beautiful spirit and great heart. Anyone who has ever had the pleasure to be in her presence doesn't want to leave her. I saw that so many times at events and things over the years. People just loved to be around her! I really think that people who have never had the chance to meet her and spend time with her have missed out on one of the greatest things life has to offer. So I hope this book will give people a little taste of what it is like to meet her personally.

DL: If you were given just a few sentences to sum her up, what would you say?

EM: She was a great mom and actress and friend. She taught me more than anyone else I have ever known. She taught me things that gave me courage and hope when I didn't have either. Of all the actors and actresses and people I've worked with throughout my life, she is number one. Of all the people I have ever met or known, she is the very best. She is the most wonderful person I've ever known in my entire life. That's really something to say about another person, but it's very true.

Chapter 19

My Dear Henry

As we go through life, we all meet people with whom we have an immediate rapport. It is kind of an amazing phenomenon that, even though you have just met and you know nothing about one another, something sparks and a connection is made. That was the case with Henry Winkler and me. From the moment we met, there was something about Henry that integrated me. Yes, he was good looking and sexy, but there was something else about him I found even more appealing. He was kind, gentle, and had an old soul.

The fact that Henry turned what was at first just this small and recurring role of Fonzie into the show's breakout character, who would launch a thousand items that bore his likeness and would become one of popular culture's and television's all-time greatest icons, was not surprising to me. He had a charm and a charisma that were just impossible to conceal.

The more I got to know Henry, the more I was fascinated with him. He was the son of Jewish emigrants who left their home in Berlin, Germany, on the eve of World

War II with nothing but a little box that contained some jewelry that had been handed down to them. He and I were also kindred spirits in that from the time we were very young, we both harbored the dream of becoming actors. Achieving that dream was much more of a challenge for Henry than it was for me due to the fact that he is dyslexic, something that went undiagnosed when he was a child. And yet, in spite of dealing with dyslexia, he went on to graduate from Emerson College and the prestigious Yale School of Drama.

I know this is hard for even hard-core *Happy Days* fans to remember, but when we first started the show, the role of Fonzie was rather insignificant and his trademark leather jacket was nonexistent. Henry was not what Garry had had in mind for that character. He had imagined him to be a blond 1950s matinee idol type. It was only after Henry got an audition, because of his part in the then yet-to-be-released film *The Lords of Flatbush*, that Garry changed his mind about who and what Fonzie would be.

As for the absence of his leather jacket, that was dictated by the brass at ABC, who felt it would make him look like a criminal. And so, for the better part of our first season, they put Henry in this god-awful green Windbreaker. He looked ridiculous wearing that jacket, and it is a great testament to Henry's charisma and acting talent that, in spite of that dorky jacket, he still established the character as the coolest guy in the room.

Garry was more than aware that the character Henry had created screamed for a black leather jacket, and so, after a bit of negotiating (the television term for arguing) with the powers that be, a compromise was struck and the network agreed to let him wear a leather jacket on one condition: he had to be either on or with his motorcycle. Garry agreed to the terms and then, in a classic Garry move, saw to it that the character of Fonzie was never in a scene without his motorcycle. That lasted until some point in our second season, when the character had become so entrenched as a leather jacket–wearing cool guy that the obligation to include the motorcycle was dropped.

I would say that during the first season of *Happy Days*, I became closer to Henry than anyone else in the cast. He really befriended me first, and we became fast pals. The writers took notice that a personal spark had been ignited between Henry and me. They saw that he enjoyed teasing me and that we had a very playful relationship with one another. As good writers do, they picked up on that and began writing more and more scenes between us. They also incorporated an interesting and brilliant little twist— that I would be the only character on the show who would call him "Arthur." They felt that would distinguish Mrs. C's relationship with Fonzie as being different and more personal than it was with any other character.

As the success of *Happy Days* grew, and Henry became such a huge star—and I mean huge, as in a way that at the time had been reserved for Elvis or the Beatles—it always amazed me that the world knew him as Mr. Cool and Mr. Perfect, and yet, to me, he was always so kind, caring, tender and sensitive.

I remember one time during a rehearsal when Henry seemed to be a bit out of sorts. He just wasn't himself, especially around me. When I asked him what was wrong, he told me that earlier that day, when he and I had been talking, I had turned away from him and had started talking to someone else. I never gave that a second of thought, but Henry was so sensitive that he thought he had said or done something I didn't like, and he was devastated. That is the Henry I know. He may have come across to *Happy Days* viewers as this sexy tough guy who was the epitome of cool, but behind that character he so perfectly created and played, he was such a tender and kind man. He was always very observant of everything going on. He was a great "people watcher," and whenever guests would show up onstage during our rehearsals, he made it a point to introduce himself (like he had to do that), ask their names, and then be so kind to them.

In this life, Henry has been, and will always be, one of my greatest pals. He is one of the most loving and sensitive human beings I have ever known, and whenever I have been asked (which I have been, about a bazillion times) what he is like, I always repeat the line he used to say when he was asked about his character: "The Fonz is everything I wasn't, and everything I always wanted to be."

"One of the great joys of my life has been getting to spend time with Marion, to work with her, laugh with her, and absorb her wisdom. Her light is so bright, you have to wear sunglasses to be around her." —Henry Winkler

David Laurell (DL): Marion has said that when you two first met, a spark was ignited that became a flame that has never been, and will never be, extinguished.

Henry Winkler (HW): Here's what happened: our souls and our humor collided and coincided, and we knew it was meant to be [laughing]. *I think that bond between us also became strong because of our characters. She was the mother the Fonz never had. I know that she gives the credit to the writers for deciding that Mrs. C would be the only one to ever call Fonzie by his given name, Arthur. But here's the truth behind that: One day on the set, when we had just started doing the show, Marion made a mistake and called me Arthur. So Garry's ears perked up and the writer's ears perked up, and right there and then it was decided that Mrs. C would always be the only one to call Fonzie by his real name.*

DL: It's amazing, by talking to all the *Happy Days* cast

members, of whom Marion was adamant that they all be a part of her book, to learn how much you all supported and loved one another.

HW: *You are right about that, David. It was, and always will be, something so unique and special. I'll tell you what is amazing: that the creators of the show—Garry Marshall, along with Tom Miller and Eddie Milkis of Miller-Milkis Productions—in casting that show, accomplished something that was truly uncanny. It was as if each person they cast was like the coupling of cars on a train. Each one pulled the other forward. And we didn't just click as characters. We clicked as performers, as actors and as people. I have never done anything in my life that gave me loving friendships like the ones that came from doing* Happy Days.

Marion always says that I'm an old soul, but the really old soul is Ron. What a career he has had, before, during and after Happy Days. *He is almost ten years younger than me, but he is easily at least ten years smarter than me. Everyone in our cast had done stage work except for Ron. So when we began doing the show in front of a live audience, that was a new experience for him. He had done more television and film work than many of us, but working in front of a live audience was not something he was familiar with. So we all came together and gave him some pointers, and you would have never known that he had never done live theater. He took to it like a duck to water. Then there was Anson. He would come in every Monday morning with a new song he had written and then sing it about two or three inches from your face.*

And Tom, I had seen him on Broadway back in the mid-1960s, in a play called Catch Me If You Can, *so I had a great respect for his work, as I did for Marion when I learned of all the theatrical work she had done before* Happy Days. *She is an extraordinary person and one of the most gifted actresses I have ever had the pleasure to work with. She is a little ditzy, and yet extremely smart and wise. She is incredibly funny and very centered and strong. And, of course, no one can imagine anyone but her playing Mrs. C. She will go down in history as one of the greatest television moms. She exuded this unique "momness" quality [laughing]. She is the epitome of momness. But, also, in my opinion, she was limitless in what she was able to do as an actress. If you look at Mrs. C and then you look at the grandma in* Brooklyn Bridge, *and then at everything else she has done in between, she defines our job. She is the definition of what an actor is. If an actor is supposed to create another being, then there is not another being she cannot carve out of whatever material she is given.*

DL: Most serious *Happy Days* fans, I'm sure, are familiar with that classic and hilarious outtake of Fonzie and Marion passionately kissing. What is the story behind that?

HW: I think that may be the most famous outtake from the entire run of the show, and it just stemmed from our doing this scene together. I don't remember if we were getting a little punchy over not doing the scene right, or if one of us blew a line or something, but it was just one of those unplanned, organic things that happen. I had been joking around with her, and something had happened that we both knew the scene was blown, but the director hadn't called to cut, so I started to nibble her neck. Then from there it grew into this passionate embrace, and the audience stared going wild with laughter, which spurred us on into doing this mock make-out scene. To this day, no matter where I go, hardly a week goes by that someone doesn't bring that up.

I love seeing that clip because, to me, it shows this beautiful side of Marion. That she was always so game to go for it. She was right there with me, or with any other cast member, for whatever was happening at the moment. She can be this very majestic woman with impeccable acting training and talent, and yet she can also be so down to earth and funny. There is such a playfulness about her that I just love. That was so very evident when we began traveling all around the world, playing softball. I know that had never been a part of the career plan for Marion, and yet there she was, all suited up, just like the rest of us, in her Happy Days *uniform. There was nothing she wasn't up for. We had all developed a strong bond by working together, but those games were like the glue that would seal our love for one another forever.*

DL: Is there a more private moment you would like to share that would provide insight into the relationship between you and Marion?

HW: I was always going to her for advice if something was bothering me, either professionally or emotionally. She was so grounded and always available to all of us, and I never came away from talking to her that I didn't have a different perspective on whatever it was I was dealing with.

DL: Perhaps the most incredible thing about the *Happy Days* cast is that as the years have passed by, you have all remained close.

HW: That is true. We have always stayed involved with one another's lives, and I think that is because, beyond our work, we were all so involved with each other's lives when we were doing the show. I have never worked with a cast in which there was so much mutual respect and a genuine love and care for one another. From the time we first started doing the show, we have all celebrated the joys and sadness of each other's lives together. And that is not only a tribute to the cast. That is a tribute to our leader. When anything as special as Happy Days *comes together, it starts with the man at the top. Garry set the standard and the tone. He and the other producers just didn't accept bad behavior on the set. He will always be my "Don." I will always bow down and kiss the ring of Garry Marshall for what he gave me.*

DL: Can you explain what your relationship with Marion is like today? How it has evolved as you have gotten older?

HW: I think we all treasure the special people in our lives more and more as we get older. I make sure I call her and that we have the chance to talk no matter where I am in the world. I may not have much of anything to tell her, but I always just want to hear her voice. It always amazes me how busy and unstoppable she is. It seems like she always has something to tell me about her children or grandchildren or what work she has done around the house. She is filled with effervescence. When you talk to her on the phone, it is almost as if she has jumped through the receiver and is sitting in front of you. There is always such joy and excitement in her voice. Even if she is complaining about something, she is even joyous about that [laughing]. One of the great joys of my life has been getting to spend time with Marion, to work with her, laugh with her, and absorb her wisdom. Her light is so bright, you have to wear sunglasses to be around her.

Chapter 20

My Funny Donny

When you purchased this book, you may have just thought it would be a nice little story about the life of a woman who played a mother in a beloved television series. Little did you know that it would also reveal the secret to maintaining youth.

While the cosmetic manufacturers, exercise gurus, nutritionists and plastic surgeons are out there promoting their products, lifestyles and services to ward off aging, not a one of them can offer my tried-and-true fountain of youth secret, which I will now reveal to you: if you want to stay young, surround yourself with young people!

Up until the time that I got the part of Mrs. C on *Happy Days*, I had done a few plays, films and television shows that included children and teenagers in the cast. I also had had my own two children at home. What I had never done in my life up until that point in time was spend the majority of every week with young people in their late teens and twenties.

Yes, it did have its nerve-racking moments, what with all the usual problems and broken hearts that come with those years, but it also gave me the opportunity to be around the most exciting, vibrant, creative, talented and funny young people I have ever encountered. That was both intoxicating and infectious for a middle-aged woman. I was swept up in their youthful exuberance about everything, and the one who made me break out in a huge smile by just walking into the room was Donny Most, who played Richie's friend Ralph.

Donny was very inventive, and Jerry Paris loved him, his character and his antics so much, he would often just give him full rein to go off on a bender and surprise us all with some improvisation he brought to his lines or actions. He was a very talented actor who had great comedic intuition. He was also a very good singer, and while he always wanted to incorporate that into the character of Ralph, Anson's Potsie had already staked that ground.

Every time I would see Donny, I would just beam. He was as cute as a button, which I always thought was appropriate, because he reminded me of Red Buttons when he would say his catchphrase "I've still got it!"

When we first started the show, Ralph was just a peripheral character—kind of a wise guy who was into girls and cars. But as he evolved, he became a jokester. I think the reason Jerry liked the character so much was because he had been a comedic actor, and I think he saw a lot of himself in Ralph.

Donny was an interesting character in his own right. He had been born in Brooklyn and at the age of nine decided to pursue a career in show business after seeing the 1946 biopic *The Jolson Story*, based on the life of Al Jolson, the singer, actor and comedian who dominated American entertainment in the first half of the twentieth century. That film had a very strong impact on him, and he became a huge Jolson fan. None of his young friends had any idea who this Jolson person was, but Donny became obsessed with him. He would buy Jolson's albums and would learn the songs and sing along to them. And then, when he was thirteen, he surprised the heck out of everyone at his bar mitzvah when he got up and sang a few Jolson songs with the band.

His friends, and even his family members, were so shocked at how good he was that he mustered up the courage to do the same thing I had done as a young girl: break the news to my family that I was going into show business. Just like with me, no one in his family was in show business, so he was rather hesitant to express his intent. But his parents understood, and they found a school in Manhattan that catered to young kids who were interested in singing and acting. Donny enrolled, and at the age of fourteen, he was tapped for his first professional gig. The man who ran the school he was attending would pick a few standout kids to be a part of a professional troupe that performed in the Catskill Mountains during the summer, and in 1968 he picked Donny to be a part of the group.

He once told me that he was kind of an odd curiosity to his friends because of that. Remember, this was 1968, when there was an explosion of all this rock and pop and folk music, which all the kids were listening to, and here was this redheaded kid who was more interested in Jolson, Bobby Darin, Frank Sinatra, Nat King Cole, Tony Bennett, Dean Martin and other crooners of the Great American Songbook, all of whom meant nothing to his friends.

Following his summer of performing in the Catskills, Donny sat down with his father and expressed his desire to seriously pursue a career in entertainment, and they found a really good acting coach and, through her, an agent and a manager. He attended college at Lehigh University in Pennsylvania, although he was back home in New York on a regular basis, going on auditions and doing some commercial work. After completing his junior year, he came out to Los Angeles and began making the rounds and getting auditions, which included one with Garry Marshall for a sitcom that had just been picked up. And that was how Donny came to *Happy Days*.

After the curtain fell on *Happy Days* in 1984, Donny continued to act. He did a few feature films and television shows, and he even carved out a niche as a voice actor on several animated productions. He has also done some directing work and returned to his first love—singing the swinging standards. He does a wonderful nightclub show, "Donny Most Sings and Swings," which I have had the pleasure of seeing, and I have noticed that audiences, who come in knowing him only as Ralph Malph, leave with a very different impression of him.

And so my funny Donny, who always made me smile, has continued the grand tradition of Brooklyn-born music makers, whose short list includes George Gershwin, Aaron Copland, Marvin Hamlisch, Neil Diamond and Barbra Streisand. But just as it is for the rest of us, his work on *Happy Days* will always hold a special place in his heart, and I think it is very sweet that during each nightblub show, he always takes the time to acknowledge the people who came to see him because they are *Happy Days* fans.

"Marion has this incredible spirit. She has such a wonderful energy and warmth about her; she lights up a room by just walking in the door." —Donny Most

David Laurell (DL): When you think back on doing *Happy Days*, what are the things that come to mind?

Donny Most (DM): I think the thing that stands out in my mind the most is the early days. I had just turned twenty, and everything was so new and exciting. During the first two seasons, we didn't have a live audience and did a one-camera shoot. When you are doing a show that

way, you finish your scenes and you're done for that day and can go home. I wasn't in a lot of scenes at first, so when they would finish with me, they still had to do the Cunningham family scenes. I rarely left when I was finished. I always wanted to stick around and watch everything that was being done. I really enjoyed watching all the other cast members do their scenes.

DL: Tell us about the relationships—the personal interactions—between cast members.

DM: It was a magical thing from a character standpoint. I mean, when anyone thinks of Happy Days, *it is almost impossible to think of just one or even two of the characters. You always think about the guys all together at Arnold's or Howard and Marion and Joanie sitting in their kitchen. I think the beauty of* Happy Days *was that the characters were perfectly matched with one another. And then, when you get beyond the characters to the actors— to the people who brought those characters to life—there was a lot of magic there, too, in the way we all worked with one another and enjoyed being with one another. I've been lucky to have worked with a lot of good people on many productions, but nothing that has ever matched doing* Happy Days. *That's something that I don't believe happens very often in show business, or any business.*

DL: Do you have any one special memory from the *Happy Days* years?

DM: Oh David, I have so many, but I think one of my fondest memories of doing the show was when we did the episodes in which the characters went from Milwaukee to Hollywood. Because we were supposed to be in California, we, of course, had to do beach scenes, and I remember we did this one scene where we were all sitting at the beach as it started to get dark. We had this roaring fire going, and we were all sitting around like we were a bunch of kids at camp. I can play that memory out in my mind so clearly: all of us just sitting there in the glow of the fire, Erin telling us these funny stories about her family, and Marion just being the delight she always was.

I also have wonderful memories of these parties that Jerry Paris would have at his house. They were really great, and we all had so much fun just being together. We really had such a great relationship with one another. Tom was like an uncle to me, and Marion was like my aunt. I used to love to go out for lunch with Marion when we were doing the show, and we have continued to do that ever since. I don't care where we go or what we eat. I just love being with her, because we have so many laughs. We really were like a family. We still are and always will be till we're all gone.

DL: When I took on this assignment to work with Marion on her book, it was decided I would talk to all the cast members about her. After that decision was made, she gave me a warning I really haven't heeded. She said, "Don't let them sound like they are giving my eulogy. Ask them to tell you the bad things about me." So far, I haven't had any success in getting anyone to give up the bad stuff on her.

DM: [laughing] *That would be Marion. I can hear her saying that. Well, there's a good reason you haven't been able to get any dirt on her, and that's because if you pleaded with me or even threatened my life, I still don't think I could come up with a bad word about her. She is one of the most unique people I have ever met. She has this incredible spirit. She has such a wonderful energy and warmth about her; she lights up a room by just walking in the door. She also has quite a sense of humor and imagination, and if you are lucky enough to be with her when that imaginative mood strikes, you will be in for a real treat.*

DL: Don, when someone mentions the name Marion Ross, what is the first thing that comes to your mind?

DM: That I have always enjoyed getting to spend time with her. And also that she was always so supportive of me—of all the cast members. When the show ended, we kept in touch on a regular basis, and every time we talked, she wanted to know what was going on in my life and career. Whenever she would do a play, I would always make it a point to go and see her, and she was so thrilled that I was there. We were all very supportive of one another's work, and since I have been doing my music, she has come to see me on a few occasions. There's nothing better than to be onstage singing and look out and, through the glare of the spotlight, see her beaming face in the audience.

DL: Is there any one special memory you have of Marion that stands out the most?

DM: I think it would have to be when we went on our softball tours. I especially remember this one time when we were in San Francisco, which is Jerry's hometown. He decided he was going to take a few of us on a tour of the city. So we piled into this convertible—Jerry, Marion, me and a couple of the other cast members. I have no recollection of learning anything about San Francisco. All I can remember is we were all laughing our heads off and having the time of our life. We had such great times doing those tours, and Marion was a real trouper. Most of us, I think, with the exception of Henry, had played since we were kids, but there was Marion, who had never played before, right out there with us as a part of the team.

DL: I have been an entertainment writer and reporter for many years. I have interviewed hundreds of actors who have been a part of ensemble casts in television shows, and in many cases, they really came to love one another and become like a family. That said, I have never seen it to the degree it seems to exist with the *Happy Days* cast.

DM: Yeah, we really grew to love and care about each other, and I have always felt that played a big part in the show's success. You asked me before about the interaction between the cast members. I think viewers perceived there was something real about the way we interacted. We had so much respect for one another, and we all worked very hard—each one of us gave it our all on that show. We supported one another, and there was a real family unity amongst us. It was the greatest thing that has ever happened to me in my life, and I'm so thankful to the people who come up to me and tell me how much Happy Days *has meant to them. I've had people even get emotional telling me how watching that show helped them get through difficult times and how they thought of all of us as a part of their family. I always feel so blessed and grateful when that happens. I am so thankful to have been a part of a show that had just a powerful impact.*

Chapter 21

My Wonderful Friend Anson

While working on this book with my collaborator, David, I introduced him to Anson Williams. One day, David called and told me he had just returned home from having lunch with Anson at a restaurant in Malibu.

"We sat and talked for hours," David told me. "I felt like we were old friends—like we knew one another forever."

That didn't surprise me in the least. That's just the way Anson is.

He treasures friendships and loves people. And he has always had this innate desire to help people. It's a part of his DNA—literally. His cousin (whom he always called "Uncle Henry") was Dr. Henry Heimlich, the thoracic surgeon and medical researcher who developed the lifesaving maneuver for treating choking victims. Dr. Heimlich had a huge influence on Anson and inspired him to found his company, StarMaker Products, which develops all sorts of wonderful things to help people—things that help their body to work better without drugs, like a completely natural topical gel that brings down a person's skin temperature when they become overheated or have a hot flash, and a natural spray that helps people stay alert by stimulating the tongue's lingual nerve.

We were very lucky to have had such a talented cast on *Happy Days*, but Anson was blessed with far more talents than the ability to act. He has always been one of the most curious people I have ever met. And I mean that in a good way. He always wanted to know what was going on with everyone, and why this was being done, or why we were doing that. I believe that is why he has the ability to establish a wonderful rapport with people very quickly: he is genuinely interested in the people he meets, who and what they are all about and what makes them tick.

I have had the pleasure of meeting and getting to work with many fascinating people during my life, but Anson is only one of a few who I would say is a true Renaissance man. Along with being an extremely talented actor, he is a good singer, director, athlete, businessman and entrepreneur. He has an ingenious mind when it comes to publicity and marketing, and he is also a very good writer. He has written a revolutionary cookbook that offers recipes for delicious comfort foods—from lasagna to apple turnovers—that can be prepared in a way that ensures perfect portion control by using a one-hundred-calorie counting system he devised with a nutritionist.

Along with the other members of our *Happy Days* family, I am so proud of all the things Anson has accomplished, especially his behind-the-scenes work as a television director of after-school specials, made-for-television movies and popular episodic television shows, including *Beverly Hills, 90210*; *Melrose Place*; *Star Trek: Deep Space Nine*; *Star Trek: Voyager*; *Xena: Warrior Princess*; *The Secret Life of the American Teenager*; *Sabrina the Teenage Witch*; *Charmed* and *7th Heaven*.

"She's calling her book My Days. *Well, I think there will be people who will read this book whose days will be better because they have read about Marion's days."*
—Anson Williams

David Laurell (DL): How did *Happy Days* come into your life?

Anson Williams (AW): I had done over thirty commercials and a lot of television shows in which they would always cast me as the concerned boyfriend (furrows his brow and gives a look of deep concern). *I had always had a desire to be a musician or to act, but I never really did much of anything to pursue it when I was in high school, or even right after I graduated. That was simply because I had no idea how to go about starting a career in show business. I had grown up in Burbank, and so a lot of my friends had family members who were in all different aspects of the film and television industry. I started asking around as to what I should be doing if I wanted to be a singer or an actor, and the answer I got was that I just needed to get out there and start doing it. So I started going to talent nights around Los Angeles. I was singing and then began going on casting calls for small parts in local theater productions, and one thing just led to another.*

DL: And one of the things it led to was an audition with Garry Marshall.

AW: Right, for the pilot that would ultimately become Happy Days. *I can assure you, when I went on that audition, I had no idea that what I was doing would dramatically change my life. At the time I was just looking for a gig to pay the rent, so to me, this was just the hope of getting a payday. But then I got the part and found out that I would be working with Ron Howard, which was unreal, because I grew up watching him on* The Andy Griffith Show. *I remember when we were shooting that pilot, there were all these whispers around the set that this would be a "sure thing" to be picked up because it was such a great premise. Well, it didn't get picked up, the pilot aired as a* Love, American Style *episode, and I didn't give it any other thought. I just went on with my life.*

But then a year later American Graffiti *came out and* Grease *opened on Broadway and became a huge hit, and all of a sudden, the 1950s were hot, and ABC gave Garry's pilot another look. Not many people know this, but when ABC decided to go with the show, they brought Ron and me back in to screen-test. That was kind of odd, because we had been in the pilot. But they were concerned that we might be too old for the roles. Something else that is not widely known is that, along with me, they were considering another actor for the part of Potsie—an actor by the name of Donny Most. He had read for Potsie, and they didn't think he was right for the part. But Jerry Paris saw something he liked in Donny, and he created the role of Ralph just for him.*

DL: Stop and think about it, Anson. Of the billions of people who have inhabited this earth, only a handful—what, maybe a couple hundred—have been a part of a successful television show and created characters that have become iconic and that will live forever. Do you ever allow yourself to think about that—that you and your cast mates are among the members of that extremely exclusive clique?

AW: I'm grateful beyond belief. The success of Happy Days *went so far beyond the scripts, which were well written, and the show itself, which was perfectly cast. There was an "it" factor with that show. There are people who live in some of the most remote parts of the world, in areas of Africa, who know nothing about American life, much less what it was like in the 1950s. And yet they related to* Happy Days *and the characters. They felt a connection between themselves and the characters, and that is because love and friendships and family are the same no matter where you go in the world. People may look different and the backdrops of their lives are different, but the message of* Happy Days *is universal to every culture.*

That is not just a phenomenon for people who loved the show. It was the same for us—those of us who did the show and created the characters. We felt that way about one another as human beings, as well as the characters each of us brought to life. I think that is why we have all remained close and stayed in touch. We all bonded in a way that really was exceptional—like it was some kind of a meant-to-be kismet. That is why, even though we may not see one another for a while, when we do, it is right back to where it has always been. We just pick up from where we left off like there has been no passage of time.

DL: You knew Marion before the other cast members, from working on the pilot, but you didn't really get to know her until the show was picked up. What was it like working with her?

AW: Professionally, she is the consummate pro. You would hear that from anyone who has ever worked with her. It would not be an exaggeration to say we were all in awe of her experience, especially as a stage actress. On the personal level, she was always so kind and positive about everything. She has always been one of those people that you feel good to be around. She has always radiated this glow of positivity, which was an inspiration to me. I would go as far as to say she was a role model who instilled the quality of positivity and the importance of positive thinking in me.

As I have gotten older, I have developed this real personal peeve about the societal definition of aging, that too many people buy into what society says about getting older, and it subconsciously limits them from doing all sorts of new things. We are such an empowered force and have so much to offer. I'm in better physical shape today than I was in my thirties. I'm more on my game than ever before when it comes to ideas. That comes with the worldliness and experience you gain by both having had successes as well as failures—from making mistakes and learning from them.

There are still so many mountains to climb as we get older, and it kills me when I see people my age, and even younger, who are on the back nine, just wandering around, not knowing what to do with themselves. I have friends who are in their fifties who look and act like old men. Their mind is aging them, because their body is following their negative thoughts. They have nothing to stimulate them. I know people who sit around wondering what they can do, and the answer is they can do anything they want to do. It's all about the power of positive thinking. You have to fill your mind with positive thoughts, and then your body follows along and gets excited about life. I have been preaching that message for a long time. It is what my business ventures have been based on. And, to a very large extent, it was Marion who sowed the seeds of embracing positivity in me many years ago.

DL: As you know, Marion is not much of a kicker or a screamer. But she may have done a tiny bit of both before finally agreeing to write her autobiography. As someone who knows her so well and has been inspired by her, what do you hope readers of this book will gain by learning more about her?

AW: *Many things. First, I would like to think that after learning more about her, and getting to know that her life wasn't all roses, people would go back and watch* Happy Days *and* Brooklyn Bridge *with a fresh perspective. I would like them to really watch her in every scene. She was a genius in the way she crafted her characters. She was also a comedic genius. I would encourage people to really watch her and to be aware of her timing, which was always right on, and her reactions and expressions. She has brought life to the characters she has played, which has made them so much more than they otherwise would have been.*

Jerry Paris recognized that, and he let her create the character of Mrs. C. He did that with all of us—allowed each of us the opportunity to contribute to who our characters became. He let us create dimensions that gave our characters life and that the writers would then take and run with. Jerry gave us all the freedom to be creative and sculpt our characters. The Fonz is 100 percent Henry. Donnie completely created Ralph. And the same was true with Mrs. C. Marion totally created that character.

DL: You sound like you are a genuine die-hard Marion Ross fan.

AW: [laughing] *I love her. Everyone who has been fortunate enough to know her loves her. Even though she has always been a strong woman, she was never the type to get in anyone's face or be obtrusive or demanding in any way. That is just not a part of her makeup. In fact, she could be very reserved and quiet. When we were doing* Happy Days, *she would sort of fall back if things ever got a little heated. She wasn't the type to be out there throwing in her two cents, unless she was asked to weigh in on something or to offer some advice on something. Then she was great—she always had something to say that was thoughtful and made sense.*

You were asking me before about what I hope people take away from this book. I think when they read about Marion's life experiences, it will be of great help to people, especially for other women who have gone through, or are going through, some of the things she has dealt with. I believe there will be people whose lives will be better by getting to see what she has been through and how she handled it. She's calling her book My Days. *Well, I think there will be people who will read this book whose days will be better because they have read about Marion's days. It will be inspiring to people, just like she has always been an inspiration to me. I have a better understanding of the world, priorities, selflessness, kindness, courage and strength because of her. She is the embodiment of the power of positive thinking—about cause and effect. When I think of her—or just hear her name—I smile. She's a white light of can-do spirit.*

Chapter 22

My Neighbor Scott

My home, which I have always affectionately called the Happy Days Farm, is located in the eastern shadow of Serrania Ridge, located between the Santa Monica Mountains and the Chalk Hills. Just to the west of the ridge, there is a beautiful formal estate where my neighbor lives—my neighbor Scott Baio.

Scott was just fifteen when he came to *Happy Days*. I was surprised to learn he was fifteen, because he appeared to be younger. He was just this cute little kid who, in what seemed like no time, grew in front of our eyes.

Another guy from Brooklyn, he was a sharp fellow who had an appealing personality. His character, Chachi, who was the younger cousin of Fonzie, joined our family during our fifth season. I can only imagine how overwhelming that must have been for him. By that time we had a major hit show on our hands, and he was immediately thrown into scenes with a cast that was entirely composed of household names.

That could have been intimidating for any actor, much less a teenager who had played the title role in the 1976 film *Bugsy Malone* but had done very little television work. But nothing seemed to faze Scott. He was polite and professional (believe me, his father would have never allowed him to be anything but) and just fit in perfectly with the rest of us.

Scott was the third child of Italian immigrants, Mario and Rose Baio. Like me, he had decided when he was very young that he wanted to become an actor. Unlike me, he was always very open about that dream, and his parents were always very supportive. When he first started out, he got some commercial work and then beat out more than two thousand other young actors for the lead role in *Bugsy Malone*, which is what brought him to Garry's attention.

After *Happy Days* wrapped, Scott went on to appear in a few feature films, such as *Skatetown, U.S.A.*; *Foxes* and *Zapped!*, and, of course, he also did the short-lived *Happy Days* spin-off, *Joanie Loves Chachi*. Not long after that he starred in his own series, *Charles in Charge*, which ran on CBS in 1984 and1985 and then in first-run syndication from 1987 to 1990.

In 2007 Scott did a VH1 reality series called *Scott Baio Is 45 . . . and Single*. At the conclusion of the first season of that show, he married his then girlfriend—a beautiful blond model, actress and Southern belle named Renee Sloan—and they soon announced that she was pregnant with twins.

Following a difficult pregnancy, during which Renee lost one of her babies, the couple's daughter, Bailey, was born five weeks premature on November 2, 2007. Initially, it was believed that she was suffering from glutaric acidemia type 1, a rare organic metabolic disorder, but extensive testing ultimately proved the diagnosis to be false, and Bailey was ultimately given a clean bill of health. With immeasurable gratefulness that their daughter was healthy, Scott and Renee took that horrific experience to heart and established the Bailey Baio Angel Foundation to raise awareness and funding for children who are dealing with metabolic disorders.

Today nothing brings a smile to my face more than to be doing something at the Happy Days Farm and to have Scott and Bailey stop by to visit while out for a walk. I always love spending a little time with them, just catching up on what they are doing. And even if some time passes and I don't see them for a while, it just makes me happy to know that they're not far away—just right over the ridge.

"I think there were times when Marion stepped in because even Jerry Paris couldn't get us to settle down with all his ranting and yelling. Those two were like the good cop and bad cop. Jerry was the bad cop, and Marion was the good cop. I swear, I really think they had that routine worked out to keep us all in line."
—Scott Baio

David Laurell (DL): It is always interesting how, in everyone's life, everything we do or don't do has an effect on where we go and who we become. Had you not been cast in *Bugsy Malone*, the chances are more than good that you would have never gotten the role of Chachi.

Scott Baio (SB): That is so true. After we did Bugsy Malone, *they screened it for the executives at Paramount, and Garry happened to be one of the executives who came in for the screening. When he saw me, something popped in his head. This is a little-known fact, but he had an idea for a spin-off of* Happy Days, *a show he created called* Pinky, *and he thought I would be perfect for it. So he arranged for me to do the pilot for that show, but it didn't go. Then, at the same time, Garry was doing a show called* Blansky's Beauties, *with Nancy Walker. He put me in that for a year, and then that is what led to* Happy Days.

DL: Tell us about your memories of doing *Happy Days*.

SB: Well, it was the real start of my career—the jumping-off point for me. It's where I learned everything about the business, about life, and I was lucky to have learned all those things from such great people. I grew up on that show. When we started out, I was a boy. I did Happy Days *from the time I was fifteen till I was about twenty-two or twenty-three. And even though I was in my mid-teens when I started, I looked like an eleven-year-old boy. So much of my real life took place while I was doing* Happy Days, *and then I went on to do* Joanie Loves Chachi—*which I shouldn't have done. That was a mistake. We did that between the tenth and eleventh seasons of* Happy Days, *and then I went back to doing* Happy Days. *After that came* Charles in Charge, *and I loved doing that. It's good to be the king, right?* [laughs].

DL: You were a part of a show that a hundred years from now, people will still know about. I don't know what sort of device they will be watching it on, but I'm betting they will still be watching it.

SB: I totally agree. I have people come up to me and mention Happy Days *all the time—kids who weren't even born when we were doing it. That just tickles me. It was a huge show, and that had a lot to do with that era—the domination of the three networks—when people eight to eighty . . . thirty to forty million people . . . watched every week. I don't know if we'll ever see any one show that will be able to get that kind of audience again. It was a beautiful story. It was well written. The characters were great. And that's the key to success in any television show. And that all goes back to Garry Marshall—his vision for the show, and how he brought all the elements together to make it work. It was a wonderful experience.*

DL: Talk about how you developed the character of Chachi.

SB: Come on, David [rolls his eyes]. *There was no character* [laughing]. *Chachi was just me, doing the dialogue the writers had written. I think every actor plays a version of themselves in whatever character they are doing, and Chachi was 100 percent me. I didn't really give it much thought—the development of that character. Chachi was just me, always was, right on through* Charles in Charge.

DL: By the time you came to *Happy Days*, the show was a hit. So you knew when you got that role, your life would be dramatically changing. Was there any moment you can pinpoint when you knew that your life would never be the same again?

SB: You know, David, I'm going to be honest. I didn't know what the hell I was doing and what was happening when I started. It was all so overwhelming that a lot of those early memories of doing the show are a big blur to me. I was just sort of winging it. But I guess there were two times that I do remember it hitting me that things would be different.

After filming Happy Days *on Friday nights, the cast would go out into the audience and sign autographs. I remember this one time, after I had been doing the show for a couple months, Henry was out there, and the people were just going crazy, as they always were. While he was doing that, I walked through the set. This roar went up from the crowd, and it scared me. I thought something had happened to someone. So I looked out at the audience, and they were looking at me. I didn't know what was happening, and then I caught eye contact with Henry, and I felt bad because I thought I was stealing his thunder. I always had great respect for him and really felt bad. So I was standing there, looking at Henry, and he motioned for me to come out into the audience. When I did, everybody was asking me for an autograph and taking pictures, and it was just crazy. I did that for about ten minutes, and then*

Henry came up behind me and put his arm around my shoulder and said, "Things are going to be very different for you from now on."

I didn't really know what the hell he was talking about. But then, soon after that, I was invited to some car show in the Midwest to sign autographs. It was at this huge convention center, and there was a catwalk around the perimeter of the hall. I remember walking there with my dad and looking down and seeing the place just packed with human beings. And I said, "Wow! This must really be a popular car show." And the guy who was with us said, "They don't care about the cars. They're all here to see you." I was sixteen. And I remember looking at my father and thinking, What is going on? He put his arm around me and said, "It's all right. You'll be all right." It was at that moment I got it—what Henry meant.

DL: Can you share some of your memories and thoughts on working with Marion?

SB: I always felt a certain amount of intimidation when I had to do a scene with Marion. Not personally, but professionally. I have worked with very few actors—and I've been lucky to have worked with some great ones—but very few that were always on the money like Marion was. She was always totally prepared, never missed a line. That is not an easy thing to do. So whenever I had to do a scene with her, I felt I had to show up with my A game. I don't mean that as a competitive thing between actors, not at all. It was just that she was always right there on cue. I think that was probably because of her theatrical training and her work in the theater, where you don't get numerous chances, like you do in television. Watching her work and working with her was a great learning experience for me, to see the way it should be done.

DL: Did you ever have any interaction with her away from the show?

SB: Oh my God, the softball games [laughing]. *We had a* Happy Days *softball team, and on weekends they played games all over the place, not just in Los Angeles, like, all over the country and even in other countries. I think Garry had this secret desire to be the owner of a professional baseball team, and there was always a running joke that people only got hired for* Happy Days *if they were good softball players. We became a real team. We would take on all these other organized teams for charities, and Marion loved that.*

When I first started on the show, I remember somebody asking me if I was going to play on the softball team, and I said, "I don't think so." Well, that must have gotten back to Garry. Not long after that, one day while we were rehearsing, my father unexpectedly showed up on the set, and I could tell something was wrong. I asked him what he was doing there, and he told me Garry had called him and wanted to see both of us. So we go into Garry's office, and I'm just scared to death. I'm sure he was going to tell me he was unhappy with something I was doing or fire me from the show.

When we walked in, he looked up at us and said, "Sit down." I was sweating like crazy. Then he got up and came around to the front of his desk and said, "You know, I love doing television shows. And do you know why I love doing television shows? Because it lets me put together a team to play softball." It was like a scene out of The Godfather *or something* [laughing]. *He looked at my dad and said, "Now, I hear your son won't play on our team. Why is that?"*

My father looked at me and I looked at my father, and then we both looked back at Garry, and my dad said, "Do you want him to play?"

Garry threw his hands up and started yelling, "Hell yes, I want him to play. That's why I called you in here!"

So my dad said, "Okay, then he plays."

And Garry said, "Good! Now, get the hell out of here and go back to work."

That was so Garry. He was the best. I loved him. We all loved him. He changed the lives of everybody who worked on that show—personally, professionally, monetarily. He was a genius, and so many people owe their careers to him. I certainly do. There were a lot of people whose talent and hard work made that show a success—we really were a team in the truest sense—but it all started and ended with Garry.

DL: Have you ever tried to analyze what it was that made *Happy Days* such a huge success?

SB: It is one of those things you really can't analyze or define. If you could somehow come up with a scientific answer as to why it all worked, then every television producer would follow the template and every show would be a hit. Obviously, that doesn't happen. So I don't know. It was the right show at the right time. The casting was just about as perfect as you could ever hope for, and there was a certain amount of magic dust that was sprinkled over us all as people that translated to what we did on-screen as characters. There were no egos at play on that show. That is very rare for a television show, but Garry and the other big players—the producers and Jerry Paris—they would have never put up with that from anyone.

DL: Has that magic dust ever landed on any other show you were in?

*SB: No. I mean, I've been in shows that have come close—*Charles in Charge *would be an example—but nothing like* Happy Days. *That show represents everything I am and everything I have. I will always be attached to that show—all of us will. Say the name Ron Howard— a child actor, a great director, an Academy Award winner—and yet the first thing people think of when they hear* *his name is* Happy Days. *That's how big that show was and continues to be. It was a wonderful experience that, I don't think for me, will ever be duplicated or matched.*

DL: Sitting here in the office of your home, do you find it a tad bit ironic that Marion's house is just over the hill?

SB: Yeah, it is. Funny thing is, that was purely coincidental. When we were looking for a house, they showed us this one, and as we were driving out here to look at it, I remember saying that I thought Marion lived somewhere nearby. So we bought it, and then I realized that she lives right around the block.

DL: Readers of this book will learn a lot about your neighbor from around the block that they otherwise would have never known. Do you think there may be some things revealed that may come as a surprise to those of you who know her?

SB: I have spoken to her about this a little bit, and she has told me she plans on being very candid and open and honest about her life. So I am going to be interested to read about her marriage, because I know nothing about it except that her husband had issues with alcoholism. She was always hesitant to talk about that, at least around me. So I would find that to be very interesting. I know she had some difficult times, and I would like to learn about just what she went through and how she dealt with it. She was always so great at helping others with their problems that I'm curious as to how she handled her own problems.

DL: One last thing. What do you know about her that you would hope readers will get to know about her?

SB: That she is the happiest person you could ever meet. She is the happiest person I've ever known in my life. I have never seen her when she wasn't upbeat and up for having a good time. This is the honest truth: I have never seen her in a bad mood—ever. Even when things might have gotten tense on the set, she always remained calm. I think that has a lot to do with the fact that she just loves what she does. She really loves the craft of acting, and I think she was always so grateful to have the chance to do it. I would say, throughout my life, along with Henry, people always ask me what Marion is like. I always say, "What do you think she's like?" They say, "I think she is bubbly and sweet." And I tell them, "You know what? That is exactly what she is like." The reason I ask that is because I know what people see by watching her, and what they see is really what she is like.

She is one of the loveliest people I have ever known, although you never wanted to mess around too much around her when we were working. Remember, she really was a mom, and she wasn't above saying, "Okay, settle down!" or "Hey! Cut it out!" And hearing that from her was like hearing it from your own mom when you were a kid. Everything just stopped [laughs]. I think there were times when Marion stepped in because even Jerry Paris couldn't get us to settle down with all his ranting and yelling. Those two were like the good cop and bad cop. Jerry was the bad cop, and Marion was the good cop. I swear, I really think they had that routine worked out to keep us all in line [laughing].

But, as far as what I would like people to know about Marion, I think more than anything it is that what you see is what you get. From the first time I met her until this day, she is one of those people who really is what she appears to be—totally genuine. You can't say that about a lot of people in Hollywood. Hell, you can't say it about a lot of people from anywhere.

Chapter 23

My Real-Life Children

Right from the start I had made the decision that there was just no way I was ever going to sit down and write the story of my life without my *Happy Days* family members being involved. They were all a part of the team that made my dream come true, and I just wasn't going to go into a project like this without my team.

But there are two other people who are members of an even more exclusive team of mine that I also had to have involved—two people whom I love so much and am so proud of—a duo that made another dream come true for me: the dream of being a mother and a grandmother. That is the team of my son, Jim Meskimen, and my daughter, Ellen Kreamer.

While I may have been revered as the model of the all-American mother for the role I played on *Happy Days*, in real life I many times questioned if I was doing a good job of raising my son and daughter. For the most part, I feel that I did. I think I even doubled up on my efforts to be as good a mother as I could because I knew their father, Effie, would be somewhat limited when it came to parenting.

On *Happy Days*, we were all very lucky to have been working with producers who recognized that, while a top-rated show demands a lot of work, the members of the cast and crew are human beings with lives outside of work. That kind of understanding and, frankly, just plain compassion are rare when it comes to television producers. But ours were a rare and wonderful bunch who realized that people needed a proper balance in life.

Our typical workweek consisted of doing rehearsals from Monday through Thursday. We usually began around 9:30 a.m. and wrapped between 4:30 and 5:00 p.m. Then, of course, Friday was the day we shot, and that was always a long one. We would usually have a call time at noon and would rarely finish before 11:00 p.m. Those are very civilized hours for a television show, and yet they did necessitate me having help with Jim and Ellen. They were no longer small children, but they did need someone to keep an eye on them, and so I had a housekeeper who came every day and made sure that the place was kept clean and that the kids were fed and did not get into any mischief. I also had a wonderful neighbor named Doris who was always available if the kids needed anything.

Along with lucking out on having decent work hours, I was also fortunate in that the school Jim and Ellen attended was just down the hill from our home, so they could walk back and forth. I was never one of those moms who was very involved with the administrative or political happenings at their school, and I never felt guilty about that. It just wasn't my thing, and even if I had not had a demanding job, I still wouldn't have ever been a PTA mom or headed up bake sales or rummage sales.

So was I a good mom? I think I was a pretty darn good one, if I say so myself. I can't begin to tell you how many times over the past thirty years or more that someone has come up to me and said, "You raised me!" or "I always wished you had been my mother." Well, that is one of the kindest things you could ever hear, and I am always deeply touched when people say those things. But there are two people whom I really did raise, and if the way any child turns out is a reflection on how they were raised, I am damn well pleased with the job I did.

Jim, who was always so kind from the time he was a baby, is a very good artist. He is a wonderful actor, voice actor and impressionist and appeared in the British version of the improvisational comedy series *Whose Line Is It Anyway?* He would also be familiar to many for having played the role of Martin Housely on the hit NBC series *Parks and Recreation* and Officer Wholihan in *How the Grinch Stole Christmas*, the big-screen version of the Dr. Seuss tale that starred Jim Carrey.

He has also carved out a successful niche doing voice-over work for commercials and video games and has voiced numerous animated characters, including doing the Robin Williams voice of the genie in Disney's *Aladdin* franchise. He is an incredible impressionist who can mimic the voice of just about any celebrity you can name, as he proved when he toured the country to perform his one-man show *JIMPRESSIONS*. He's also well known on YouTube for several viral hits featuring his impressions (www.youtube.com/user/jimmeskimen).

In 1987 Jim married Tamra Shockley, an actress who has appeared in feature films, including *Apollo 13*, *Absence* and *What Would Jesus Do?* She is also the founder of an excellent acting school in Los Angeles, The Acting Center (www.theactingcenterla.com). In 1990 Jim and Tamra teamed up to provide me with the most wonderful gift: my first grandchild, Taylor Brooke Meskimen, who has kept the family tradition alive for the third generation by appearing in independent films, commercials and music videos. As a narrator of audiobooks, she has already won prestigious awards.

Ellen, who always had a far more independent streak than her brother, has also achieved a wonderful level of success in television as a producer and writer. She has also carried on the family tradition by being associated with a legendary hit show, *Friends*. She was a writer for *Friends* and then went on to write for the show's spin-off, *Joey*, with Matt LeBlanc, and for *The New Adventures of Old Christine*, which starred Julia Louis-Dreyfus.

In 2008 Ellen married Scott Kreamer, who is also a talented television writer and producer and has done work on numerous animated and children's programs. Ellen and Scott have also given me two more beautiful grandchildren, Roxane Marion, who was born in 2010, and her little brother, Hap Henry, who is just a year younger.

I guess, like any parent, I could ramble on and on about how I raised my kids and where I feel I did good or failed in my parenting style. But, I think, as with my *Happy Days* family, it would be far more interesting to turn it over to David and let him go directly to the source: the products of my parenting style.

"As a mother, she may not have done everything perfect and right like Mrs. C, but she did a whole lot more right than she did wrong, and I'm forever grateful to her for that."
—Jim Meskimen

David Laurell (DL): You know that your mom was very hesitant about writing this book, and, frankly, had it not been for your pushing her to do it, she never would have done it. Now that she has not only been persuaded but has actually done it, what are your feelings about her candid honesty, especially in regard to what she has shared about your father?

Jim Meskimen (JM): I knew if she ever did a book, she would be very honest and open about who she is and what she has gone through in her life. That is just her. I have no problem in having her tell her story, because I believe it is one that will help people who may be in a similar situation. I also think that by her telling the story of her relationship with my father, readers will learn that one of my mother's greatest qualities is that she has always been a helper. She tried to help my father, just like when she was a young girl, she tried to help her mother raise a child who was physically handicapped. She also helped her brother, Gordon, directly in many ways, right up until his death in 1995. She saw herself as a helper. I have seen her go out of her way to help many people over the years.

Maybe she didn't have all the perfect tools for being married to an alcoholic. But it was different in those days. There was not the kind of understanding and help and support like there is today. As for my dad, the fact is he was an alcoholic, and trying to help an alcoholic is a very tough thing to do. Very few people succeed at it. It's just a bigger problem than most people are equipped to handle. Why? Because it doesn't make sense why the person you are so greatly trying to help continues to fail—why they continue to drink even when they are aware of the damage it is doing to themselves and their family.

In my dad's case, here was this handsome and intriguing man that she wanted to share her life with. She found him mysterious and interesting. She admired him and loved the fact that they had similar interests. All she ever wanted was for him to be a great success, whether that be as an actor or in whatever field he wanted to pursue. She wanted to help him to achieve that success and to have a stable family life. But he just wasn't capable of that, and he never really wanted children. My mother thought that with her help and support, she could change him and help him have this great life. I totally understand that, because, as a child, I tried to do the same thing. I always wanted to amuse him. I wanted to give him a reason to live. But that was impossible, because it was beyond anything I had the power to do. It took a couple of decades for me to understand that.

DL: You know that your mom has said that for many years she never really got it, that your dad was an alcoholic.

JM: I can understand her not getting it. She grew up in that era in which people drank . . . a lot! It was just a part of life for many people in the 1950s and '60s. I had never really noticed anything up until I was around eight years old. He had left us, and I would go and visit him. It was when I saw him outside of our home, in his own place, that I slowly became aware that he had a problem. But it was very confusing for me. Anyone who has ever dealt with alcoholism in their family knows it is very typical to be dealing with two distinctly different personalities. That was the way it was with my dad, and it was what confused me. During a certain time of day, he would be easy to get along with, and then, usually around nightfall, he would start to drink more heavily and would turn into a dangerous kind of person.

DL: While your mother ultimately had to give up trying to be helpful to him and on trying to make their relationship and marriage work, it seems she also always harbored feelings for him. What was your relationship like with him? Did you feel he tried to be a good father?

JM: Maybe he tried to some extent, but not being able

to take responsibility for his alcohol problem trumped all the good things he may have tried to do. But I understand where my mother is coming from. I'm very grateful to him for giving me an appreciation for the arts, music and theater and poetry. He knew a lot about movies, and he shared that information with me.

As for the guidance and parenting part, that was his weakness. I think he was also conflicted and confused about being a parent. He had sought treatment with psychologists and psychiatrists. He seemed to have an aversion to being a parent. Maybe he equated being parental with being responsible. That was a bad word for him because he wasn't a responsible person. He was always going out of his way to not be parental. He kind of treated me like an equal or a friend. Which isn't in itself a bad thing. The bad part was in that he wasn't always the kind of friend you would ever want to have. He was always wary about giving any sort of advice or guidance. He had so little trust in his own vision of what was right and what was wrong that I don't think he could have ever been of help to himself, much less anyone else.

DL: Did you continue to have a relationship with him till the end of his life?

JM: Our relationship dwindled considerably in his later years because as I got older, I did what my mother had tried to do: help him. I wanted to at least help him get cleaned up physically, but he flat out turned me down. At that point in time, when I really wanted to try and help him and he snubbed me, it was like, "Okay. Look, if you're not even going to reach out for help when it is being offered, then I don't know what else to do." So from then on, I just kind of gave up on him and kept our relationship on a friendly basis. I visited him last in 1991, four years before he died. He was living in Texas, and I had to be there for an event, so my wife and I brought our daughter, who was just a baby, out for him to see her, and we stayed with him for a few days. After that, we would talk on the phone every now and then. We were always sociable.

DL: While your mother has become the quintessential "perfect all-American mom," she sometimes questions if she was the best parent she could have been for you and Ellen in real life. Your witness, Mr. Meskimen.

JM: Well David, there was always some irony there for sure. While the world had come to know her as this wonder mom, in reality, by playing that role, it took her away from her own home and kids. I was kind of a snarky teenage boy when she was doing Happy Days, *and I used to laugh about that. But, as far as her success as a mom, I think it's important to remember, when we look at classic television moms—Mrs. C, Shirley Partridge, June Cleaver, Carol Brady—we are looking at a creation, a symbol of what we consider that job to be and what we considered that role to be. I have talked to a lot of people over the years that have told me that they considered my mom to be like their mom, like she raised them. I know my mother has heard that from a lot of fans over the years. I kind of understand that is an endearing way for them to tell her, or me, that they viewed her as the mom they wished they had—that we all wished we had.*

But it is important to remember that Mrs. C was a character, and that there was a real person behind that character, with the flaws that every real person has, and that the fans who loved her as Mrs. C never had any personal relationship with her. My mom was a mom—a working mom. When she finished doing her job—which was to play the perfect mom—she would come home to us, and as far as I'm concerned, she was an excellent mom in a lot of ways, although a very different one than Mrs. C.

I would say the most important thing she gave me was a gift that only as I got older did I really appreciate, because I came to learn how rare it is, and that was the gift of artistic encouragement. I am well aware that many kids who have artistic talents never get that from their parents. My mother always had a great appreciation of my artistic expression and a true respect for that. I know a lot of kids who had parents that said, "Look, if you are going to waste your time drawing or being a figure skater or playing your guitar, you had better have something else to back that up." My mom was never like that. She was always so supportive and so openly admiring of my creations that it actually opened me up to pursue the career I have had. To me, that may have been her best quality.

DL: Your lives changed when she got the role on Happy Days. Can you talk about how it changed her?

JM: All for the good. We were always struggling financially before Happy Days, *which seemed to always have her on edge. She was the one who was financially responsible for our family, as well as caring for me and Ellen. I know how tough that is with two parents, let alone one. I do remember times when she would cry or when she would get angry about the situation we were in. I was a kid and would sometimes say something snarky, and she would burst into tears. It is a dynamic that plays out in every family, no matter what their situation is.*

But I would say things did change after she got Happy Days, *and especially when the show became a hit. She became much more confident and seemed to have solutions to all the things that went into the making of a family. With that financial establishment in place, that was the biggest difference I saw in her, that she had great confidence. Remember, she had been aiming for that goal—to become an established actress—ever since she was a young girl. So she had accomplished that, and by doing that, she also was making a good living to support her family.*

I think she was greatly nourished by success. That wasn't to say things were perfect. She was gone a lot, although she would always find ladies from the church or neighbors or a housekeeper to take care of us. We were by no means latchkey kids, and we were never left wanting for anything. We were living in this very comfortable upper-middle-class environment and had nothing to complain about. As a teenager, I actually started to like the freedom I had, which most of my friends didn't have. When she wasn't around, I got a taste of being on my own and living by my own rules. Then, when she was back and all of a sudden wanted to enforce some rules, well, that didn't work for me at times [laughing], and that turned into a point of friction.

But the big overriding thing was that she always took great care of us, and we were always well provided for, even before Happy Days. *Then, when she got the show and it became really big, she was finally able to relax a bit. As the seasons of* Happy Days *went by, she took the time to expand her knowledge of things she was interested in, she grew as a person, she traveled, she became open to having a love life again, and, of course, she didn't have to worry about making the car payment or the mortgage payment.*

DL: Everyone has a few special memories of something they did with their mother at some point in their life. Is there one you would like to share?

JM: [laughing] *This was so embarrassing, but it also gives you a look into the psyche of Marion.*

When I was a senior in high school, we had this art fair. I was one of the kids in charge of setting up the performance part of it, and it was kind of a big deal. There was a showing of drawings and paintings, and then there was a performance and monologue part of it. Anyway, they had asked my mom to be a celebrity judge—the only judge. So I performed, including a monologue from a Shakespeare play. Well, my mother the judge awarded me first place. I'll never forget what she said: "I want to award the first prize to my son, Jim, because I taught him everything he knows."

I had no inkling that such a thing could happen. But it happened, and I was completely mortified. I was sure there would be all sorts of protests from the other kids' parents [laughing]. But they just let her get away with it, and when I look back on it now, I see that it was a totally lovely thing to do on her part. My mother didn't care how it looked. She never even gave it a thought that it would look bad. All she cared about was encouraging me and my artistic goals. She has always rewarded my artistic expression. If I had an art project to do, she was right there with me. She would make hot cocoa, and we would stay up and work on the project together. I was always one of her projects, and I think I turned out pretty well. As a mother, she may not have done everything perfect and right like Mrs. C, but she did a whole lot more right than she did wrong, and I'm forever grateful to her for that.

"My mom is a thorn in my side that I couldn't live without." —Ellen Kreamer

David Laurell (DL): As the daughter of America's mom, tell us what your childhood was like.

Ellen Kreamer (EK): Well, I wasn't Marion Cunningham's daughter. I was Marion Ross's daughter, and I really had a great childhood. I know that when I was young, my mom was struggling a lot, trying to be an actress, having her marriage fall apart, with two young children, provid-

ing for my brother and me. She was dealing with things that caused her a lot of anxiety. But I was a little girl and wasn't really aware of those things.

I was never a coddled child. That would not have been my mother's style. She wasn't a Mrs. C kind of a mom who would slave over the stove, making dinners. For the most part, Jim and I would fend for ourselves. She always made sure we had plenty of provisions, or the neighbor up the street would send dinner down to us. But to us, that was just normal. She was a working mother, and we understood that. We certainly never suffered because of that. In fact, it was just the opposite. It was because she was working that we had the lifestyle we did once Happy Days *became successful.*

It was great to grow up as my mother's daughter. She was always such a moral person. We really were raised with a strong sense of right and wrong. And she has always had this amazingly wonderful adventurous spirit about her. We had a lot of great adventures when we were kids. We would get into our Grand Prix and take off to go camping somewhere. There would be no planning. We would just go. We did things like that on a whim. What kid wouldn't love that? So, I had a great childhood, but it wasn't a Cunningham childhood.

DL: You were young when your parents separated and then divorced. As a child, were you at all aware of your father's problems?

EK: I remember the exact moment I became aware that my dad was an alcoholic. I was six years old, and Jim, who is four years older than me, was always a really good artist. I remember he did a drawing of this odd amphibian-like creature trying to crawl out of a glass with liquid in it. I remember sitting and looking at it, and my mom said, "Do you know what that means?" I told her I didn't, be-

cause I didn't. To me, it was just some sort of a lizard crawling out of a glass. And then she explained to me that Jim's drawing depicted an alcoholic. "That is what your daddy is, you know," she told me.

Even though I was young, children are perceptive of things, and I remember piecing things together in my mind. I remember being aware that there were problems in our family, but I just figured every family had the same sort of problems. So yes, I was aware that my father had problems, but when you are young, you just love your parents, no matter what. But I also did know things weren't good. Even as a little girl, I had heard my father yelling and shouting at times, and I totally related to that drawing Jim did.

DL: You mother would be the first to admit she was rather Pollyannaish about your father's drinking and the difficulties she dealt with in her marriage for a very long time.

EK: My mother is a born optimist. So I don't think it was odd that she was rather blind to his issues. When we were young, my mother was never the type who would bash my dad. Jim and I could tell that there was this underlying tension between them. I mean, we weren't stupid. But I never had the feeling that she was ever trying to take him down or make him look bad in front of us. In fact, she was just the opposite. She would have done anything to help him and to change him, and when they separated, she knew it was important for us to still see him and spend time with him—to have some sort of a relationship with him, even though it was sometimes hard to have any conversation with him.

I know my mother felt she had failed in her attempt to help him and that she couldn't save her marriage, but there is one thing people should know about her: my mom is the kind of person who gets over things quickly—very quickly [laughs]. *I have seen it happen over and over: something bad will happen, and she takes it in stride and then basically just moves on. I have to believe that kind of resilience, that capacity to bounce back, has a lot to do with the overdose of optimism she was born with. I sure wish I could be more like that.*

I think that along with being an optimist, she is also extremely good at compartmentalizing things. I have seen her handle deaths of people very close to her in that fashion, and I wouldn't consider it to be an unhealthy way to deal with the loss of someone if you are capable of doing that. She has all the normal feelings and emotions we all have, but she has this ability to not just get over things quickly, but then to suffer no ill effects from doing that. Maybe that comes from a great blend of optimism and inner strength. My mother isn't one to linger on sadness— never has been. She doesn't let it grab hold of her. I've seen her cry and become very emotional, but then, once it's out of her system, she dusts herself off, and it's just like, "Okay. Enough of that. Let's move on." Maybe that comes from the rugged ancestral Canadian blood she inherited [laughs].

DL: You said that your life growing up was not like the Cunninghams'. Were there kids you went to school with or friends of yours who did think that was what your life was like because Mrs. C was your mom?

EK: No. Her role on Happy Days *wasn't really an issue at all. I had a tight group of girlfriends, and they had all known my mom before she did* Happy Days, *so they were quite aware of who she really was. And then, as I got older—to be honest—there were people I met and knew, some who were even friends, that didn't know my mother was Marion Ross. When the show had become this smash hit, I always wanted to make sure people wanted to be*

around me or be friends with me because of me, not be-
cause of who my mother was. It also seemed braggy to tell
anyone who she was, so unless it came up, I usually
wouldn't say anything.

DL: Thanks to you, your brother and your respective
spouses, your mother is now a three-time grandmother.
Can you draw any parallels to or point to the differences
of how she relates with her grandchildren as opposed to
the relationship she had with you and Jim when you were
kids?

EK: She is completely different [laughing]*! I mean, com-*
pletely! She doesn't have a disciplinary bone in her body
when they are around. She lets them do whatever they
want to do. If they are at her house and want cake for
breakfast, which they always do, they get cake for break-
fast. She really is a fantastic grandmother. The kind of
grandmother every kid would want. And her grand-
children really adore her. In many ways, she was very
strict with us when we were kids. As I mentioned before,
she was always very moralistic and big on teaching us
right from wrong. Of course, just like all kids, we had our
rebellious moments, but overall, we were always pretty
darn good kids, and I think that stems from that strong
moral center she instilled in us.

DL: The first thing that will always come to mind with
people when they see your mom or hear her name is
Happy Days and Mrs. C, but you have seen her in so many
roles, onstage as well as on television. Of everything she
has done professionally, is there anything that is a particular favorite with you?

EK: Of every role she has ever done, I love her as So-
phie Berger in Brooklyn Bridge *the most. That was a role*
she had to fight for, and she was absolutely brilliant in it.
As far as I'm concerned, that was the performance of her
career. Of course she was great in Happy Days—*that goes*

without saying—but it is as Sophie that you see what an insanely skilled actress she is. Because of that show, to this day, people think she really is Jewish.

DL: Do you have any outstanding memory of your mom—something she said or did, or that you did together—that will always stick out in your mind?

EK: One of my favorite stories about her is, ironically, one that neither she nor my brother remembers, but it is one of my favorite memories. Jim and I were very young, and for some reason, we got this idea in our heads that we wanted to dig this giant hole in our backyard. I don't know why—maybe we thought there was some sort of treasure to be found or something—but we were kind of obsessed with it, and my mom would never let us do it. So one Christmas, we woke up and began to open our presents, and one of them was a scroll that looked very courtly and very official and that read: "You may dig a hole in the backyard" [laughing]. It was the best Christmas present ever! It was like getting the go-ahead to be bad [laughing]. After that, we just ignored all the other gifts and ran out back, grabbed our shovels, and started digging this huge hole. It just kills me that neither Jim nor my mother remembers that, and I just wish I still had the scroll to prove that I'm not crazy or didn't dream it. It was a great present and a great memory for me.

I also have one other story about my mother that I'll never forget, and that says a lot about her. When I was young, because of the issues with my father, I felt unsafe at times. Like I wasn't on solid ground. After my father left, I was afraid something would happen to my mother and then wondered what would happen to me and my brother. During their separation and divorce, my mom was tense and would get uncharacteristically upset about things. It was just sort of chaotic. I would lie awake at night and my mind would play all sorts of tricks on me and I would panic and think she might die. I will tell you, I was truly crazy with panic at times over her dying.

I would go to her and say, "I'm worried that you are going to die. Are you ever going to die?" I would be in tears, and my mother would hold me and say, "I will never die. Never! That will just never happen!" She would be so convincing that I would totally believe her, and this great sense of peace and relief would come over me. That lie was such a great lie! The best lie! She could have been real with me and said something like, "Well, you know, we're all going to die someday, but that will be a long, long time from now." But she didn't say that. She sensed that I needed full assurance that she would never die. She knew in her heart that I wasn't ready to deal with anything other than knowing everything would be okay and that she would never die. I will always love her for lying to me like that [laughs].

DL: I guess it could also be said that your mother perpetuated the lie for years that she would never write an autobiography. Or maybe she was always telling the truth all along and then had a change of heart. Whatever the case, now that she has documented her life story in a book, what do you hope people will come away with from reading it?

EK: I would hope that they will see that she is incredibly bright. I mean, she is really smart. She has also always been a very reasonable human being. She is an incredibly good listener. She'll take all sides of an argument and hear them out. She is also ambitious beyond measure. I wish I had a fraction of the drive and fight that she has. I would also hope they would see what a unique and shining star she is. That may sound corny, but it's the truth. Yes, I may be a bit jaded because she's my mom, but I have met a lot of people throughout my life, and I can tell you without hesitation, there is something special about Marion Ross.

She drives me crazy sometimes, but she is special, and I'm grateful to be her daughter.

DL: If you had to summarize your mother in one sentence, what would you say?

EK: [laughing hysterically] *My mom is a thorn in my side that I couldn't live without.*

Chapter 24

My Right-Hand Woman Gwen

I couldn't bring myself to write this book without my team—my cast mates from *Happy Days* and my two children—and there is one more person who also must be included: my longtime personal assistant, confidant, traveling companion and dear friend, Gwen Berohn.

In the early 1990s, while I was doing *Brooklyn Bridge*, my assistant, who had been with me for many years, got married and decided she needed to spend time taking care of her husband instead of me. I thought, *All right. That's no problem. I can handle all my business affairs and obligations, answer fan mail, run my household, take care of all my personal business, from paying bills to food shopping, and still continue to work on a demanding show.* At least I thought that for about twenty-four hours.

Once I came to my senses and realized I desperately needed help, fast, I started putting the word out. That word spread, and it eventually led me to a woman named Gwen who had been working on the game show *Concentration*. We spoke on the phone, and she sounded lovely. Even more important, she sounded like she really understood the inner workings of show business.

I invited her to come to Paramount, where we were doing *Brooklyn Bridge*, and as soon as I saw her, I just loved her face. She was so sweet looking that I put my hands on her cheeks and just kept telling her how much I loved her dear face. I couldn't help myself! I think she thought I was kind of nuts, and later she told me she was sure I was going to give her a big kiss. Well, I didn't, but I did think she just had the sweetest face.

So that little meeting went well, at least from my standpoint, and I guess I didn't scare her too badly, because she agreed to come out to my home for a second meeting. When she arrived, I showed her around the house and grounds, and at one point she sheepishly asked me if I had a typewriter. That kind of caught me off guard, but I told her I thought there was one around somewhere, and if we couldn't find it, we would surely get her one. Gwen took it all in stride, or should I say, she took me in stride, and I was very thrilled when she accepted the offer to come work with me.

If there was a typewriter around the house, we never found it, so we got her a nice new one, and within a very short time, I came to realize that bringing Gwen on board was one of the smartest things I'd ever done. She had worked in the entertainment business for quite a while and was well versed in how things worked. She understood the language of the business and the people of the business. She wasn't the type to go all gushy and gaga when the phone rang and it was Henry Winkler or Ron Howard or Anson Williams. She was extremely professional and savvy and really worked well with everyone, from high-level studio executives and big stars to fans hoping to get an autograph or representatives of charitable organizations asking if I could attend their event. She treated everyone with the same professional courtesy, no matter who they were, and I quickly learned she was as genuinely sweet as her face, and a good, honest, hardworking person to boot. Within no time she became so valuable to me that I had no idea how I had ever gotten along without her.

Anyone who knows me knows I rarely go a week without having workers of some sort doing something at the Happy Days Farm. Gwen had no problem with that. She was great with the workmen. She knew how to handle them, how to handle any professional issues that needed to be dealt with, and, most importantly, she knew how to handle me and keep me going in the right direction.

Over the years—going on almost a quarter of a century now—Gwen hasn't just become a valued assistant and close friend; she has become a member of our family. She comes to my house every day for however long it takes to get done what we have to do that day. She has become my travel companion, and I would say she knows more about me than anyone else. She has also been an invaluable resource to me in writing this book, so much so that I can emphatically say, without her, you would be reading someone else's book at this very moment, because this one wouldn't exist.

"Marion is one of those people who is goal oriented about each day. Just spend a day with her and you'll get that. Every day she has things planned to be handled that day, and she makes sure those things happen. She's the type of person who gets things done." —Gwen Berohn

David Laurell (DL): So, just what is the career path that leads one to becoming Marion Ross's personal assistant?

Gwen Berohn (GB): Well [laughing], *it's kind of a long story, so here goes. I began my career in entertainment in the late 1960s as a tour guide at 20th Century Fox. Unlike Universal Studios or Warner Bros., they only had tours of 20th Century Fox for a short time. There had been various*

productions that weren't happy that the public was being brought on to the lot, but they put up with the tours until the summer of 1969, when they were doing scenes from Hello, Dolly! *there. Barbra Streisand was upset about the tours. She felt they were disruptive and even invasive, and to be honest, we tour guides did really push it at times. From what we were told, one day, while they were in the middle of a scene, a tour came through and Streisand had enough. "If I see one more tour come through here," she supposedly told the studio's operation people, "I'm walking off of the set." Well, that was that. Not long after Streisand made that threat, the tours came to an end, and I was out of a job.*

So, because I had experience as a studio tour guide, a friend of mine and I just drove over to NBC in Burbank, because we knew they were doing tours there. They were impressed that I had experience, and I got hired . . . as only the second girl to ever be hired as an NBC page up to that time. They didn't even call me a page. They called me a "guidette." So I was "Guidette Gwen." At that time, the NBC page system was just an eighteen-month gig. After doing it for a year and a half, you either had to find another job within NBC or look elsewhere. So when there was a job available, they interviewed the pages first. I ended up getting a job in program merchandising. I worked on Hollywood Squares *and many other shows. It was a great time to be at NBC. They were doing all the great shows of the time:* Laugh-In, The Dean Martin Show, *the Bob Hope specials. It was just a lot of fun.*

But then they had all these cutbacks, and I got laid off. After that I moved on to work for the Screen Actors Guild, in their residuals department. That was the only job I have ever had that I absolutely hated. It was far too regimented for me. Right around that time I had gotten married, and then, after my son was born, I was talking to a friend who was working as a game show broker. She mentioned that she was going to be moving on in her career and asked me if I wanted her job. I was interested, and so I went down to meet her boss, who, like my friend, was also moving on to work on Sale of the Century. *She liked me, and instead of interviewing me for the job I went for, she asked if I would like to come along with them instead. I did, and I really enjoyed working on* Sale of the Century. *I was in charge of getting the prizes, which entailed going to Beverly Hills and buying everything. After that I went to work for Mark Goodson, who was producing* Concentration. *I worked there for two years, until 1991, when the show was canceled.*

That was when I got a call from my sister's boyfriend, who told me he had heard that Marion Ross was looking for an assistant. My job with Concentration *was ending on Friday, and that Wednesday was when my sister called and told me about Marion. I told her I was very interested and that led to me meeting Marion. She was doing* Brooklyn Bridge *at Paramount at that time. When I got over to the Paramount lot to meet her—for what I thought would be a formal job interview—all she did was come up to me, put her hands on both sides of my cheeks, and put her face right up to mine. My eyes were crossing, we were so close. She told me I had a sweet face and that I would do just fine. It was the weirdest job interview I've ever had. She didn't ask me one question. She just gave me her home address and told me to come to her house on Friday night so we could talk.*

When I showed up on Friday, she showed me around the house and the property but never asked me one question about my qualifications. Then she led me into the kitchen, where we sat down, and she said, "So, what is it that you do?" I told her I had been working on game shows, and she thought that was great. And that was that.

*We never talked about money or even about what it was I
would be doing. She just told me I would be starting the
following week and that my hours would be 10:00 a.m. to
2:00 p.m. It all happened so fast that I never even asked
about the salary. Actually, I was too shy to ask about the
salary. I was excited, but I was also concerned that I would
not be making enough money. Well, I ended up making
more money than I ever had made before. That was in
September of 1991, and we have been together ever since.
We are both in agreement that my coming to work for her
was meant to be.*

**DL: Your job entails a rather diverse set of duties. What
would you say is the most important thing to be on top of?**

*GB: My duties have changed many times over the years
depending on what project or show Marion is doing. But
the number one thing that has never changed is to always
make sure that nothing gets out of hand. Marion is one of
those people who stays on top of things, especially when it
comes to her home and property. She gets things fixed
right away—sometimes before they even need to be fixed
[laughs]. She believes if you let anything go, it snowballs
and becomes a much bigger thing to deal with. That is
why it is pretty rare to have a day go by when there aren't
workmen doing something at the Happy Days Farm. I
think there is something about having work going on
around the house that makes her happy. She likes to see
activity taking place all the time, and every day she asks
me who will be coming on that day and what they will be
working on. She loves that so much, I had a little sign
made up for her that reads A DAY WITHOUT WORKMEN IS
LIKE A DAY WITHOUT SUNSHINE.*

**DL: Everyone has an issue with their boss from time to
time. Have you and Marion ever had a disagreement?**

*GB: We have honestly never had an argument. There
have been times when I have put my two cents' worth in*

about something, but whenever that has happened, she knows that it was just because I was trying to be helpful.

DL: There are few people who have spent as much time with Marion as you have. So spill the beans. What is she really like?

GB: I know that most people, those who don't know her personally, think of her as Mrs. C. Well, she is not completely that character, but she does have a lot of Mrs. C's qualities. She is kind and caring. But I think the thing most people don't know is that she is smart—very smart. She may seem to be somewhat hands off on certain things—work being done around the house or handling some of her business dealings—but that is only because she is intuitive about the people she works with and the ones who work for her. She has a high level of trust in them to handle things. She may seem to be hands off, but she is always very aware of what is going on.

I remember the first time I went with her to get her taxes done. She went out of the room for something, and the tax man said to me, "You know, Marion already knows everything I'm about to tell her. I have very few clients who keep track of things like she does." So that's really it. She is smart, kind and very ambitious. She is a dream to work for, and she has really taught me a lot, especially about accomplishing things. Marion is one of those people who is goal oriented about each day. Just spend a day with her and you'll get that. Every day she has things planned to be handled that day, and she makes sure those things happen. She's the type of person who gets things done.

Chapter 25

My Happiest Days

Right after we completed the last episode of *Happy Days*, the entire cast went off together to fulfill some obligations not pertaining to the show but to playing softball. When I returned from that last softball tour, it was the first time in over a decade that I didn't have a commitment for the next day, the next month or the next season.

Over the years, I have had friends—actors—who, after finishing a long run in a play or a show, are craving some downtime. That wasn't the case with me. By the time *Happy Days* had wrapped, Jim and Ellen were adults, with lives and careers of their own, and I was a tad bit obsessed with one thing: What's next for me? For the first time in my life, making a paycheck was not the driving force to finding my next gig, but there was still something pushing me just as forcefully: my love of acting.

As the final months of 1984 trickled down, I kept thinking about what I wanted to do next. I let the holidays pass and was then off to work again. I had done a few guest roles on shows like *Night Court*, *MacGyver* and *Burke's Law*, which was a revival of the 1960s series. But there was one thing that kept tugging at me: the stage. And so, with the kids gone and the house empty, I once again returned to my refuge: the Old Globe. I ended up doing a few shows there, and for other companies, as well, maybe a half dozen or more. During that time, I also returned to Broadway, where I costarred with Jean Stapleton in *Arsenic and Old Lace*.

During that time, I did date a few men, but by that time I was far worldlier and wiser than the young woman who all those years ago ran off to get married on a romantic whim. After Effie and I divorced, I really threw myself into fending for myself and my children, and then *Happy Days* hit. Once our divorce was final, I saw Effie only on rare occasions, such as at a few milestone events, like Ellen's first wedding. When we did see one another, we were always cordial, but seeing him was always a reminder to me that I was far better off not having a man in my life. It was for that reason that I rarely gave any of my postdivorce suitors much of a chance. All I had to see was one tiny flaw—a bit too much to drink at dinner one evening, a less-than-polite quip to someone who approached me for an autograph, or even the briefest flash of temper—and I was done with them.

To say my dating was casual would be an understatement. The more accurate term would be "almost nonexistent." I was just not interested in a man coming into my life and invading the relationships I had with Jim, Ellen and my friends. I just didn't need that, although, while I wouldn't admit it to anyone, not even to myself, for the most part, I was lonely.

I was turning sixty that year, and there were times I would think about facing the rest of my life alone, without anyone really special to share things with. I had achieved my lifelong dream, had built a wonderful career for myself, had raised two beautiful children, had the greatest friends a person could ever hope for, and had bought, decorated, and remodeled houses. I was proud of what I had accomplished and was living my life as a big, brave and strong woman, and yet that old loneliness thing kept nagging me.

And then, in 1988, in the middle of a writers' strike that brought every film and television actor's work to a complete standstill, I attended a play at the La Mirada Theatre, located down near Disneyland. I went with a group of friends who were joined by another group of friends, and as we sat having dinner that evening, I found myself seated next to a man who had no idea who I was. It is, perhaps, a sixth sense that people who are famous and in the public eye develop. You become so accustomed to complete strangers knowing who you are, and in some cases, knowing so much about you, that when you encounter someone who has no clue who you are, you are very attuned to it, and I was attuned to the fact that the gentleman seated next to me was one of those encounters.

Although we were seated next to one another, we had not been formally introduced, but once we were—and I know this will sound corny—I felt some sort of a jolt hit me. Instead of shaking hands, we embraced. He just held out his arms, and I fell into them—the arms of Paul Michael.

As the evening went by, we learned we were both actors. He began his career back in the 1950s, doing operas, and he appeared with Judy Holliday in the Broadway musical *Bells Are Ringing* in 1956. From there he went on to do quite a bit of theater work: the title role in the musical *Zorba* (a role he was born to play), Tevye in *Fiddler on the Roof*, and the barber in *Man of La Mancha*. He also appeared in a few feature films and many television shows, including in the role of the king of the Gypsies, Johnny Romano, on the gothic soap opera *Dark Shadows*.

Before the night was over, I also ferreted out that he was originally from Providence, Rhode Island, had served as a sergeant in the U.S. Army in the South Pacific during World War II, had earned a degree in English literature from Brown University, had grown children and, most importantly, was single. When I told him about my background, he seemed to be rather nonplussed about *Happy Days* in a way I found to be charming. It's always a healthy thing to get knocked down a peg or two whenever you start thinking the whole world knows who you are, you know.

During our first meeting, there was clearly a two-sided flirtation at play, and that intensified when, shortly thereafter, we did a play together called *The Whole Half*, in which I played a stately widow and Paul played an uncouth plumber. Well, before the run of that play was over, I just thought Paul was a great guy—the cat's pajamas, as my mother used to say. He would make me laugh like no one else I had ever met. He had this quirky and charming sense of humor, which I was very attracted to. I was also attracted to him physically.

Paul was Lebanese, with blue-gray eyes and a beaming smile. He was a real man's man—big, strong, hairy, and just oozing with sex appeal. He was also very talented, smart and charming, and he was a great cook. He was so many things that I wasn't. I have always been a bit reserved, cautious, thrifty and prudent. He had a big personality. He was gregarious—always joking around—and had this wonderful devil-may-care attitude toward things.

I could make it work with a man like that, I remember thinking not long after we met. That was not just the romantic longings of a sixty-year-old woman; it was also a testament to where I was in life as a person. There was a time when a man like Paul would have been too much of a man for me. But I was in a good place. I was strong, sure of myself, and ready for a guy like him.

When the play we were doing ended, I was worried that I might not see him again. I remember sharing that concern with my assistant, who, after some coaxing, convinced me to call him and invite him to my home. From that time on, Paul and I were inseparable. I decided to do a one-woman show as the poet Edna St. Vincent Millay, called *A Lovely Light*, down in San Diego. Paul went with me, and we stayed at this little hotel, where our romance flourished. Everything about him charmed me. We would get into the car, and I would say, "Do you love me?" He would look at me with those eyes of his and say, "I love you more than when we got into the car!" We began building a relationship the likes of which I had never had or thought I would have. He was my soul mate, and every day with him was romantic, adventurous and fun.

He eventually moved to the Happy Days Farm with me and quickly became the resident chef. He loved to cook, and he would go to the market and buy all these groceries and make every kind of food you can imagine, from Lebanese to Asian. He loved the process of creating a meal, and he was a sensual eater. He savored food as he savored everything in life. He loved to cook so much that you would think that by being with him, I would have learned to cook, but that didn't happen. He never wanted me in the kitchen. That was his domain, and he was the master of it.

As the years went by, our love grew. We did more theater work together, and he never minded that I always got top billing and the big entrance and the curtain call applause. He also never minded when we would be out and fans would come up to me and ask for an autograph and gush over how much they loved *Happy Days* and Mrs. C. He was very secure with himself and proud of me. He didn't mind in the least that I got more attention, and within our circle of friends, it wasn't long before he was getting far more attention than me. He just had such a big dominating personality that couldn't be kept in the background.

I know there were some people who were surprised over my relationship with Paul, but I wasn't. I felt that I had been through a lot in my personal life and that I deserved love—that I deserved him. I don't think a day went by that, at some point, I didn't look over at him and think, *This is perfect! It's just so perfect!*

Here I was, this woman in her sixties, having a hot romance. It was a whirlwind of eating, laughing, traveling, sharing so many wonderful experiences, and being happy like I had never been happy in my life. Paul and I began posing for pictures during our travels, which we would use for our annual holiday card. We would hold up this sign we carried with us that said SEASON'S GREETINGS, and it got to the point where all our friends would wait in anticipation for our card. We were like a couple of kids in love. He made me feel like a young girl, and I remember my son, Jim, would roll his eyes because I just couldn't keep my hands off Paul, even when the family was visiting. "My gosh!" Jim would say. "You two are going to burn down the house!"

It may have taken until I was in my seventh and eighth decades, but my life in the 1990s and early 2000s was truly my happiest days. Not only was I sharing every day with the love of my life, but I also had the opportunity to do what I consider to be some of my finest acting work.

In 1991 producer Gary Goldberg, who had created *Family Ties*, was given the green light by CBS to move forward with a new show, *Brooklyn Bridge*, his semiautobiographical sitcom about a Jewish family living in 1950s Brooklyn. I didn't know Goldberg, but Henry Winkler did, and he was the one who told me about the series. He also told Goldberg that he thought I would be great as the obstinate, iron-willed Jewish matriarch Sophie Berger.

I was more than intrigued with the role, and after my people had talked to their people, as they say in the television biz, I was asked to come in and read for the role. I was well aware that my name immediately conjured up the image of the all-American mom, and I knew I would have a hurdle in convincing the producers and the network that audiences would buy Marion Ross as a Jewish woman. To prepare for my audition, I made myself a little costume and brushed up on a dialect I thought would fit the character.

As was the case with so many auditions I had been on since I was a young woman, this one was at Paramount. When I arrived on the lot, I was directed to a room, where, in front of a group of men I didn't know, I took a deep breath and, in this little accent I had invented, began my reading.

A few moments in, someone said, "Okay, the accent is too heavily Russian, so we'll have to hire a dialect coach for you."

I was taken aback. I had been told that the producers were far from being sold on me and that, in fact, I would really have to step up to the plate if I were to change some minds. And now someone was saying they would be hiring a dialect coach for me. *Does that mean I got the job?* I thought to myself.

What I ultimately learned was that they were still looking at other actresses but thought it was worth me coming in for another audition after working with the coach. That made me feel good. It meant that at least they were serious about me, and I wanted this role so badly.

A few days after my audition, I got a call telling me a dialect coach had been secured and she would be calling to arrange a time to work with me. Her name, I was told, was Jessica Drake.

"Jessica Drake," I said. "That's funny. I know a Jessica Drake who is the daughter of the character actor Ken Drake and my old friend Sylvie Drake, who I had acted with when we were in our twenties and was the theater critic for the *Los Angeles Times*."

"Yes. That's her," the voice on the other end of the phone told me.

"What!" I replied. "That won't work! I need an older woman, preferably a Jewish one."

"Don't worry," I was told. "Jessica is a real professional."

I was still picturing Jessica as this little girl I had met years earlier, and so I was surprised when this beautiful woman showed up at my door, claiming to be her. We hit it off well, and she was in fact a real pro. She would read my lines into a tape recorder with the right dialect and then have me listen to the tape over and over and then mimic her.

Armed with my new accent, I again auditioned . . . and again . . . and again. The producers just couldn't seem to make up their mind, and they kept bringing in other actresses to read, mostly Jewish actresses from New York. I had never worked so hard for a part, not even when I was an unknown, and it seemed like every time I got discouraged and was about to give up on getting it, I would get a call to come in for another reading.

Finally, I had enough. I had allowed my emotions to get out of hand in regard to getting this role, and I was fed up with the roller-coaster ride of it all. I told Paul, Jim, Ellen and Gwen that I was finished—that there would be no more auditions. I just let it go and did what I do: moved on.

Then, one evening, we were eating dinner out on the patio and the phone rang. Paul went to answer it and then came out and told me it was Gary Goldberg for me. I took the phone and said, "Yes. I see. Okay. Yes," and then I started to cry. Paul was looking at me with this concerned expression, and when I hung up, I said those three beautiful words every actor loves to say: "I got it!" Gary had told me he had just gotten back from a meeting with the CBS executives in New York and had gotten what he went in asking for: that sweet mother from *Happy Days* to play Sophie.

I was elated. It was a role I wanted so badly—one that I had really fought for. From the moment I hung up with Gary, I began immersing myself in all things Jewish. Paul and I became regulars at Canter's, the famous Jewish delicatessen and restaurant down by CBS Television City in the Fairfax District of Los Angeles. We would sit at one of their tables, and while we were eating, I would study their menu, ask the servers questions about dishes I wasn't familiar with, talk to other diners, and intensely watch people. I just sopped it all up like the last few drops in the bowls of matzo ball soup we became accustomed to devouring.

Although I knew the role of Sophie would be challenging (which is why I wanted it), when we actually began work on *Brooklyn Bridge*, I found it to be easier than I had expected. To a large extent, that was due to our wonderful director, Sam Weisman. Every actor knows that working with a talented director makes all the difference in the world, and Sam was as good as they get. He was playful, and he would let me try different things and then pull me aside and whisper a couple of words only to me about what he thought had worked and what he thought we could do differently. He was just marvelous!

I had loved every moment of work I put in on *Happy Days*, but doing *Brooklyn Bridge* was a totally different experience—a very emotional one. I came to love Sophie, and doing that role would sometimes strike me with such strong feelings that I would cry. Sophie just touched something deep down in my core—in my spirit. That didn't happen with any other role I had ever played. I felt so fortunate that I got to play her and to be a part of what I thought was a beautifully done show. There is no doubting the fact that I had much more of an emotional attachment to Sophie than I ever did to Mrs. C, or any other character I have ever played. I will, of course, be forever grateful that I got to portray both of those wonderful women, but to me, on a very deep and personal level, I loved Sophie more than any other.

Although *Brooklyn Bridge* was a masterfully done show, it was, unfortunately, never a ratings winner and was canceled after two seasons. I hated to see that show go, but it opened the door for me to get a role I otherwise would have probably never been considered for, in the 1996 Lifetime film *Hidden in Silence*, which told the real-life story of a Catholic woman who sheltered Jews from the Nazis in her home during World War II.

Having had the opportunity to appear in that film, and to play Sophie in *Brooklyn Bridge*, meant the world to me. I had wanted to prove that I was more than just Mrs. C— that I could be viewed as a serious and respected actor— and *Brooklyn Bridge* and *Hidden in Silence* put me in that class.

As the last few years of the twentieth century slipped by, I continued working on a very regular basis. While I did a role in the feature film *The Evening Star*, which starred Shirley MacLaine and was the sequel to *Terms of Endearment*, most of my work was in television. As the new century came in, I did roles on numerous shows, including *Touched by an Angel*, *That '70s Show*, *Gilmore Girls*, *Brothers & Sisters* and *Two and a Half Men*. After Drew Carey told the producers of his show he could imagine only one person playing the role of his mother—*me!*—I took on that role on *The Drew Carey Show*. I also made a foray into what was somewhat uncharted territory for me—animation—by providing the voice of SpongeBob SquarePants's grandmother. And I also continued to perform in my highly charted world of theater, including an Old Globe performance of Joe DiPietro's play *Over the River and Through the Woods*, which I did with Paul.

When I look back at that time, it seems like I worked a lot during the first decade of the 2000s, and when I wasn't working, Paul and I ate and traveled and laughed and had such a marvelous time living our lives together that if I could have hit a pause button at any one time in my life—to make one moment last forever—that would have been it.

During that time, I knew Paul had some health issues. He had been in and out of the hospital a few times and had had heart bypass surgery, which was a great success. But in spite of that, he always seemed healthy to me, and he certainly never let any ailment hold him back from his enjoyment of life. When he would go to see his doctors, he would always just brush off those visits as no big deal, saying they were nothing but routine checkups to make sure everything was still working as it was supposed to. Having been extremely blessed with good health all my life, I never really gave it much thought when his doctor's appointments became more frequent. He looked great, ate with the same gusto as always, and seemed to me to be the picture of health for a man in his eighties.

In early July of 2011, I was scheduled to ride in a Fourth of July parade in Cardiff-by-the-Sea, a beach community in San Diego County. As we prepared to drive down to Cardiff, Paul didn't seem himself. He was irritable and said he didn't feel like going. He did end up accompanying me, but he was rather crabby during the drive down, and by the next day, when we went to a beach party that had been arranged by the parade's organizers, he was really not himself at all. At the party they had tables set up in the sand, very close to the water, and he was making this totally out-of-character fuss about his shoes getting wet.

That evening, we returned to the Happy Days Farm, and by the time we got home, he seemed to have calmed down a bit. The next morning, whatever it was that had been bothering him seemed to have passed, and we went out for breakfast. After we ate, we returned home, and I told him I was going to run a few errands. He was doing what he always did when we returned from breakfast: sitting out on the patio, smoking a cigar. I remember it was a very hot day, and as I got ready to leave, he came inside to answer the phone. It was one of his sons, who told him he had made plans to come and see him for his upcoming birthday.

After he hung up, he mentioned something about the heat and said he was feeling a little light-headed and was going to lie down on the couch. That was not like him at all, but I figured that it was awfully hot out and that perhaps if he took a short nap, he would be feeling better when I returned.

A few hours later, when I arrived back home, I was surprised to see he was still asleep on the couch. "*Hey!*" I yelled at him. "What are we doing? Sleeping the day away? What's that all about?"

Having heard me return, Gwen came downstairs from the office and began going over some messages that had come in. As she was talking, I stood watching Paul, who had never responded to me. I felt a wave of panic rush through my body.

"Gwen! I don't think Paul is breathing!" I yelled as I ran over to him.

She immediately called 911, and they gave us instructions on how to perform CPR. I frantically followed their directions until the paramedics arrived and took over. I had gotten no response from him, and neither did the paramedics, who finally made the decision to transport him to the hospital. Once he was there, they managed to get his heart started again. I don't know how long it had been that his heart wasn't beating, but it had to have been at least forty minutes by that time, and he was incapable of breathing on his own. When they let me see him, they had him plugged into everything imaginable and his condition was dire. To be honest, I think if it were not for the machines, he would have really already been gone. And yet I was convinced, in spite of what the doctors told me, that he would somehow pull through. They kept him on the respirator for two days, and then, when it was clear that there was no evident brain activity, we let him go.

It was July 8, 2011, and for the first time in twenty-three years, I returned home without the welcome of that big grin, hug and kisses from Paul. I was completely numb, and I have only the foggiest recollection of that night and the following few days, as we informed friends of his passing and made his funeral arrangements. His funeral service took place the following week at Our Lady of Mt. Lebanon Church near Beverly Hills. I don't remember much about that week or even the service. I have always been the type to accept things and move on, but this was different, something like I had never before experienced. I felt as if things weren't real, and when I would come out of my numb fog, I would feel such pain that I didn't see how I could move on, or even know if I wanted to. I was as broken as I had ever been.

I do have this foggy memory of sitting in the church, listening to Paul's son Matt give a beautiful eulogy and seeing all the people who had come to pay their respects to Paul. There were so many people—dear friends of ours and even friends of his whom I had never met. They seemed to have come from everywhere. Along with Paul's son, he also had five great nieces who were there, and they were just wonderful to me. That's what I remember. Beyond that, it is all a blur, as was much of the remainder of 2011. I had experienced loss in my life—my mother, my father, and my brother, Gordon, who had died in 1995—but the loss of Paul truly broke me in a way I didn't think I could be broken. He was truly my soul mate, and there was no doubting the fact that when he went, he took half of my soul with him.

The holiday season of 2011 was especially difficult for me. Paul loved the holidays—all the decorating and cooking and family and commotion. That was his thing, and having that first Thanksgiving and Christmas come without him was unbearable. I really have no idea how I got through it all, and had it not been for Jim, Ellen, Gwen and a few other close friends, I don't know if I would have. I was physically and mentally in a place that I had never been before. And yet I knew that, just as in many other instances throughout my life, somewhere deep down inside of me, I did have the strength to be able to eventually accept Paul's death and heal and move on. It wasn't easy to muster up that strength; in fact, it was the most difficult thing I have ever had to do in my entire life. But as the weeks became months since Paul's passing, I could feel that strength gradually returning and clearing away the fog.

As 2011 gave way to 2012, I began to think about returning to work. In fact, I actually started looking forward to it. I had committed to doing a play in Canada—Neil Simon's *Lost in Yonkers*—before Paul died. The plan was that he would accompany me, but heartbreakingly, that was not to be. I knew it would be good for me to get out of the house and to be back on the stage. The preparations to leave for Canada, rehearsals, opening night and the run of the show diverted my thoughts, and for the first time in eight months, I felt life creeping back into my body.

During the final week of the play, Gwen flew up to meet

me, and we prowled around Toronto for a few days before heading on to New York, where we spent a few days before taking a train up to Connecticut to visit Gillette Castle, the home that was commissioned and designed by William Gillette, the actor best known for his numerous theatrical portrayals of Sherlock Holmes from 1899 to 1932. The reason I wanted to see Gillette's residence was to do some research. I had committed to doing another play, *The Game's Afoot*, in the fall in Kansas City. It was a comedy about William Gillette that took place at his grand mansion overlooking the Connecticut River.

After doing that play, I returned home to Los Angeles and continued to take on roles in various television series and made-for-television films. Doing what I loved, and being with people that I loved, was all a part of the healing process for me.

I have often said that the nice thing about life is that within our one life, we can have many very different ones. For so many years, the love that I so desperately hoped to find—that all of us hope to find—had eluded me. But I was lucky. It took me sixty years to finally find it, but I did, and my years with Paul were truly the happiest of my life. I just wish they could have lasted longer. No, let me take that back. I wish they could have lasted forever.

Chapter 26

My Days (Which Just May Never End) at the Happy Days Farm

From the time I finally decided to write this book until I finished telling the tale of my days, I added two more years to my life. In 2016 I decided I would pull back from actively pursuing work, especially in live theater, with its high physical demands. I figured if something came along that interested me—a film or television role in a production being done here in Los Angeles—I would consider it. But as for actively knocking on doors, those days were over.

As much as I always truly loved to work, I am also enjoying my quiet and relaxing days at my home, which I also love. I love to be at home, and my days here are as lovely as one can imagine. Gwen still comes to work every day, and we both have a grand old time dealing with all the workmen who are here at the Happy Days Farm, so much that one would think I'm some sort of a modern-day Sarah Winchester, the eccentric woman who became obsessed with constant work taking place at her mansion up in San Jose.

Although I have never cut the wood, hammered the nails, poured the cement, or done any other part of the physical remodeling of my home, I love to proudly state that I did build the place. I honestly feel that to be true, because everything that exists here does so because I imagined it and designed it . . . with a little help from a wonderful architect. My home reflects my personality in every way. When people come to visit me, one of the first things they notice is that I have very few curtains or drapes in the house. I love things to be very open and bright. I love when the sunshine boldly bathes each room in light.

The architect who helped me envision what the Happy Days Farm would look like was very good at getting into my head and my thought process. He spent a tremendous amount of time with me and wanted to know a lot of details as to how I live, what I like, what I need, what I do, the type of environment I prefer—all sorts of things. It was very exciting to watch this house come together. We knocked out walls and put in beautiful stained-glass windows. And then I filled the house with things I love, like a drawing of Paul in the role he was born to play, Zorba the Greek; a magnificent chandelier from Austria; and a wonderful old grandfather clock that was a part of the set in a play I once did in Maine with Gavin MacLeod. I just fell in love with it, bought it, and had it shipped to California.

I also have these beautiful oriental rugs I bought somewhere in Asia during one of our *Happy Days* softball tours. I just fell in love with these beautiful rugs when I saw them, and yet the old prudent side of me kept debating whether or not I should buy them, because they were ridiculously expensive, and on top of the price, I found it was going to cost me another fortune to have them shipped to the United States. As I was standing there debating with myself over whether or not I should get them, the man who was showing us around came up and whispered to me, "I think there may be a chance we can get the U.S. Army to transport them for you." How the heck he planned on doing that, I didn't know. I still don't, and maybe it's best that I don't. All I do know is that his offer was enough of an incentive for me to buy them, and the army did come through.

One of my more recent acquisitions is a cuckoo clock I bought in Bavaria. It was another outrageously priced item that, like those rugs, just reached out and pleaded with me to take it home. It was a totally crazy impulse buy, but what the heck. I wanted it, and it looks beautiful in my sunroom, which, by the way, is my favorite room in the house. It's open and airy and has lots of light. I love to sit there when I read. It is also where I love to sit and chat with visitors, and I always know the time, thanks to that little cuckoo bird.

I will sometimes sit there in the late afternoon, when Gwen and all the workmen have gone, and just think back over my life. I would imagine that is something most people do when they are in their late eighties and have so many wonderful memories to recall.

I also think about the world as it is today. I am truly shocked and awed at the advances, in just about everything, that have taken place during my lifetime. Today's world is one that would be very foreign to my parents and totally incomprehensible to my grandparents. In many ways, the world today is one that moves too fast for me. I am really rather out of touch with a lot of it, especially the technology, which, at least from what I see, seems to change on a weekly basis, if not quicker. I just don't know how people keep up with it all.

I do keep up to date on the news of the day, depressing as it sadly seems to be. But I'm not obsessed with knowing about everything that's going on. I think the constant bombardment from all these news and information sources just sucks the happiness and creativity and optimism—even the very soul—out of people. I know there are a lot of horrible things happening out there, and while I'm not one to completely stick my head in the sand, I think everyone would be a hell of a lot happier, and a lot less stressed, if instead of spending so much time watching the cable news networks, sitting at the computer, and checking the phone, they took some time in the late afternoon to sit quietly in their favorite room thinking about their past with a little dog by their side.

I know that some of my friends have overwhelming concerns about the world their grandchildren are inheriting. Well, I have concerns, too. But I don't fixate on them, and frankly, I don't worry about it all that much. This planet has a history of bad times—horrible times—and it seems that there are always enough good, decent and smart people who come along to figure out how to fix things and keep it all going in somewhat the right direction, until someone else comes along and messes it all up again. I think that is just the cycle of this world.

I am an extremely optimistic person—always have been—sometimes to the point of being viewed as a Pollyanna. I am, by all means, aware that we are in a period of time that is terribly chaotic, not just in foreign lands and third world countries, but right here in the United States. But I travel a bit, and when I do, I still see how much beauty exists in our world and how many lovely people there are everywhere. I don't lose sleep about the world my grandchildren, and even their children, will live in. I believe they will be just fine. They will have some tough times, like all of us have had. But their generation will produce wonderful people who will lead them through to the time when, I would expect, as elderly people, they will also worry about the world their grandchildren will inherit.

I am now of the age that causes people to think I have

lived long enough to have figured it all out and to have some sort of sage advice and wisdom to share. Well, I may have learned a couple of things along the way, but I don't think any of us really ever figure it all out. We just have to do the very best we can.

I do think we have to be more willing to let people be who they are, instead of trying to mold them into what we think they should be. When I was the mother of two young children, I was very keen on enforcing rules and a moralistic code so that they would be imprinted on my children and would make them the way I wanted them to be. Of course, just like any parent, I did that out of love and to try to help them be the best they could be. But as I got older, and a little more wisdom started to creep in, I gradually began to let go and let them be who they were, which resulted in the wonderful people they have become. Oh, and as far as my grandchildren go, well, they can do no wrong, so I just give them free rein to do whatever they please. That is, and always will be, the best and only advice you can give to other grandparents. Offering anything else would just be a waste of breath.

But I must say, I am always intrigued and curious about the connection people make with age and wisdom. I don't know. . . . It seems to me that in my life I have met some extremely wise young people and some awfully foolish old people.

Another thing I have found you are frequently questioned on once the age of eighty is in your rearview mirror is if you have adopted any philosophy on aging.

Well, my answer to that is a simple one: "No!"

I am so lucky to be in great health, and there is nothing about me that feels old. I don't even know what "old" is supposed to feel like. I know some people who say they have made peace with their age. That's not for me. How can you make peace with something you aren't at war with?

I would say that the only philosophy I have to offer has nothing to do with my age. I believe that the most important thing a person can have in their life is a dream that they never lose sight of and that they work as hard as they can to achieve it. That's my philosophy today, and it was my philosophy when I was a little girl, one who did just that.

One of my favorite lines from Shakespeare is one he wrote for *Julius Caesar*: "Men at some time are masters of their fates: the fault, dear Brutus, is not in our stars, but in ourselves, that we are underlings."

To me, that line says that just believing in destiny and not acting toward the accomplishment of your goals will lead you nowhere. Is there such a thing as destiny? I believe there is. But I also believe, to a large extent, we can and do control it.

I decided very early on what my dream was, and then I worked like the blazes to follow a path that would make that dream come true. It wasn't some sort of a sprinkle of fairy dust from some benevolent godmother that made it happen. Even when I was very young, I knew there would be no godmothers or fairies or brownies or wood sprites, or whatever you want to call them, who would come swooping down on Albert Lea in search of me and would make my dream come true. I knew there was only one person who could make it happen: *me*!

I think the reason I thought that way from the time I was very young was that that concept was instilled in me by my mother. She was a strong and self-reliant woman who always taught me that I could be whatever I wanted to be. When you are told that over and over from the time you are a child, it becomes a part of your DNA. I believed that with all my heart because I heard it so often. We are all being inspired or being discouraged constantly by the things we are told or that we hear or read, or by talking to other people. Having that kind of positive inspiration is so important when it comes to fulfilling our dreams and our destiny.

I cannot recall a time in my life when I didn't wake up in the morning and say to myself, *I've got to do this today, and I've got to do that tomorrow, and I've got to start working on something else next week.* This was all geared toward making my dream a reality. I was like that because of the gift I received from my mother: an inner strength, determination and strong will to do whatever needed to be done. I think that this, along with unconditional love, just may be the greatest gift a parent can give to their children. It was because of that gift that a lot of things happened to me throughout my life—good things, bad things, great things, unbelievable things—and I take full responsibility for making every one of them happen.

Another dreadful question that is always posed to octogenarians (and I'm sure to nonagenarians also, as I will learn soon enough) is how they would like to be remembered. I don't think, as the years go by, that I'll be remembered much. Oh, I may get a fleeting mention from time to time when the history of television is reviewed in some retrospective and when classic shows like *Happy Days* are remembered. But I'm not one of the giant icons of the industry, like Marilyn, who even all these years after her death is still known to people of all ages by just her first name. That is just fine with me. I have always had the healthy ego of an actor, but I have never been an egotistical person (there's a great difference, you know). So it doesn't bother me that in fifty years, the image of me in a perfectly pressed dress and with immaculately coiffed hair, serving a platter of cookies to teenagers, won't immediately come to mind if anyone just says the name Marion.

I have no great need to be remembered, but if I am, it would be nice if the thoughts that came to mind were pleasant ones. Perhaps if I had lived a more worldly and exotic life, rife with all sorts of juicy love affairs and scandals, I would be better remembered. But that never was me. I didn't just choose to be a solid, steady and moralistic person who believes in goodness and kindness; it was just a part of who I was from as long back as I can remember. If there is anyone who is a product of their sturdy Midwestern upbringing, it's me. And because of that, being a good person with a code of morals has always been very important to me.

So how would I like to be remembered?

Whenever I'm asked that, I think about a time when I was traveling through Scotland and we went to this old cemetery by the sea where my great-grandfather is buried. There was a beautiful chapel in the cemetery; and inside, under a stained-glass window, there was a little bronze plaque with a man's name on it; and underneath his name were three simple words: *A good man.* That really struck me, and I'll never forget it. I have no idea who he was, but when he shuffled off his mortal coil, he left people behind who remembered him for his goodness. Is there really anything better that any of us could ever hope to be remembered for?

As I sit here in my sunroom, putting the final touches on this story of my days, I have already lived well over thirty-two thousand of them, and each one served as the stage for its own unique twenty-four-hour scene. All those scenes have made up the story of a life—a happy life, for the most part—in which I saw my secret dream, my destiny, fulfilled. I've lived a life filled with happy days—not all of them, but more happy ones than otherwise. I can't imagine anyone asking for anything more.

As for what else I have to do in life, there isn't much. My bucket list is pretty well complete. I'm comfortable and happy, and there is almost no place I can go on the planet where, because of *Happy Days*, doors don't open for me and people don't warmly welcome me with love and affection. Isn't that wonderful! I mean, what could be more rewarding and lovely than that?

I'm at peace, and I know that I did what I was supposed to do during my days on this planet. I am so grateful for all I have, and yet, if for some reason it was all taken away from me tomorrow, I could manage and survive—I really could. I have proven that to myself over and over again: that no matter what happens, I have the strength and resilience to carry on.

There is one last question older people are constantly asked: What do you think happens when we die?

My answer: "I don't know. I have no idea at all, and frankly, I don't care, because I never think about it." I think having life means dwelling on life—what we can be doing in the here and now—not on what may or may not be looming out there in the great beyond. I heard a saying once: "Don't die until you're dead." I don't know who said it, but I thought it was good advice, and it resonates with me even more as I prepare to enter the tenth decade of my life.

And as for dying? I don't know. I guess it may be nice if I was given a dignified little send-off by my family, perhaps with the overture from Richard Strauss's *Der Rosenkavalier* playing as some friends file in to pay their final respects. Wouldn't that be lovely? I also think it would be nice to have my ashes buried side by side with Paul's in the San Diego cemetery where the other members of the Ross family peacefully rest in our family plot.

Yes, that would all be lovely. But, I'm beginning to think that none of those things are going to happen. As a matter of fact, I just may not bother to do it at all—die, that is.

You know, when Ellen was a little girl, she would have nightmares and would run into my room and say, "Mommy,

Mommy, I'm afraid you are going to die. Are you going to die?"

I would hold her and assure her, in the most convincing way, that dying was not, nor would it ever be, a part of my plan.

"That will never happen!" I would promise her. "I will never die! Never! I can assure you." And when I told her that, she would calm down, smile, and go back to sleep in peace.

So maybe that will be the next big dream I will chase. My next goal will be to never die (I mean, I *did* promise Ellen, and a promise *is* a promise). I know that may sound ridiculous—like the most crazy, outlandish and far-fetched dream a person could ever have. But is it?

You know, there once was this little girl who wrote a far-fetched dream in her diary book:

> *When I become a great actress—and I will—I will act in theatres [and will] have all the people in the world clamoring to talk to me and gush over me.*

And guess what? That far-fetched dream came true.

So here I am, all these years later, writing in another book. So how's this?

> *When I have lived forever and ever—and I will—I will become known as the woman who never died, and all the people in the world will clamor to talk to me and gush over me.*

Some may read that and think, *My God, the poor thing has gone mad in her old age.* But, when you think about it, is that really any more far-fetched than a little nobody from Albert Lea, Minnesota, dreaming of becoming an actress; meeting and getting to work with some of the greatest legends Hollywood has ever produced; starring in films and television shows, including one of the most beloved shows of all time; becoming a mother of two wonderful children; finding a soul mate and having one of the world's most passionate romances; and even getting a star on Hollywood Boulevard's Walk of Fame to boot?

I don't think it is. I really don't.

My Epilogue and Acknowledgments

There are some people in the public eye who write their autobiography when they are in their thirties or forties and then, as the years go by, come to regret some of the things they shared with the world. Not me. I waited until I was old enough to know I would have no regrets.

Over the course of my days on this earth, I have learned many things, including how it takes many working parts, carried out by a team of talented people, to bring a theatrical production, a television show or a feature film together. What I had no idea about until I was well into my eighties was how a book comes together.

I always dreamed I would become an actress, but never dreamed I would someday write a book—any book—much less one about my life. In fact, at times I had been adamant that I would never do such a thing. And yet, over the years, I have had many people suggest that I document the story of my life—my son, Jim, and my daughter, Ellen, at the forefront—but it just didn't seem like something I would ever do . . . until I did.

The genesis for this book actually began without my even knowing about it when an enterprising entertainment producer named Jackie Lewis, the president of Jackie Lewis Productions, arranged for a meeting between my son, Jim, and writer David Laurell at a Studio City, California, restaurant. I am told that Jackie, Jim and David sat and talked for hours and all agreed that the story of the days I have lived was worthy of being documented. And so, shortly thereafter, Jackie and David met with me at the Happy Days Farm to do what may have been the most difficult part of putting this book together: convincing me (a) to do it and (b) that anyone would care to read it. "I don't have any juicy gossip to share," I argued. "I have no scandalous or tawdry tales to tell."

When I shared that same concern with my literary agent, Jennifer De Chiara (who, by the way, is the best in the business), she listened to me intently.

"You do know that I'm not going to have any salacious stories about devious plots to undermine anyone," I told her. "There will be no sexy tales of clandestine affairs or romps or orgies or trysts, or whatever they call them nowadays . . . no airing of dirty laundry—"

Jennifer cut me off. "Marion!" she said sweetly. "Don't worry. There's still plenty of time for you to do all those things before the book comes out."

And with that, she made me laugh and also convinced me . . . I would write a book.

Once I did decide to tell my story, I had one question— a big one: How and where do I start?

What I quickly learned is that writing a book, even if it is your book, about your life, is like doing a television show, a film, a play or anything else in life; it takes the collaborative effort of a team. And just like with *Happy Days*, I once again lucked out by having a most wonderful team, who all worked so hard to make this book a reality.

Taking the lead on that team was David Laurell, who spent days and days and days (all happy and enjoyable ones, I may add) with me at the Happy Days Farm, plotting out how I should approach this task and asking me about things I hadn't thought about in many years or—in some cases—ever. He was a godsend to me and has become a very special person in my life.

Doing this book, which I had been so hesitant to do, turned out to be a really lovely experience because of the people involved. And even though I am now "a writer," I really don't think I can come up with the proper words to express my deep gratitude to all of them for helping me tell the story of my days. And while there are so many people— many whose names have been included in this book—who are responsible for helping me make my dream come true, so that there would even be a reason for me to write a book, there are those who all really pitched in over the past two years and made this happen. I am used to doing projects that, as they end, acknowledge those who made it happen in credits. So, here we go. Let the credits roll. With heartfelt love and thanks to:

Garry Marshall and his executive assistant, Heather Hall, and all my beloved *Happy Days* family members: Ron Howard and his assistant, Louisa Velis; Erin Moran; Henry Winkler and his assistant, Sarah Chiaravalle; Anson Williams, Donny Most, and Scott Baio.

My family: Jim, Tamra, Taylor, Ellen, Scott, Roxane and Hap.

My assistant: Gwen Berohn.

My agent: Jennifer De Chiara, and everyone at The Jennifer De Chiara Literary Agency.

My writing collaborator: David Laurell.

My transcriber: Maxine "Max" Andrews.

My publicist: B. Harlan Boll.

And all the wonderful and talented people at Kensington Publishing Corp: Publisher Lynn Cully, editor in chief John Scognamiglio, publicity director Karen Auerbach, director of communications Vida Engstrand, art director

Louis Malcangi, director of social media and digital sales Alexandra Nicolajsen, production editor Robin Cook, copy editor Rosemary Silva, and copy chief Tracy Marx.

And, finally, to Jackie Lewis, who sparked the entire thing.

To all of you, I thank you and wish you a lifetime of health and happy days!

Connect with Us

Visit us online at
KensingtonBooks.com
to read more from your favorite authors, see books
by series, view reading group guides, and more.

for sneak peeks, chances to win books and prize packs,
and to share your thoughts with other readers.

facebook.com/kensingtonpublishing
twitter.com/kensingtonbooks

Tell us what you think!

To share your thoughts, submit a review,
or sign up for our eNewsletters, please visit:
KensingtonBooks.com/TellUs.